ELEMENTS OF TRANSPORT MANAGEMENT

A study course for
the Certificate of
Professional Competence

by
DON BENSON
FInstTA, MCIT

CRONER PUBLICATIONS LIMITED

Croner House, London Road,
Kingston upon Thames, Surrey KT2 6SR

Telephone 081-547 3333

Elements of Road Transport Management

First Edition
June 1980

Second Edition
December 1983

Third Edition
April 1985

Fourth Edition
October 1986
Reprinted May 1987

Fifth Edition
March 1989

Sixth Edition
1990
Reprinted 1990

ISBN 1 85452 068 7

© Croner Publications Ltd 1980, 1986

All rights reserved. No part of this publication may be reproduced, stored in a retrieval system, or transmitted in any form or by any means, electronic, mechanical, photocopying, recording, or otherwise, without the prior permission of Croner Publications Ltd.

Printed by Whitstable Litho Printers Ltd,
Whitstable, Kent.

Contents

Introduction 5
Preface to the fifth and sixth editions 6

PART I - National Section

Chapter 1 - *(Module A)*
The CPC examination — your questions answered 7

Chapter 2 - *(Module B)*
Drivers' hours 11
Community regulated 12
Hours of work records 13
Driving licences 21

Chapter 3 - *(Modules A & B)*
General traffic regulations; Speed limits 29
Parking, loading and unloading 31

Chapter 4 - *(Modules A & B)*
Traffic offences and legal action; Endorsement and disqualification 37
Powers of goods vehicle examiners, etc 40

Chapter 5 - *(Modules A & B)*
Accidents, insurance and safe loading; Procedure in case of traffic accidents 43
Compulsory vehicle and passenger insurance 44
Safe loading of vehicles 45
Specialist vehicles, etc 45
Hazardous and dangerous goods 47

Chapter 6 - *(Module B)*
Technical standards and aspects of operation 52
Vehicle weights 53
Maximum dimensions of vehicles 54
Overloading 56
Long and wide loads 56
Abnormal indivisible loads and special type vehicles 59
Attendants 60
Vehicle selection 61
Mechanical conditions 62

Chapter 7 - *(Module B)*
Plating and testing, checks and prohibitions 69
Type Approval 71
Vehicle marking regulations 72
Vehicle lighting 76
Vehicle checks and prohibitions 80
Vehicle maintenance 84

Chapter 8 - *(Module B)*
Licensing requirements for goods vehicle operations; Existing legislation 88
Operator licensing 88
Trade Licences 93
Recovery Vehicle Licences 94

Chapter 9 - *(Module A)*
Company law, business and financial management; Business units 95
Financial management 97
Elements of costing 100
Purchasing and stock control 107

Chapter 10 - *(Module A)*
Commercial conduct of business 109
Other services; The advantages and scope of insurance 113
Banking services 117
Methods of operating 120

Chapter 11 - *(Module A)*
Structure of the law 123
Law of business and carriage 125

Chapter 12 - *(Module A)*
Social legislation 136
Industrial relations 136
Social security 152
Discrimination 155
Company Safety Policy 159

PART II — International
Chapter 13 - *(Module D)*
Law, Legislative sources 163
EC hours and conditions of work 166
AETR hours and conditions of work 168

Chapter 14 - *(Module D)*
Access to the international market 170
International transport documentation 175
Fiscal charges 179

Chapter 15 - *(Module D)*
Business and financial management of the undertaking 181
Consignment notes and carrier's liability 181
Insurance abroad 188
Customs practice and formalities 190
Customs entry and clearance of imports 194
TIR Convention 198
Systems and services 202

Chapter 16 - *(Module D)*
Vehicle construction, weights and dimensions 206
Harmonisation 206
Traffic restrictions and special requirements 207
Dangerous goods 210
Perishable goods 212

PART III
Self-examination tests 217
Answers to tests and examinations 266
Index 269

PASSING THE TRANSPORT OPERATOR'S CERTIFICATE OF COMPETENCE

Introduction

This book has been written to assist applicants in passing the examination for the Certificate of Competence required by the EC directive on admission to the occupation of road haulage operator. It will be particularly useful to those people who find it difficult to attend classes but it is also designed to assist lecturers and students at colleges offering classes, by providing a textbook which will eliminate the need for taking copious notes and providing ready-made exercises.

Chapter 1 deals with the background to the Certificate of Competence and the examination. It gives answers to the questions "Who must hold a licence?", "Who must take the examination?", "Is anyone exempt?" and many others which people in the road transport industry are asking.

Chapters 2–16 deal with the subject matter of the examination and at the end of the book there are objective questions for each chapter to enable the reader to assess to what extent he has mastered the subject matter of the examination. The questions are similar to those which will be used in the actual examination. By answering these questions during his study, the student will become thoroughly familiar with the kind of questions he will be called upon to answer during the examination and will be able to tackle them with greater confidence.

When the student has finally worked his way through the book to his own satisfaction he should test himself by answering the Specimen Examination Papers to be found at the end of the book.

Wherever possible the subject matter has been broken down into a series of questions and answers. This has been found to be a more interesting way of presenting information and helps the student to learn more easily. It also enables friends or members of the family to "test" the student's knowledge by asking the questions and checking the answers.

Hints to the student on studying for the Certificate of Competence examination

The type of material to be learned for this examination does not call for long periods of study but for frequent periods of, say, up to 30 minutes. It will also be found that odd 10 or 15 minute periods can be used to great advantage. Constant revision is the secret of success, so make sure that you revise the previous section of work each time before starting on a new topic. In addition, try to devote one long period each week to going over all that you have studied before.

In this way you consolidate what you have already learned and do not fall into the trap of forgetting what you thought you had learned thoroughly several weeks before. Whenever possible get a friend to test you, as suggested in the last section.

Try to avoid reading the questions covering each chapter until you feel confident of your knowledge of that chapter. When you do the test, write your answers on a separate piece of paper, then check them against the answers at the back of the book. Do *not* mark the answers in your book, then, if you are not satisfied with your results, you can re-study the chapter and repeat the test without seeing your previous answers.

Throughout this book, for the sake of simplicity, the word "he" is used to represent both male and female gender.

The law as stated in this book was correct at the time of going to press but as transport legislation alters very rapidly readers should ensure that they have access to the monthly amendments to *Croner's Road Transport Operation*, either at work or through their local libraries, to make certain that all their information is up-to-date.

I am indebted to the publishers of *Croner's Road Transport Operation* for allowing me to make extensive use of their book in the compiling of this work and to Geoffrey Whitehead for permission to quote from his book *Elements of Overseas Trade*.

Don Benson

Preface to the 5th Edition

Although the National Examinations have been divided into three parts, viz:

    Module "A" 20 questions covering parts of the syllabus which are common to both goods and passenger vehicle operations;
    Module "B" 40 questions specific to goods vehicle operations;
    Module "C" 40 questions specific to passenger vehicle operations;

it was decided to retain the existing format of the book as it was felt that to attempt to separate the contents along modular lines would have resulted in a very disjointed narrative.

However, in order to assist students to cope with the examinations in their new form, the single Trial Examination (National) paper, incorporated in previous editions, has been replaced by two papers corresponding with Module "A" and Module "B".

Don Benson

Preface to the 6th Edition

Since publication of the 5th Edition, a number of requests have been received to re-organise the book to correspond with the modular form of the examination. As mentioned in the Preface to the 5th Edition this would lead to a very disjointed narrative as questions on some topics can be legitimately asked in both Modules A and B, eg on maximum speed limits. Since most candidates take both Modules A and B at one sitting it seems logical to continue to present the material for study in the manner most convenient for the majority. However for the guidance of those taking the modules separately or revising for a re-sit, this is how the chapters correspond with the examination modules.

Chapter 1	}	Chapter 3	}	Chapter 2	}
Chapter 9		Chapter 4		Chapter 6	
Chapter 10	} Module A	Chapter 5	} Modules A and B	Chapter 7	} Module B
Chapter 11		Chapter 7		Chapter 8	
Chapter 12	}				

This information is also given under each chapter heading.

Don Benson

PART I
CHAPTER 1
(Module A)

The Certificate of Professional Competence Examination — Your Questions Answered

Background
Originally the Transport Act 1968 (Part V, s.65) established a legal requirement for a person to be nominated as a transport manager, ie the holder of a transport manager's licence, for each goods vehicle operating centre.

Schedule 9 to the Act provided for a test to be prescribed before the issue of a licence but this part of the Act was never implemented (and has since been revoked).

Following a meeting of EC Transport Ministers in 1974 an EC directive (74/561) was issued laying down conditions for admission to the occupation of road haulage operator in national and international operations. Amongst other things the directive requires road hauliers to be of good repute, of appropriate financial standing and professionally competent.

Before formulating the scheme to be introduced in Great Britain, the Department of Transport highlighted the issues to be resolved in a consultation paper in August 1975 and invited the views of the main representative organisations of the road freight industry. After further studies of comments from the industry, draft legislation was circulated among interested bodies — trade associations, professional bodies, etc — and in the light of their comments some alterations were made. This legislation was submitted to the EC for approval and was finally laid before Parliament on September 8, 1977.

How many certificate holders must there be in a business?
There should be one certificate holder for each operating unit. The directive requires only one certificate in each business, but this is clearly an ineffective approach for large, diverse undertakings when the aim of the scheme is to encourage more direct individual responsibility for transport operations. Therefore the approach in the 1968 Act is more appropriate, with the Licensing Authority being fully encouraged to use its discretion on what constitutes an operating centre to give, in effect, an operating unit, eg when in the area of a Licensing Authority, two or more centres are within such distance of each other that one transport manager is continually and effectively responsible for the operation and maintenance of vehicles, they would be designated an operating unit.

What were the effects of this legislation?
The effects were two-fold. It introduced:
    (a) a new system of operator licensing
    (b) a test of competence for those responsible for goods vehicle operation, officially entitled The Certificate of Professional Competence. For the sake of brevity it is usually referred to as the Certificate of Competence or CPC.

How does this system of licensing work?
Briefly, it means that there are two types of operators' licences:
  (a) Standard Operator's Licence — covering hire or reward operations, which is subdivided into national and international, or national only
  (b) Restricted Operator's Licence — covering own account operations only.

Are both kinds of operator affected by the Certificate of Competence requirement?
No! Own account operators and/or their managers are not required to hold a Certificate of Competence.

Are own account operators and managers able to obtain Certificates of Competence if they wish to do so?
Certainly! Many will wish to keep their options open. For example, an own account operator may wish to apply for a Standard Operator's Licence to enable him to carry for hire or reward should the need arise. Similarly, a manager may consider it wise to obtain a Certificate of Competence in case he needs it in order to change jobs or in case the firm's policy changes and they decide to engage in hire or reward operations.

Are there any other exemptions from the Certificate of Competence requirement?
Yes! Where operators are exempt from the operator's licence requirement under the Transport Act 1968, they are similarly exempt from the Certificate of Competence requirement, eg an operator of small vehicles having plated weights not exceeding 3.5 tonnes, or an unladen weight not exceeding 1525kg, if unplated.

How long will the Certificate last?
The Certificate of Competence is valid for life, subject to revocation or suspension.

What happens to the business if the operator or manager dies or becomes incapacitated?
To allow the business to continue, the Licensing Authority is allowed to grant dispensations for a period of 12 months, extendable if necessary at the discretion of the Authority by a further six months.

Who sets the examination?
An independent body is responsible for recognising "the possession of skills" referred to in the directive. This body is the Royal Society of Arts (RSA) who prepare and mark examination papers and arrange for examinations to be held at convenient centres.

What kind of examination is it?
It is a written examination, by objective testing. This method requires a minimum of writing, eg the marking of a number of possible answers to a question. This ensures, as far as possible, that it is a test of knowledge and understanding and does not require the ability to write elegant prose.

Is a high level of education required?
No! The level of knowledge required is within the grasp of those persons whose education corresponds to the level normally reached at school-leaving age.

How often are the examinations held?
The examinations are held on a national basis, usually in March, June, October and December.

Are there different levels of examination for different size fleets?
No! Different examination levels for different size fleets would create difficulties when a fleet exceeded the threshold. It is hoped, however, that operators and managers will be encouraged to progress to higher qualifications on a voluntary basis.

Does the examination cover operators engaged in international transport operations?
There are two examinations, one for national operations and another for international operations. The latter follows on from the examination for a national certificate and refers specifically to international requirements.

Does possession of any existing qualifications exempt applicants from the examination?
Yes! A list of these qualifications has been approved by the Department of Transport.

Can an operator or manager who has qualified in this country engage in similar operations in other EC Member States?
Yes! A qualified person may obtain a Certificate of Qualification from a Licensing Authority, covering good repute, professional competence and, where relevant, financial standing.

How can the knowledge to pass the test be acquired?
The knowledge required may be obtained by:
  (a) attending courses
  (b) practical experience
  (c) private study
  (d) a combination of the above methods.

Which organisations offer courses?
There are no restrictions on who may run courses. The Road Transport Industry Training Board, Group Training Associations, Trade Associations and Technical Associations and Technical Colleges all offer courses.

Are courses readily available?
The RSA try to ensure that courses are available nationally. But in some areas of the country there is a marked absence of transport education facilities and students in those areas may find that they have to travel to intensive residential courses, or rely on written material.

What subject areas does the RSA examination cover?
The topics covered by the examination are:

National Examination Syllabus	*International Examination Syllabus*
Driver's hours and records	Law
Driving licences	Hours and conditions of work
Traffic regulations	Use of tachographs
Procedure in case of accidents	Permits, quotas and tariffs
Vehicle and passenger insurances	International transport documentation
Safe loading of vehicles	Fiscal charges
Vehicle weights and measures	Consignment notes and carrier's liability
Vehicle selection	Insurance abroad
Mechanical condition of vehicles	Customs practice and formalities
Operator's licensing	Financial aspects of operation
Financial management	Route planning
Costing	Vehicle construction, weights and dimensions
Commercial conduct of business	Traffic regulations
Company law	Traffic safety, accident prevention and procedure
Social legislation	
Taxation	

CHAPTER 2
(Module B)
Drivers' Hours and Records

It is essential, in order to operate within the law and, incidentally, to pass the CPC examination, for a transport operator or manager to have a thorough knowledge of the regulations governing drivers' hours and records.

Drivers' Hours

Do the regulations cover only those people employed as drivers?
Under the regulations a driver is *any person* who drives a goods vehicle in the course of his employment.

This means not only those people who drive regularly but also part time drivers such as maintenance staff and technicans, and employees who have to use a goods vehicle as a means of transporting themselves and their equipment or carrying out errands in the course of the owner's business.

Is there a precise meaning to "driving", for the purpose of these regulations?
Driving means sitting at the controls of a goods vehicle for the purpose of controlling its movement when it is either moving, or stationary with the engine running.

What are the regulations concerning drivers' hours, rest periods, etc?
Drivers' hours of work are governed by EC Regulation 3820/85 and British domestic regulations in the form of the Transport Act 1968 and statutory instruments arising therefrom.

Do these regulations cover all types of goods vehicle operations?
Goods vehicles operations fall into four basic categories:

1. Community regulated operations
2. International operations outside the scope of the "Community regulated" operations
3. Domestic operations
4. Mixed driving

and the regulations apply, in some form or another, to drivers of all goods vehicles.

What operations do each of these categories cover?
1. Community regulated operations are covered by EC Regulation 3820/85 and apply to goods vehicles exceeding 3.5 tonnes gross plated weight, including the weight of any trailer drawn, engaged in commercial operations in Great Britain and other Member States of the EC.
2. International operations using goods vehicles exceeding 3.5 tonnes gross plated weight, including the weight of any trailer drawn, between Great Britain and those countries party to the AETR agreement who are not also members of the Community (see pages 168-9).
3. Domestic operations are covered by the Transport Act 1968 and apply to vehicles which are exempt from EC regulations, including those below 3.5 tonnes gross

plated weight and specialised vehicles used by public authorities, unless also exempt under some other legislation.
4. Mixed driving regulations apply when drivers are engaged in a mixture of either of the above operations during the working day or week.

What aspects of operation are covered by the regulations?
The aspects covered are: maximum driving periods and breaks; daily driving periods; fortnightly driving periods; daily rest periods; and weekly rest periods.

Community Regulated

1. Maximum driving periods
No driver may drive for more than a total of **4½ hours** after which a break must be taken.

How long must a break last?
A break must last for at least **45 minutes** after a total of 4½ hours' driving. It can, however, be split into two or three shorter periods of not less than 15 minutes duration, totalling 45 minutes, if this is preferred and spread over the driving period or immediately following it. During a break the driver must not do any other work. Waiting time, however, and time spent in the passenger seat of a vehicle in motion, on a ferry or a train, is not regarded as other work.

2. Daily driving periods
The daily driving period must not exceed **nine hours,** but this may be extended to **10 hours** on two days per week.

3. Weekly and fortnightly driving periods
After **six** daily driving periods a driver must take a weekly rest period. Therefore, if he takes advantage of the concession to increase his total driving time twice in the week, he can total **56 hours** driving but over a fortnight he must not exceed **90 hours.**

Are there any exemptions from these regulations?
There are a number of exemptions and modifications to these regulations but generally these apply only to specialised vehicles or special traffics and to include them at this point would only confuse and complicate your studies.

4. Daily rest period
(a) A driver must have a daily rest period of not less than **11 consecutive hours** in 24 hours.
(b) This period may be reduced to a minimum of **nine consecutive hours** in 24 not more than three days a week.
(c) Any reduction in the daily rest must be made up before the end of the following week.

The daily rest may be taken in the vehicle provided it is fitted with a bunk and the vehicle is stationary.

NB As a concession, on days when the rest is not reduced, it may be taken in two or three separate periods (minimum one hour) during the 24 hours, one period of which must be of at least **eight consecutive hours**. When the daily rest period is split in this manner the minimum length of the daily rest must be increased to **12**

Are there any exceptions to the daily rest period rules?
Yes! Where a vehicle is double-manned each driver must have a rest period of not less than **eight consecutive hours** during each period of **30 hours.**

5. Weekly rest periods

During each week a *daily rest period* must be extended into a weekly rest period which must total **45 consecutive hours**. This may be reduced, however, to **36 consecutive hours** if taken where the vehicle is normally based, or to a minimum of **24 consecutive hours** if taken elsewhere. Each reduced rest period must be made good by the driver taking an equivalent rest period *en bloc* before the end of the *third week* following the week in question.

A weekly rest period beginning in one week and continuing into the next can be attached to either week.

Any compensatory rest period taken for the reduced daily and/or weekly rest periods must be attached to another rest period of at least **eight hours** and be granted, at the request of the driver, at the vehicle's parking place or driver's base.

NB A week is a fixed week commencing 00.00 hours Monday to 24.00 hours Sunday.

What provisions are there for journeys involving the use of ferries or trains?

Where journeys involve the use of ferries or trains, crew members may interrupt their daily rest periods not more than once, provided they comply with the following conditions:

   (a) that part of the daily rest period spent on land may be taken before or after that part of the daily rest period taken on board the ferry or train

   (b) the period between two parts must be as short as possible and must not exceed **one hour** before embarkation or after disembarkation and completion of custom formalities

   (c) crew members must have access to a bunk or couchette during both parts of the rest period

   (d) where the daily rest period is interrupted in this way, it must be increased by two hours

   (e) when time spent on a ferry or train is not counted as part of the daily rest period it will, instead, be regarded as a break.

Is there provision for unavoidable delays?

In the event of an emergency or in circumstances outside a driver's control the driving and rest periods may be waived to allow a driver to reach a suitable stopping place but only to the extent necessary to ensure the safety of persons, the vehicle or its load. Details of the occurrence must be noted on the tachograph chart.

What differences are there for vehicles operating under "Domestic" regulations?

Maximum daily driving is 10 hours. Maximum daily duty is 11 hours.

"Off the road" driving

Driving done off the road, eg on a farm, at a quarry or building site, does not count as driving time but as part of the working time.

Hours of Work Records

What records of drivers' hours must be kept?

Drivers of most goods vehicles over 3.5 tonnes permissible maximum weight are required to keep records of the time they spend driving, taking breaks and rest periods and other periods of work.

Can a vehicle, normally used for the carriage of goods, be used for non-business purposes without the need to keep records?
Whenever a driver is driving a vehicle which comes within the scope of the EC regulations, even if it is being driven for recreational purposes, a record must be kept of that driving and the hours taken into account when assessing daily, weekly or fortnightly driving periods.

What is the prescribed method of keeping drivers' hours of work records?
Unless exempted, all goods vehicles exceeding 3.5 tonnes gross weight (including the weight of any trailer drawn) must be fitted with an EC approved tachograph to record not only the driver's hours but also, if a second driver is carried, his working periods.

Do tachographs fulfil any purpose other than recording drivers' hours?
In addition to providing useful management information, the record they provide may be used as evidence in prosecutions for driving offences. They may also be used to rebut allegations, eg by showing that a vehicle could not possibly have been in a certain location at a specific time, or that waiting times or speed limits had not been exceeded.

What law governs the fitting and use of tachographs?
The appropriate law is contained in EC Regulation 3821/85.

Exactly what information does the tachograph record?
It records the following:
    (a) the distance travelled by the vehicle
    (b) the speed of the vehicle
    (c) the driving time
    (d) periods of other work and the availability of driver(s)
    (e) breaks in work and daily rest periods
    (f) the opening of the tachograph case.

Does the tachograph record all these things simultaneously?
Yes! The instrument combines clock, speedometer and distance recorder mechanisms. A permanent record of time, speed and distance is made by separate styli pressing on a special chart. The chart rotates with the clock, while the styli are actuated by the vehicle's movements.

How do these styli mark the charts?
The record charts (discs) are composed of several layers. Under the white surface layer is a coloured layer which is revealed as the sharp point of each stylus presses through the surface layer.

How are these different records made?
Each stylus records on a separate field or zone of the tachograph chart (disc) and makes its own distinctive trace as follows:

    (a) the distance stylus moves up and down within a specific field on the chart, making a series of Vs. Each upwards or downwards stroke equals 5km

(b) the speed stylus moves upwards within its field as speed increases and downwards as speed decreases, producing an irregular trace. When the vehicle is stationary a continuous level line is recorded
(c) the driving time, periods of other work, breaks in work and rest periods are all recorded by the same stylus but on different tracks within the same field. When the vehicle is moving a thick trace is made; when stationary the trace is quite distinctly thinner, even if the engine is running
(d) when the tachograph case is opened each of the styli makes a slight mark at right angles to the direction of the trace made when the vehicle is stationary.

See page 16 for an example of a tachograph disc.

How is the stylus moved from the "driving track" to a track recording other work?
The driver turns a knob or key (depending on the type of tachograph) which causes the driving time stylus to move to the required track.

What period of time does one record cover?
Each record covers 24 hours.

Should a driver adjust the tachograph clock when entering another time zone?
No! The time shown on the clock must remain on the time zone of the country where the vehicle is registered.

When there are two drivers, can both their times be recorded?
Yes! In fact this is a specific requirement. A separate chart inside the tachograph records the time of the second driver.

Does the driver have to insert any information on the record chart?
Since the charts are personal logs, each driver must complete the chart by inserting the following information in the space provided in the centre field of the chart:
(a) surname and first name
(b) date and place of commencement and finish of chart
(c) registration number of each vehicle used
(d) the odometer reading at:
   (i) the start of the first journey recorded on the chart
   (ii) the start of each working day
   (iii) the end of each working day
   (iv) the end of the last journey recorded on the chart
   (v) if more than one vehicle is used during the working day, the respective readings on each vehicle
(e) the time of any change of vehicle.

What happens if the driver changes vehicle during a period of work?
He must take his record chart with him and insert it in the tachograph of the new vehicle.

Illustration of a Completed Tachograph Chart

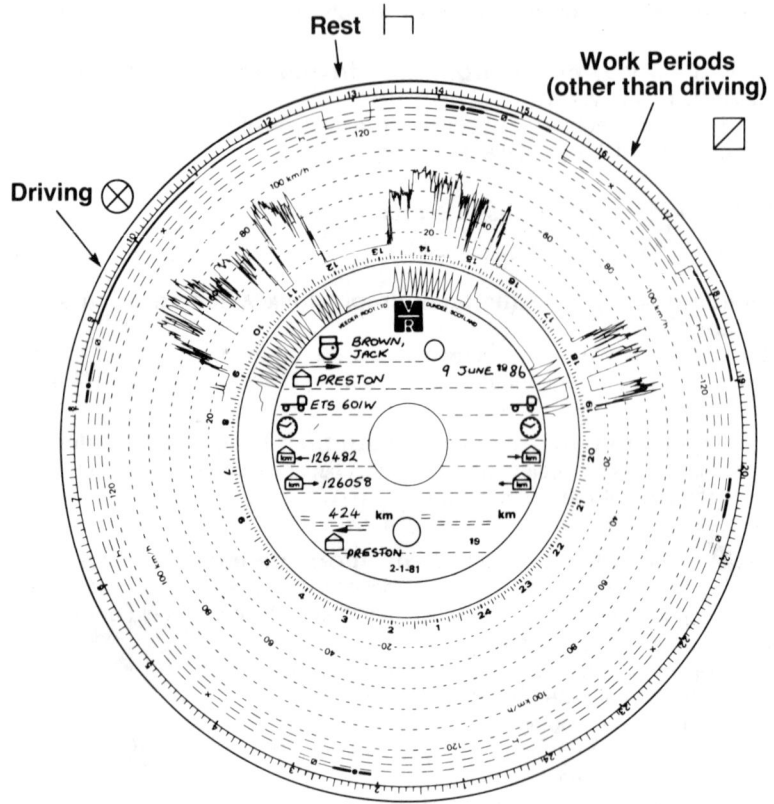

Suppose the new vehicle is fitted with a different type of tachograph which will not accept the type of chart he is using?
If his chart is not compatible he must insert one which is and retain both charts as a record of his day's work.

How can the driver keep records if his tachograph breaks down?
If the tachograph is inoperable the driver must mark on the record chart or on a temporary sheet attached to the record chart all pertinent information as required by the regulations.

For how long should a driver retain his completed record charts?
He must retain completed charts for the current week and also for the last day of the previous week on which he drove. He must give them to his employer within 21 days.

What does the employer do with the charts?
He must make periodic checks to ensure that the regulations are being observed and file them in a safe place for at least one year.

What are the regulations regarding inspection of tachograph records?
A Department of Transport examiner or uniformed police officer can inspect the tachograph and employee's record charts and detain a vehicle for as long as is necessary for this purpose. He may also remove charts for further examination.

Premises in which vehicles and records, etc are kept may be entered at any reasonable time for inspection purposes. Records suspected of being false may be removed and can be held for up to six months.

What should a driver do if his record chart is removed by an authorised person?
It is recommended that a receipt be obtained showing the date, time and name of the person. He should also be asked to record the circumstances on the replacement chart in case further checks take place during the working period.

Is it possible for an authorised person to inspect a tachograph chart without removing it from the instrument?
Yes! The EC regulations require the tachograph to be designed in such a way that an inspecting officer, after opening the equipment, can read the recordings for a period of nine hours preceding the check without handling the tachograph disc.

Who is responsible for ensuring that a tachograph is in working order?
The employer and driver(s) must ensure that the equipment is in working order and that seals remain intact. Seals may be broken only in cases of absolute necessity, which will have to be proved.

What is the position when a driver has more than one employer?
He must notify each employer of the name and address of the other and all charts used must be returned to his first employer, regardless of who issued them.

Can a driver obtain copies of his tachograph charts?
Employers have a duty to provide copies of the charts to drivers if they request them.

What happens in the event of a breakdown or faulty operation of the tachograph?
Repairs must be effected by an approved tachograph centre as soon as circumstances permit but if the vehicle is likely to be away from its depot for more than a week the instrument must be repaired en route.

Where, in the vehicle, is the tachograph fitted?
It is usually fitted on the vehicle's dashboard but if this is not possible it must be fitted in some other convenient visible position.

Can any mechanic fit a tachograph to a vehicle?
No! Only persons who are officially approved, ie at approved centres, are able to install and repair the instruments.

How is this checked?
All work must be sealed by the person carrying it out and a statutory register is maintained of approved workshops and their respective seal identification marks.

Why is it necessary to have approved workshops for the installation, calibration and repair of tachographs?
It is essential that the information recorded is accurate and, therefore, instruments must be calibrated before they can legally conform with EC regulations.

What degrees of accuracy are required of the tachograph when in use?
It must be accurate:
   (a) to plus or minus ($\pm$) 6 kph of the actual speed at all speeds
   (b) to 4% more or less than the real distance when that distance is at least 1km
   (c) time, ± 2 minutes per day or ± 10 minutes per 7 days.

How is evidence supplied that a tachograph fitted to a vehicle conforms with the regulations?
When a tachograph carries an installation plaque and has been sealed by an approved centre, it is presumed to conform with the EC regulations.

When must a tachograph be re-calibrated?
Whenever repairs to the vehicle necessitate breaking the seals, if the instrument fails, or if different size wheels or tyres are fitted which alter the circumference of the tyres, re-calibration and re-sealing will be necessary. In the unlikely event that none of these things occur re-calibration will be necessary every six years.

Are any other forms of inspection necessary?
In addition to routine checks by the driver and/or fitting staff to ensure that the instrument is in apparent good working order, the regulations require the instrument to be checked every two years and this work must be carried out at an approved tachograph centre. A "two yearly inspection" plaque will be attached to the inside of the tachograph head when this work has been carried out.

Should the vehicle be laden or unladen when sent for tachograph calibration or repair?
The vehicle should be unladen.

Which vehicles are exempt from the requirement concerning the fitting and use of tachographs to record drivers' hours, etc?
The following exemptions apply:

A. Exemptions which apply to both national and international journeys
1. Goods vehicles not exceeding 3.5 tonnes maximum permissible weight (including any trailer or semi-trailer).
2. Vehicles used for the carriage of passengers constructed or equipped to carry not more than nine persons including the driver.
3. Vehicles with a maximum authorised speed not exceeding 30 kph.
4. Vehicles used by or under the control of the armed services, civil defence, fire services and forces responsible for maintaining public order.
5. Vehicles used in connection with the sewerage, flood protection, water, gas and electricity services, highway maintenance and control, refuse collection and disposal, telegraph and telephone services, carriage of postal articles, radio and television broadcasting and the detection of radio or television transmitters or receivers. **Note:** Vehicles used for the carriage of postal articles on national transport operations must have tachographs fitted *except* for Post Office vehicles used for the carriage of letters.
6. Vehicles used in emergency or rescue operations.
7. Specialised vehicles used for medical purposes.
8. Vehicles carrying circus and funfair equipment.
9. Specialised breakdown vehicles.
10. Vehicles undergoing road tests for technical development, repair or maintenance purposes and new or rebuilt vehicles which are not yet in service.
11. Vehicles used for the non-commerical carriage of goods for personal use.
12. Vehicles used for milk collection from farms and the return to farms of milk containers or milk products intended for animal feed.

B. Exemptions which apply to national journeys only
13. Vehicles used for the carriage of passengers and constructed or equipped to carry not more than 17 persons including the driver and intended for that purpose.
14. Vehicles which are being used by a public authority to provide public services which are *not in competition with professional road hauliers*.
15. Vehicles being used by agricultural, horticultural, forestry or fishery undertakings to carry goods within a 50km radius of the place where they are normally based, including local administrative areas, the centres of which are situated within that radius. **Note:** where fishery undertakings are concerned this only applies to the carriage of live fish, or a catch which has not been processed or treated (other than frozen) from the place of landing to the place where it is to be processed or treated.
16. Vehicles carrying animal waste or carcasses which are **not** intended for human consumption.

17. Vehicles carrying live animals between a farm and a local market or from a local market to a local slaughterhouse.
18. Vehicles being used as shops at a local market, for door-to-door selling, mobile banking, exchange or savings transactions, for worship, for the lending of books, records or cassettes, or for cultural events or exhibitions. **Note:** such vehicles must be specially fitted for the use in question.
19. A vehicle carrying goods having a permissible maximum weight not exceeding 7.5 tonnes and carrying material or equipment for the driver's use in the course of his work within a 50km radius of the place where the vehicle is normally based and provided driving the vehicle is not the driver's main activity.
20. Vehicles operating exclusively on an island not exceeding 2300 square kilometres in area and which is not connected to the rest of Great Britain by a bridge, ford or tunnel.
21. A vehicle propelled by gas produced on the vehicle or a vehicle propelled by electricity, having a permissible maximum weight not exceeding 7.5 tonnes.
22. A vehicle being used for driving instruction with a view to obtaining a driving licence. **Note:** this does not apply if the vehicle or any trailer or semi-trailer attached to it is carrying goods on a journey for hire or reward or for, or in connection with, any trade or business.
23. Tractors which are used exclusively for agricultural and forestry work.
24. Vehicles being used by the Royal National Lifeboat Institution for hauling lifeboats.
25. A vehicle manufactured before January 1, 1947.
26. A vehicle propelled by steam.
27. A vehicle being used for collecting sea coal. **Note**: this exemption applies to the fitting and use of tachographs only.

Does this mean that drivers of these vehicles are exempt from all requirements to keep "hours of work" records?

No! Although exempt under EC regulations from fitting tachographs and keeping records, British domestic legislation applies to drivers of many of these vehicles operated wholly within Great Britain and drivers must observe the requirements of the Transport Act 1968, Part VI, unless they are covered by some other exemption.

What "other exemptions" are there from British domestic legislation?

Exempt from having to keep written records are:
  (a) drivers operating tachographs. Although exempt under EC regulations from the necessity to fit and use tachographs, many operators prefer to do so rather than keep written records and also to standardise procedures when they also operate vehicles to which the EC regulations do apply
  (b) drivers operating under the British domestic rules of the drivers' hours regulations in the following circumstances:
    (i) part time driving for not more than four hours on any day of the week and not going outside a radius of 50km from the operating centre
    (ii) driving goods vehicles not requiring an "O" licence (this does not apply to vehicles of the Crown which would normally require an "O" licence had they not been Crown property).

What kind of written records must be kept by those who are not exempt?
Drivers are required to keep individual record books in duplicate format.

Is the employer required to check the record book?
Yes. The driver must return the book within **7 days** of each week for checking, countersigning, and removal and filing of the duplicate sheets.

What happens to the book when it is full?
After the last entries have been checked and countersigned the book is returned to the driver who must retain it for **14 days**. After this the book must be returned to the employer, to be filed together with the duplicate sheets and retained for at least **one year**.

Driving Licences

Who must hold a driving licence?
To drive any particular class of motor vehicle a person must hold a driving licence which authorises him to drive that class (Road Traffic Act 1972).

How are driving licences obtained?
Driving licences are granted upon passing the statutory test of competence to drive, or upon having held a licence, not being a provisional licence, for the previous 10 years either in Great Britain, Northern Ireland, the Isle of Man or the Channel Islands and not being, at the time of the application, disqualified from holding a licence.

What types of licence are there?
The types of driving licences include:
  (a) the provisional licence
  (b) the ordinary or full driving licence
  (c) the Public Service Vehicle Drivers' Licence
  (d) the Heavy Goods Vehicle Drivers' Licence
  (e) Visitor's Driving Permit
  (f) International Driving Permit

but see page 27 for information on the changes in the licensing system due to take effect at the beginning of 1991.

What is the purpose of a provisional licence?
The purpose of a provisional licence is to allow a vehicle to be taken on the road by a person learning to drive and taking the regulation driving test.

What specific regulations apply only to "learner" drivers?
The holder of a provisional licence may drive a vehicle only when accompanied by and under the supervision of a qualified driver. The vehicle must display "L" plates which are clearly visible within a reasonable distance from both front and back of the vehicle.

What are the minimum age limits for driving motor vehicles?
No person under the age of 16 is allowed to drive a motor vehicle on the road. The minimum ages for driving the various classes of vehicles are:

Moped, engine capacity n.e. 50cc...................................... 16 years
Motor scooter, motor cycle and *three-wheel car* .... 17 years

Small passenger vehicle, ie constructed or adapted to carry not more than nine persons including the driver or *small goods vehicle* ie constructed or adapted to carry or to haul goods and not adapted to carry more than nine persons including the driver and not exceeding 3.5 tonnes permissible maximum weight (including any trailer) .... 17 years
Medium-sized goods vehicle, ie constructed or adapted to carry or to haul goods and not adapted to carry more than nine persons including the driver and exceeding 3.5 tonnes but not 7.5 tonnes permissible maximum weight (including any trailer) .... 18 years

Other motor vehicle, ie goods vehicle exceeding 7.5 tonnes permissible maximum weight (including any trailer); articulated vehicle........ 21 years*

The age limits do not apply to vehicles owned or driven under orders of HM Forces.
*See "Young HGV Driver Training Scheme" (page 26).

Is there any age limit for drivers' mates?
Yes! EC Regulation 3820/85 specifies that drivers' mates must be at least 18 years of age.

What are the regulations regarding notification of disabilities?
All licence holders are obliged to notify the Driver and Vehicle Licensing Centre (DVLC) at Swansea of the onset (or the worsening) of any disability which is, or is expected to become, relevant to safe driving.

Are sufferers from heart conditions permitted to drive?
Persons subject to sudden fainting or giddiness, who have not previously been allowed to drive, may be granted a driving licence provided that this liability is corrected by the fitting of a cardiac pacemaker and that other conditions are satisfied, ie that the person is unlikely to be a source of danger and that adequate arrangements have been made to receive regular medical supervision by a cardiologist (such supervision continuing throughout the period of the licence) and that such arrangements are being complied with.

When must a driving licence be produced?
1. An ordinary driving licence must be produced:
    (a) on request by a police officer or, if it cannot be produced at the time, within **seven days** at a police station nominated by the driver
    (b) at a magistrate's court when endorsement is ordered following conviction of an offence
    (c) when applying for an HGV licence
    (d) on request by a traffic warden employed at a car pound if he has reason to believe an offence concerning obstruction, parking, loading or unloading a vehicle on a road has been committed.

2. An HGV licence must be produced:
    (a) on request by a police officer or, if it cannot be produced at the time, within **seven days** at a police station nominated by the driver
    (b) on request by a Department of Transport examiner or, if it cannot be produced at the time, within **10 days** at the office of the examiner or at an office of a specified Licensing Authority (LA)

(c) on the request of the Licensing Authority, within **10 days** together with the driver's ordinary driving licence
(d) when applying for a renewal of an HGV licence.

NB Documents may be produced later if it is not reasonably practicable to produce them within the specified times.

What are the regulations governing the licensing of drivers of heavy goods vehicles?

No person may drive a heavy goods vehicle unless he is the holder of a driving licence appropriate to that class of vehicle, in addition to his ordinary driving licence.

What are an employer's responsibilities in connection with the licences held by his drivers?

It is an offence to cause, or permit, any person to drive a motor vehicle without a current driving licence, or a licence for a particular class of vehicle, or if disqualified from driving. Both *drivers and employers* must, therefore, know and understand their respective responsibilities.

The law states that drivers must not be allowed to drive vehicles under the above quoted conditions, nor under the specified age limits. There is no redress against a charge of employing drivers under these circumstances. Employers should, therefore, exercise strict documentary checks on the recruitment or employment of drivers and institute periodic checks to ensure that the licences are still valid, e g that the driver has not been disqualified; or that because of penalty points accumulated a further conviction could result in disqualification.

How is a heavy goods vehicle defined?

A heavy goods vehicle is defined as:
 (a) an articulated vehicle **exceeding 7.5 tonnes** permissible maximum weight
 (b) a large goods vehicle, ie a motor vehicle (not being an articulated vehicle) constructed or adapted to carry or haul goods and having a permissible maximum weight (including any trailer) **exceeding 7.5 tonnes.**

What are the application procedures for HGV licences and driving tests?

Applications for a licence should be made on the appropriate form and should be submitted to the Licensing Authority in the area in which the applicant lives not more than two months before the date from which the licence is to commence.

What is the duration of an HGV licence?

A full HGV licence is valid for 3 years. A provisional HGV licence is valid for 6 months.

Is the applicant required to prove his fitness?

Yes! The application form for a licence includes a medical certificate which must be completed by a registered medical practitioner.

Who pays for the medical examination?

This must be paid for by the applicant.

How often must medical certificates be provided?

The Licensing Authority (LA) will call for further medical certificates at the age of 60, on each renewal after that and at every other time if there is any reason to doubt the driver's fitness.

NB The Department of Transport is proposing to reduce the age for medical certificates from 60 to 45 and this is due to take effect from the beginning of 1991.

Who issues the application forms?
These can be obtained by applying to the Department of Transport Traffic Area Offices.

Can the Licensing Authority refuse to grant an HGV licence other than on medical grounds?
Yes! The decision whether the applicant is a fit person to hold an HGV licence rests entirely with the Licensing Authority.

In reaching its decision the LA will take particular note of any convictions during the previous three years for motoring offences, drivers' hours and records offences relating to the road-worthiness or loading of vehicles and offences connected with driving under the influence of drink or drugs within 10 years of the application. The driver must declare particulars of these convictions on his application form for an HGV licence. Failure to declare them, or any false statement made in connection with the application, can incur a fine, or four months' imprisonment, or both.

Can the LA suspend, revoke or disqualify an HGV driver at any other time?
The LAs have the power to suspend or revoke HGV licences and to suspend persons from holding such licences on the grounds of misconduct or physical disability.

Is there any appeal against the LA's decision?
If the LA refuses to grant an application for an HGV licence, or revokes, suspends or limits it, the aggrieved person is entitled to appeal against the decision under the Road Traffic Act 1972. He may either appeal in writing to the LA to reconsider its decision and then, if this is refused appeal to a magistrate's court (or to the Sheriff in Scotland) or he can appeal direct to the magistrate or Sheriff.

Can a driver, disqualified from holding an HGV licence, apply to have the disqualification removed before the disqualification period has expired?
Yes! In the same way and after the same periods of time that a driver disqualified from holding an ordinary driving licence may apply (see page 40), except that in the case of HGV licences the application must be made to the Licensing Authority.

Are there different classes of HGV licences?
In order to take account of the varying skills and degrees of skill required to drive different types of heavy goods vehicle, there are six classes of heavy goods vehicle licence:

For the purposes of the definitions below:

(a) where a vehicle is fitted with two wheels in line transversely and the distance between the centres of their respective areas of contact with the road is less than 18 inches they shall be regarded as only one wheel

(b) a vehicle with automatic transmission shall mean a vehicle in which the driver is not provided with any means whereby he may, independently of the use of the accelerator or the brakes, gradually vary the proportion of the power being produced by the engine which is transmitted to the road wheels of the vehicle.

Class	Definition	Additional classes
1	an articulated vehicle, without automatic transmission	1A, 2, 2A, 3 & 3A
1A	an articulated vehicle, with automatic transmission	2A & 3A
2	a heavy goods vehicle, without automatic transmission, other than an articulated vehicle designed and constructed to have more than four wheels in contact with the road surface	2A, 3 & 3A
2A	a heavy goods vehicle, with automatic transmission, other than an articulated vehicle designed and constructed to have more than four wheels in contact with the road surface	3A
3	a heavy goods vehicle, without automatic transmission, other than an articulated vehicle designed and constructed to have not more than four wheels in contact with the road surface	3A
3A	a heavy goods vehicle, with automatic transmission, other than an articulated vehicle designed and constructed to have not more than four wheels in contact with the road surface	

Who provides the test vehicle?

The applicant for a test must provide a vehicle of the appropriate class, which must be unladen and have an enclosed cab.

What are the age limits for HGV drivers?

The applicant must be at least 21 years old at the starting date for the licence, except a participant in the Young HGV Driver Training Scheme when a lower age limit applies.

Are there any special requirements in respect of trainee drivers?

Trainees driving heavy goods vehicles with a provisional licence must be accompanied by a fully qualified licence holder. The holder of a provisional licence may not drive a heavy goods vehicle towing a trailer and must display "L" plates.

Can a driver who has not passed his test for an ordinary driving licence take an HGV test?

He can take both tests simultaneously but while under instruction must display both ordinary and HGV "L" plates. (This arrangement will cease in 1991 when a new licensing system is due to come into force – see page 27.)

What is the effect of disqualification on a driver's HGV licence?

When a driver is disqualified from driving he loses his *ordinary* driving licence and is therefore not allowed to drive any class of motor vehicle on a public road. It does not matter what class of vehicle he was driving at the time of the offence (Road Traffic Act 1972 s.93).

What happens to his HGV licence?
An HGV driver who has been disqualified must notify details of the disqualification and deliver the HGV licence to the Licensing Authority in whose area he resides.

What must he do to obtain the return of his HGV licence when the period of disqualification is over?
At the end of the disqualification period, the driver should produce his ordinary driving licence and request the restoration of the HGV driving licence.

Will his HGV driving licence be automatically returned to him?
The Licensing Authority may, if it considers it desirable, call the applicant before a public inquiry into the events which led to the disqualification, after which it may decide that the applicant must wait a further period before applying again, or that he must take an HGV driving test before he can regain his licence.

A driver aggrieved by the Licensing Authority's refusal to restore his HGV licence may appeal to the magistrate's court (RTA 1972).

Are HGV licences obtained in other EC countries valid in Great Britain?
There are reciprocal arrangements for journeys to and from Community countries and many other countries, although some non-Community countries insist upon an International Driving Permit. The situation is different when a driver, qualified in another Community country, wishes to take up permanent residence in Great Britain. He need not take a British HGV test provided that he satisfies certain conditions.

What conditions must be satisfied?
He can obtain a British HGV licence without having to take a test, provided that:
- (a) he is qualified to drive heavy goods vehicles having taken a test in a Community country or holds a Community licence for vehicles of the equivalent class
- (b) he has been granted an ordinary British driving licence
- (c) he has been resident here for not more than 18 months.

He must also be able to satisfy the authorities that at the time he took up permanent residence in this country he had been in the habit of driving vehicles of the type for which he is making application:
- (a) for at least six months during the last 18 months
- (b) for at least one year during the last three years
- (c) for periods which, taken together, satisfy the requirements in either (a) or (b) above.

What is the Young HGV Driver Training Scheme?
This is a scheme which enables young drivers between the ages of 18 and 21 to undertake training as heavy goods vehicle drivers.

Who operates the scheme?
The training scheme is administered by the National Joint Training Committee which consists of representatives from the Department of Transport, the Road Transport Industry Training Board (RTITB), the Road Haulage Association (RHA), the Freight Transport Association (FTA), the Training Services Department and the trade unions involved in road transport activities.

What conditions must be satisfied by an applicant for a trainee heavy goods vehicle licence?

A person between the ages of 18 and 21 may apply for a trainee heavy goods vehicle licence provided that:

(a) he holds a clean ordinary driving licence
(b) he has entered into an agreement with an approved employer, ie one registered with the National Joint Training Committee, to undertake practical training by a qualified instructor in accordance with a recognised syllabus.

NB The licence can be withdrawn if the driver is convicted of road traffic offences which result in his ordinary driving licence being endorsed with more than three penalty points.

When can the trainee drive heavy goods vehicles?

The trainee HGV licence entitles the holder to drive heavy goods vehicles:

(a) *only* for his employer, *or*
(b) when on a full time course at an approved training establishment.

The names and addresses of both the employer and the training establishment will be shown on the licence.

How does the scheme work?

Trainees progress at yearly intervals from four-wheeled rigid (Class III) vehicles at age 18, to multi-wheeled rigid (Class II) vehicles, to articulated (Class I) vehicles, provided each part of the training course is completed and the driving test on each class of vehicle has been passed.

A driver may not drive a vehicle (including an articulated vehicle) which draws a trailer until he is 21, except under supervision.

In addition to training for his licences, the programme includes an element of further education. This lasts for a period of one year or, if desired it can be spread over a longer period. This is designed to teach the trainee the basic information a driver must know to carry out his duties legally and safely. The opportunity is taken to reinforce the elements of reading and writing in a job related manner. The further education section of the programme also includes the elements of transport engineering, ie basic servicing, maintenance and fault-finding and a short course on first-aid.

An examination is held on the further education aspects of the programme and a certificate is awarded to successful candidates. Failure in the examination does not disqualify the trainee from obtaining an HGV licence.

Unified Driver Licensing System

The types of licences posed by the question "What types of licences are there?" on page 21 and listed under (a) to (d) will change in 1991 when a new unified driver licensing system will operate. The ordinary driving licence and vocational licences will be replaced (although holders of the existing ordinary licence will not receive a new style licence unless it has to be returned to DVLC for alteration or amendment) by a single document which will show the categories of vehicle the holder is entitled to drive. These categories are as follows –

Category A – Motor cycles with or without sidecar
Category B – Motor vehicles with a maximum authorised mass (weight) not exceeding 3500kg and having not more than nine seats including the driver (cars and light vans)

Category C – Motor vehicles other than those in category D and whose maximum authorised mass exceeds 3500kg (goods vehicles, etc)

Category D – Motor vehicles used for the carriage of passengers and having more than nine seats including the driver (minibuses, buses, coaches)

Category E – Combinations of vehicles of which the tractor is in a category or categories for which the driver is licensed (B, C and D) but which are not themselves in that category or categories (articulated vehicles, vehicles towing trailers, etc where the trailer exceeds 750 kg maximum authorised mass).

A trailer up to 750kg maximum authorised mass may be drawn by vehicles covered by categories B, C and D.

Category C may be sub-divided to cover vehicles exceeding 3500kg up to 7500kg maximum authorised mass, eg category C1.

Category D may be sub-divided to cover vehicles exceeding nine but not exceeding 17 seats, eg category D1.

Each category has its own test standards and applicants must have passed a category B test before they can apply to drive larger vehicles.

Categories C, D and E will cover the existing HGV/PSV drivers' licences and as mentioned above categories C and D may be sub-divided to differentiate between the lighter and heavier vehicles on mass (weight) or seating capacity. Also, holders of licences for categories C, D and E will be authorised to drive such vehicles up to the age of 45 after which renewals will have to be applied for every five years up to the age of 65 and yearly thereafter. All renewals from age 45 onwards will have to be accompanied by a medical certificate.

CHAPTER 3
(Modules A and B)
General Traffic Regulations
Speed Limits

What are the speed limits at present in force on Britain's roads?
Speed limits vary according to the class of road and the category of the vehicle.
  Motor vehicles may not be driven on restricted roads at speeds exceeding the specified limits, usually 30 mph, but these may be increased on particular roads in which case this will be indicated by appropriate traffic signs. Speed limits apply to roads and vehicles; where these are different the lowest applies.
  The maximum speed limit on motorways and dual carriageways is 70 mph and on single carriageway roads 60 mph, unless lower speeds are in force and unless the class of vehicle is already restricted to lower limits.

What are the speed limits which apply to goods vehicles?
The following is a general summary of the limits relating to goods vehicles:

Class of vehicle	Motor-ways	Dual Carriage-ways	Other roads
Passenger vehicle, motor caravan or dual-purpose vehicle not drawing a trailer being a vehicle exceeding 3.05 tonnes unladen weight **or** adapted to carry more than eight passengers:			
(a) if not exceeding 12m in overall length	70	60*	50*
(b) if exceeding 12m in overall length	60	60*	50*
Passenger vehicle, motor caravan, car-derived van or dual-purpose vehicle drawing one trailer	60	60*	50*
Rigid goods vehicle not exceeding 7.5 tonnes gross vehicle weight and not drawing a trailer	70	60*	50*
Articulated goods vehicle not exceeding 7.5 tonnes maximum laden weight or rigid goods vehicle drawing one trailer where the aggregate maximum laden weight of vehicle and trailer does not exceed 7.5 tonnes	60	60*	50*
Articulated goods vehicle exceeding 7.5 tonnes gross train weight, rigid goods vehicle exceeding 7.5 tonnes gross vehicle weight without trailer or when drawing a trailer the aggregate maximum laden weight of vehicle and trailer exceeds 7.5 tonnes	60	50*	40*
Motor vehicle drawing more than one trailer	40	20	20

*Provided the dual carriageway or other road is not subject to a lower limit.

Class of vehicle	Motor-ways	Dual Carriage-ways	Other roads
Motor tractor (other than industrial tractor), light locomotive or heavy locomotive:			
(a) provided they are equipped with suitable and sufficient springs between wheels and frames and unless the body affords protection, they are fitted with wings, etc for trapping mud or water thrown up by the wheels (if drawing a trailer to which the foregoing provisions also apply)	40	30	30
(b) in any other case	20	20	20
Works truck	18	18	18
Industrial tractor	n/a	18	18

Maximum speed on any road

Vehicles other than track-laying vehicles, not fitted with pneumatic tyres on all wheels:
  (a) motor vehicle or motor vehicle drawing one or more trailers where:
     (i) every wheel of the vehicle or combination is fitted with a resilient tyre   20
     (ii) at least one wheel is fitted with a resilient tyre and the remainder are fitted with pneumatic tyres   20
     (iii) any wheel of the vehicle or vehicle combination is not fitted with either a pneumatic or resilient tyre   5

Locomotives, engineering plant, dump trucks and other earth moving machinery are permitted to use motorways provided they can attain a speed of 25 mph on the level when unladen.

On motorways a goods vehicle exceeding 7.5 tonnes gross weight (2540kg unladen weight) and any vehicle drawing a trailer, is not allowed to use the outside lane of a motorway having three or more lanes, except when passing an abnormally wide load.

Are there particular speed limits for "Special Type" vehicles?

The maximum speeds depend upon the class of road and the category* of the special type vehicle, viz:

	Motor-ways	Dual Carriage-ways	Other roads
Category 1	60	50	40
Category 2	40	35	30
Category 3	30	25	20
Vehicles carrying wide loads exceeding 4.3m but not exceeding 6.1m	30	25	20

*See Chapter 6.

Are there any exemptions to these speed limits?
Yes! Vehicles being used for fire brigade, ambulance or police purposes are exempt from speed limits if such limits are likely to hinder their use.

What are the special rules of conduct regarding driving in conditions where visibility is seriously reduced?
If visibility is poor during the daytime due to adverse weather conditions such as fog, snow, heavy rain, mist or spray, drivers of all moving vehicles must switch on both side and headlamps or side lights and a matched pair of fog lights.

Parking, Loading and Unloading

What regulations govern the parking, loading and unloading of goods vehicles?
Unfortunately, like so much other legislation governing the operation of goods vehicles, the regulations are not to be found in a single convenient source but in various pieces of legislation, Ministerial orders and local by-laws.

Are there any general requirements which must be observed?
There is a complete prohibition on stopping on uncontrolled pedestrian crossings or in the approach zone of a crossing (distance normally 45 feet).

Although a vehicle which is stationary while loading or unloading is not normally causing an obstruction if it is complying with any regulations in force concerning parking, loading and unloading, it must be parked in a proper manner. It is an offence to park heavy commercial vehicles on road verges, footpaths, or any land situated between two carriageways unless permission has been obtained from a police officer in uniform, or there is an emergency.

In what other situations is a vehicle likely to be adjudged to be in an area where it is likely to cause danger or obstruction?
The highway code lists the following areas where a parked vehicle may cause obstruction or danger:
    (a) in a "no-parking" area
    (b) on a clearway
    (c) alongside yellow lines
    (d) where there are double white lines
    (e) near a road junction
    (f) near a bend
    (g) near the brow of a hill
    (h) near a humpback bridge
    (i) near a level crossing
    (j) near a bus stop
    (k) near a school entrance
    (l) near a pedestrian crossing
    (m) on the right-hand side of the road at night
    (n) where the vehicle would obscure a traffic sign
    (o) on a narrow road
    (p) on fast main roads and motorways

(q) near entrances and exits used by emergency service vehicles
(r) near road works
(s) alongside or opposite another parked vehicle.

This is a formidable list but it is by no means exhaustive. Drivers must always use common sense when parking and must try to ensure that their vehicles are parked in a way that will cause the least inconvenience to other road users.

What other restrictions apply to the parking of goods vehicles?
The restrictions can be split into two parts — those which apply at all times and those which operate at night-time only.

General parking restrictions
It is an offence to leave a vehicle unattended without stopping the engine and securely applying the handbrake.

A vehicle or trailer must not be left on a road in such a way as to cause an obstruction.

Vehicles parked on the road at night
The Road Vehicles Lighting Regulations 1989 (SI 1989 No. 1796) allow goods vehicles not exceeding 1525kg unladen weight, motor cars and motor cycles to be parked at night without lights on any road, including a road with marked out parking spaces, subject to a 30 mph speed limit or less provided:
 (a) no part of the vehicle is within 10m of a road junction and
 (b) the vehicle is parked with its nearside close to and parallel with the kerb, except when standing in a recognised parking space or in a one-way street.

On all other roads the obligatory side and rear lights must be lit.

Goods vehicles exceeding 1525kg unladen must have their side and rear lights illuminated when parked at night on any road and this requirement also applies to vehicles of any weight if they have trailers attached.

Are there any exceptions to these requirements?
Yes! A vehicle which would normally be required to have its side and rear lights illuminated need not do so if it is parked in an area on part of a highway on which road works are being carried out and it is outlined by lamps or traffic signs (cones) in order to prevent the vehicle, its load or equipment being a danger to persons using the road.

Are there any other restrictions on parking at night?
Yes! In London most boroughs prohibit commercial vehicles from parking in residential streets. The restrictions apply to vehicles over 2½ tons unladen weight from 18.30 hours to midnight and midnight to 08.00 hours seven days a week. Other towns and cities have, or are, introducing similar schemes.

Drivers should be instructed to check whether any restrictions exist before parking overnight anywhere other than at an authorised parking place.

What special regulations apply to parking on clearways and motorways?
With the exception of vehicles used in connection with demolition, building and special services, no parking is allowed on clearways. Roads are not usually designated as clearways unless there is off-street access to buildings. Therefore undue difficulty should not arise for goods vehicles collecting and delivering.

On motorways vehicles must not be parked except in an emergency. If vehicles have stopped for any special reason they should be driven onto the hard shoulder and then only for as long as particular circumstances dictate.

Do the "No parking" restrictions apply 24 hours per day?
They apply on rural clearways but on urban clearways the restrictions usually apply to peak hours only.

How are no parking (waiting) restrictions indicated?
1. A single unbroken yellow line parallel with the kerb — No waiting for at least eight hours between 07.00 hours and 19.00 hours on four or more days of the week.
2. Double unbroken yellow lines parallel with the kerb — No waiting for at least eight hours between 07.00 hours and 19.00 hours on four or more days of the week, plus some additional period outside these times.
3. A single broken yellow line parallel with the kerb — No waiting during any other periods.

A convenient way of remembering these markings is:
    (a) during the working day
    (b) more than the working day
    (c) less than the working day.

What restrictions are there on loading and unloading?
In most large towns and cities throughout the country, regulations are in force to control vehicles stopping to deliver and collect goods.

How are these restrictions indicated?
The measures in force are indicated by yellow markings on kerbs and in gutters showing the various forms of prohibitions for loading and unloading. These markings are:

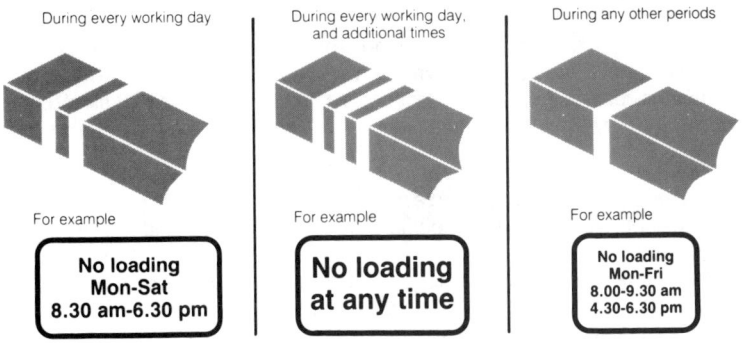

No loading or unloading at times shown on nearby plates. If no days are indicated on the sign, the restrictions are in force every day including Sundays and Bank Holidays.

During every working day

For example

No loading
Mon-Sat
8.30 am-6.30 pm

During every working day, and additional times

For example

No loading
at any time

During any other periods

For example

No loading
Mon-Fri
8.00-9.30 am
4.30-6.30 pm

1. *Single marks at right-angles to the kerb:* Loading bans at peak hours (actual times shown on lamp-post signs).
2. *Double marks at right-angles to the kerb:* Loading ban throughout the working day (normally 08.30 hours to 18.30 hours).
3. *Treble marks at right-angles to the kerb:* Loading bans for more than the working day (eg London theatre land — 08.30 to midnight).

Times of the respective prohibitions are indicated by a sign fitted to posts on the roadside or at the extremities of roads. The top portion of the sign indicates times of "No Waiting" and the lower half times when loading and unloading are prohibited. "No Waiting" instructions sometimes refer to unlimited parking when one side of a road is restricted on alternate days.

These schemes invariably contain exemptions allowing vehicles to pick up and put down goods — usually for a maximum period of 20 minutes. The exemption does not permit waiting for other purposes such as drivers' breaks for rest and refreshment.

Restrictions for "No Waiting" can vary in different towns and it is wrong to assume that the provisions always have the same meaning.

Generally speaking, loading and unloading are not completely banned but, as previously indicated, are subject to a time limit. Drivers should be made fully aware of the requirements and instructed to read the signs and act upon them.

To avoid infringement of the instructions and the possibility of causing an obstruction, drivers should be advised to co-operate with local police.

Who is responsible for enforcing these regulations?
In the first instance the responsibility lies with the police but, in assisting the police with their duties, traffic wardens have taken over many parking and obstruction duties.

In connection with which offences are traffic wardens empowered to enforce the law?
Traffic wardens may enforce the law for offences in connection with:

(a) obstruction, waiting, parking or loading
(b) leaving a vehicle parked at night without lights or reflectors
(c) parking meter schemes
(d) failure to display a current excise licence.

In addition to these enforcement duties they engage in supervising school crossings and regulating traffic and may be employed in making enquiries about the identity of a driver. They can also, when employed at a car pound, request production of driving licences if they have reasonable cause to believe that an offence has been committed by the vehicle obstructing, waiting, being loaded or unloaded on a road.

What is the fixed penalty system?
It is a system of fixed fines for specific traffic offences to avoid the necessity for court proceedings.

The fixed penalty system is in general operation in most towns and cities and, although operated mainly by traffic wardens, tickets for the listed offences may be issued by both police and traffic wardens.

What are the listed offences for which traffic wardens may issue fixed penalty tickets?
The offences are:
- (a) leaving a vehicle parked at night without lights or reflectors
- (b) contravening waiting, parking or loading restrictions
- (c) contravening controlled parking zone regulations
- (d) failure to display a current excise licence

In addition to these offences further mainly moving traffic offences, are included in the fixed penalty system and for the majority of these only the police may issue tickets.

How is the fine imposed and collected?
Tickets may be handed to the driver or affixed to the vehicle. The recipient then has the option of paying the fixed penalty **within 28 days**.

What happens if the driver of the vehicle is not its owner?
Under the Road Traffic Regulation Act 1984 the registered owner of a vehicle (whether a company or individual) is ultimately responsible for payment if the driver of the vehicle at the time of the offence does not pay the fine within the specified period, ie 28 days for a fixed penalty, or seven days for an excess parking charge.

Suppose the owner was not aware that a fixed penalty ticket had been issued and had not been paid?
In cases where a fixed penalty or excess parking charge has not been paid within the prescribed period, a statement setting out details of the alleged offence must be sent to the registered owner within six months of the fixed penalty notice being issued. The statement obliges the owner of the vehicle either to pay the fine or complete a "statutory statement of ownership".

What is the purpose of the statutory "statement of ownership"?
This is to enable a person who was not the owner of the vehicle at the relevant time to make a statement of the facts, eg he had not at that time acquired the vehicle, or he had sold it.

The owner of the vehicle is also entitled to prove that although he was the owner of the vehicle at the time of the alleged offence, the vehicle was in the possession of some other person without the consent of the owner.

What is the penalty for not paying a "fixed penalty" within the specified period?
If the payment is not made and the statement of ownership is not given within the time limit allowed (usually 14 days) a fine can be imposed; where false information is given the fine is much heavier.

Are the owners of hired vehicles liable for offences committed while vehicles are on hire?
No! Provision is made in the regulations for vehicles hired out under a hiring agreement for fixed periods of less than six months. If a statutory statement is served on the hiring company it is sufficient for the company to declare, in the appropriate manner, that the vehicle is on hire and to attach a copy of the hiring agreement together with a statement of liability signed by the hirer acknowledging responsibility for any fixed penalty and/or excess parking charges incurred.

NB The list of fixed penalty offences was extended to cover some of the less serious moving traffic offences such as failure to comply with traffic directions and various minor vehicle defect offences. Included in the list are endorsable offences such as speeding, etc and a police constable may offer a fixed penalty to a driver as an alternative to prosecution. However, he must be satisfied by looking at the licence that there would be no liability to disqualification by the accumulation of 12 or more penalty points (see next chapter) if the licence is endorsed for the offence in question.

CHAPTER 4
(Modules A and B)
Traffic Offences and Legal Action
Endorsement and Disqualification

What do the expressions endorsement and disqualification mean?

Endorsement means writing the details of an offence on the licence of the person convicted of the offence.

Disqualification means that the person convicted of the offence or offences is forbidden to hold or obtain a licence to drive during the period laid down by the court.

For which offences is a court obliged to endorse a driving licence on conviction?

The Road Traffic Offenders Act 1988 (schedule 2) lists the offences for which endorsement is obligatory and provides for obligatory disqualification for certain of the more serious offences. Courts can, however, disqualify for other offences at their discretion, if they consider the offence or offences serious enough.

The Act also lists the offences for which penalty points are awarded if the driver is not disqualified.

Offence	No. of points
Use of special road contrary to scheme or regulations	3
Contravention of pedestrian crossing regulations	3
Not stopping at school crossing	3
Contravention of order relating to street playground	2
Exceeding speed limit	3
Causing death by reckless driving	(a)
Reckless driving	(b)
Careless and inconsiderate driving	3-9
Driving or attempting to drive when unfit to drive through drink or drugs	(a)
Being in charge of a vehicle when unfit to drive through drink or drugs	10
Driving or attempting to drive with excess alcohol in body	(a)
Being in charge of a vehicle with excess alcohol in body	10
Failing to provide a specimen for breath test	4
Failing to provide specimen for analysis or laboratory test	(b)
Motor racing and speed trials on public ways	(a)
Leaving vehicle in dangerous position	3
Failing to comply with traffic directions	3
Failing to comply with traffic signs	3
Contravention of construction and use regulations	3
Driving without a licence	2
Driving with incorrected eyesight, or refusing a test of eyesight	2
Failing to comply with conditions attached to a provisional or full licence	2

Offence	No. of points
Driving while disqualified–	
where offender was disqualified as under age	2
where offender was disqualified by order of court	6
Using motor vehicle without insurance	6-8
Failing to stop after accident and give particulars or report accident	8-10
Taking, etc, vehicle without consent, driving it or allowing oneself to be carried in it	8
Manslaughter or, in Scotland, culpable homicide	(a)
Stealing or attempting to steal a motor vehicle	8
Going equipped for stealing, etc, motor vehicles	8

(a) 4 points if under exceptional circumstances disqualification is not imposed.
(b) 4, or 10 points, depending on circumstances, if disqualification is not imposed.

NB If an employee driver is charged with not complying with compulsory third party insurance, he has a valid defence if he can prove that the vehicle did not belong to him and that he had no reason to believe it was not insured (Road Traffic Act 1988 s.143).

What is the limit referred to in drinking and driving offences?

Breath analysis is the primary means of determining a person's alcohol concentration. The statutory limit for breath alcohol concentration is 35 micrograms of alcohol in 100 millilitres of breath (equivalent to the alcohol limit of 80 milligrams of alcohol in 100 millilitres of blood or 107 milligrams of alcohol per 100 millilitres of urine).

Is there any right to require a check on the level determined by breath analysis?

A person has a right to a blood test to replace breath analysis when the breath analysis indicates a level which does not exceed 50 microgrammes of alcohol per 100 millilitres of breath.

Does a police constable need a warrant in order to arrest a person suspected of a drink/driving offence?

If a police constable has reason to suspect that a person has committed an offence relating to alcohol or drugs, he may arrest without a warrant. He may also enter (by force if necessary) any place where that person is, or where the constable suspects that person to be.

How does the penalty points system work?

If 12 or more points are accumulated within *three years* the driver will be disqualified.

In what circumstances can courts exercise their discretion in connection with "obligatory disqualification" offences?
Only in exceptional circumstances connected with the offence, eg if a driver, over the prescribed limit of alcohol, drove a vehicle in order to save a life because there was no other alternative, the court would probably exercise its discretion.

If disqualification is not imposed for an "obligatory disqualification" offence, are any penalty points incurred?
Yes! Either four or ten penalty points are incurred depending on the circumstances.

Can the court exercise discretion once 12 penalty points are incurred?
Unlike the situation with "obligatory disqualification" offences, here the court can exercise discretion after taking into consideration the circumstances of the driver, eg the court may decide not to disqualify, or disqualify for a shorter period, a person for whom a licence is essential, such as a doctor or an HGV driver.

What happens if a driver is convicted of more than one offence committed on the same occasion?
In that case he will incur the highest number of points awarded for one of the offences.

How is the three year period calculated?
The three year period is a rolling term, ie it is measured on each occasion backwards from the date when the latest offence was committed.

What is the period of disqualification?
This varies — for "obligatory offences" the minimum period of disqualification is one year (unless the court exercises discretion), a second conviction for a driving offence related to drink or drugs within 10 years incurs a minimum disqualification of three years.
Disqualification in connection with the "totting-up" procedure is:
six months, if there has been no previous disqualification within the three years
one year, if there has been one previous disqualification within the three years
two years, if there has been more than one disqualification within the three years.

Does a disqualified driver have to take a driving test to regain his licence?
Not usually, but courts disqualifying a driver for any of the specified offences do have the power to require him to undergo another driving test prior to the re-issue of his licence. In the case of HGV licences the Licensing Authority has the power to require a new HGV driving test before reissuing this particular licence.

When and how can a disqualified driver apply to have the disqualification removed?
Applications for removal of a disqualification may be made to the Clerk of the Court which imposed the disqualification:
  (a) if the disqualification is for less than four years, when two years from the date on which it was imposed have expired

(b) if the disqualification is for less than 10 years, but not less than four years, when half the period of disqualification has expired
(c) in any other case when five years have expired from the date of disqualification.

If the first removal application is refused, others may be made at three month intervals.

For how long must an endorsement remain on a licence?
Endorsements are not removed from a driving licence until **four years** after the conviction, except in the case of drinking and driving offences when the endorsements remain for **11 years**.

Following a disqualification, what happens to the penalty points accrued?
After a disqualification the penalty points accrued will be cancelled but the endorsements will remain on the licence, as explained above.

NB See Chapter 3 for extensions to the fixed penalty system to cover some of the less serious moving traffic offences such as speeding, failure to comply with traffic directions and various minor vehicle defect offences.

Powers of Goods Vehicle Examiners, etc

What are the powers of goods vehicle examiners, certifying officers and police examiners?
The Road Traffic Act 1988 s.68(1) empowers the Secretary of State to appoint goods vehicle examiners for the purpose of ensuring that goods vehicles are maintained in a fit and serviceable condition.

Any reference to goods vehicle examiners in s.68 also applies to certifying officers. Under these and other sections of the Act, considerable powers are given to authorised examiners.

When may a goods vehicle examiner inspect a vehicle?
Under s.68(3) a goods vehicle examiner may:
(a) at any time, on production of his authority, enter and inspect any goods vehicle and detain the vehicle for the time required for the inspection
(b) at any reasonable time enter any premises in which he has reason to believe a goods vehicle is being kept.

Can a goods vehicle examiner be refused entry to premises because it is not convenient, or for any other reason?
Yes. Under regulation 74 of the Road Vehicles (Construction and Use) Regulations 1986 an examiner must obtain the consent of the owner of the premises or give him 48 hours' notice before the time of the proposed test or inspection (72 hours if notice is sent by recorded delivery service).

It should be noted that examiners normally apply the powers given them under s.68 of the Road Traffic Act for inspection purposes.

Can an examiner require a vehicle to be moved to a suitable place for the purposes of an inspection?

Under s.68(5) a goods vehicle examiner or a police constable in uniform may, at any time, issue a form GV3 requiring any person in charge of a stationary goods vehicle on a road to drive the vehicle to a suitable place, not more than five miles away, for the purpose of an inspection.

What is the procedure if the vehicle is found to be unfit?

Under s.69 if, on inspection or examination, it appears to a goods vehicle examiner that the vehicle is unfit, or likely to become unfit for service, he may prohibit the driving of the vehicle on a road either absolutely or for a specified purpose. (The system of prohibition notices is covered in Chapter 7.)

Can a goods vehicle examiner order a vehicle to be weighed?

Under s.78 an authorised officer, ie a Department of Transport examiner, a Trading Standards Officer or a specially authorised police constable, is empowered to require a motor vehicle or trailer to be weighed and can instruct the person in charge of the vehicle to proceed to a weighbridge for this purpose.

What happens if the vehicle is found to be overloaded?

If the vehicle is found to exceed the relevant construction and use weight limits any of the above-mentioned authorised officers is empowered to issue the relevant prohibition notice — GV 160.

(The GV 160 procedure is covered in Chapter 7.)

What happens if the vehicle is found not to be overloaded?

If the weighbridge to which the vehicle was ordered was more than five miles from the place where the requirement was made and the vehicle is found to be within the limits authorised by law, the Highway Authority, on whose behalf the requirement was made, shall pay any loss suffered.

A certificate in the prescribed form will be issued and if the vehicle was not overloaded this will enable the driver to complete his journey with the same load without further weighing.

NB The Secretary of State for Transport has powers to designate areas in Great Britain in which the five mile limit is increased to any greater distance he may specify.

What other powers do the police, examiners and certifying officers have?

Under ss.164 and 165 police constables are given powers to require the production of driving licences, to obtain statements of date of birth, names and addresses of drivers and to require production of evidence of insurance or security and vehicle test certificates. Examiners and certifying officers are given the same powers under s.166.

When can a police constable exercise these powers?

Under s.164 a constable can require the production of a driving licence and where relevant, a statement of date of birth from:

(a) any person driving a motor vehicle on a road

(b) any person believed to be the driver of a motor vehicle at a time when an accident occurred owing to its presence on a road
(c) any person believed to have committed an offence in relation to the use of a motor vehicle on a road
(d) any person supervising, or believed to be supervising, a learner driver when an accident occurred or an offence was committed.

Under ss.164 and 165 in cases (a), (b) and (c) above the constable has power to: obtain the names and addresses of drivers and owners of vehicles; require production of certificates of insurance or security; require motor vehicle test certificates and goods vehicle test certificates, if relevant.

In case (d) above, the supervisor must give his name and address and the name and address of the owner.

In relation to traffic offences what do the expressions "forgery and false statements" mean?

Under s.173 of the Road Traffic Act 1988, a person shall be guilty of the offence of *forgery* if he, *with intent to deceive:*
(a) forges or alters, or uses or lends to, or allows to be used by any other person, a document or other thing to which this section applies
(b) makes, or has in his possession, any document, or other thing so closely resembling a document, or other thing to which this section applies, as to be calculated to deceive.

"Documents and other things" are licences, test certificates, plates containing plated particulars, maintenance records, certificates of insurance, etc.

A *false statement* is one which is untrue, which is made knowing it to be untrue, or believing it to be untrue, or made recklessly not caring whether it be true or false.

Making such a statement to obtain a licence, etc is an offence, as is making use of a document which is known to be false, believed to be false or used recklessly not caring whether it be true or false.

When is the owner of the vehicle, though not at the relevant time the driver, liable for offences committed?

In addition to his ultimate liability for fixed penalty offences (see Chapter 3) an employer is liable in respect of the following offences:
(a) permitting or causing a person to drive when under age
(b) contravention of an order relating to street playgrounds
(c) contravention of construction and use regulations by using, or causing or permitting the use of, a goods vehicle so that it is likely to cause danger:
  (i) by its general condition, or the weight, distribution or packing or adjustment of the load
  (ii) by breach of requirements as to brakes, steering gear, tyres, or its unsuitability
(d) employing and allowing a person to drive without a licence or without a licence appropriate to the type of vehicle in question
(e) permitting the use of a motor vehicle uninsured or unsecured against third party risks.

CHAPTER 5
(Modules A and B)
Accidents, Insurance and Safe Loading
Procedure in Case of Traffic Accidents

What is a driver legally bound to do if he is involved in an accident?
In any accident resulting in:
- (a) personal injury to another person
- (b) damage to another vehicle
- (c) injury to an animal other than one in the vehicle or trailer causing the accident
- (d) damage to any other property on or adjacent to the road

the driver must:
- (i) stop
- (ii) give his name and address, the name and address of the owner of the vehicle, the identification marks and insurance details of the vehicle to any person having reasonable grounds for requiring them.

What should the driver do if he does not give the particulars at the time of the accident?
If, for any reason, the particulars are not given at the time of the accident, the circumstances must be reported to a police constable or to a police station as soon as possible and in any case within 24 hours.

What is meant by "animal" in the regulation?
For the purpose of this regulation, "animal" means any horse, cattle, ass, mule, sheep, pig, goat or dog.

Can the driver be required to furnish any other information or documents at the time of the accident?
A police constable (and in the case of a goods vehicle, a certifying officer or goods vehicle examiner) has the power to require the driver to produce his driving licence, certificate of insurance, vehicle test certificate and plating certificate, if relevant.

Suppose the driver is unable to produce the documents at the time of the accident?
In that case he must produce his driving licence in person at a police station nominated by him at the time its production was required, within seven days. In respect of other documents they must also be produced within seven days but need not be produced "in person".

Can anyone else require details of the certificate of insurance?
It is an offence under s.165 of the Road Traffic Act 1988 not to give details of a certificate of insurance on demand by or on behalf of a person making a claim, *without reasonable excuse*.

For example, an employee driver might not know the name of his employer's insurance company. In that case it would be sufficient for him to give his own and his employer's names and addresses.

An owner-driver whose insurance company operated a "knock for knock" policy would not wish to disclose his insurance company's name in circumstances where the other party was clearly to blame, but instead would wish to pursue his claim himself without involving his insurance company as that might prejudice his "no claims" bonus.

What instructions should employers give their drivers to follow in case of accidents?

The legal duty to stop, give names and addresses, etc as discussed at the beginning of this chapter should be thoroughly impressed on every driver. He should be advised to adopt the following routine.

1. If any person is injured, seek assistance and send for the police.
2. Try to obtain the names and addresses of witnesses.
3. Do not admit responsibility for the accident to the other party or witnesses.
4. Obtain the following information:
   (a) name and address of the other driver
   (b) name and address of the vehicle owner
   (c) registration number of the vehicle, type and colour
   (d) name and address of the other driver's insurance company.
5. As soon as possible, while the events are still clear in his mind, prepare a rough report indicating:
   (a) the extent of the damage
   (b) the time the accident occurred
   (c) where the accident occurred:
      (i) the locality
      (ii) names of streets and roads adjacent
      (iii) position of the vehicles at the time of the accident
      (iv) visibility at the time of the accident
   (d) the cause of the accident (including any information about whether signals were given)
   (e) a rough sketch to emphasise the general situation.

It is essential to obtain the correct information at the time of the accident as the true facts are difficult to obtain once the parties have dispersed.

If the employer does not issue his own accident report forms, drivers should carry a copy of the insurance company's accident form to act as a guide to the information required.

The driver should be instructed to report the accident to his employer at the earliest opportunity.

Compulsory Vehicle and Passenger Insurance

What are the legal requirements in respect of motor vehicle insurance?

In accordance with the requirements of the Road Traffic Act 1988 (ss. 143–158) users of all motor vehicles used on roads in the United Kingdom must be insured with an authorised insurer against liability at law in respect of death, compensation for injury caused to another person and also the cost of any emergency medical treatment resulting from the accident, and damage to property.

This is the legal minimum; in practice most policy holders insure for third party, fire and theft.

Who is an "authorised insurer"?

The Road Traffic Act 1988 s.145 provides that an authorised insurer must be a member of the Motor Insurer's Bureau.

Must the insurance cover liability for injury to passengers carried in the insured party's vehicle?
Yes! All passengers must be covered and any "own risk" agreement concluded between passengers and the owner or user of the vehicle is of no effect.

Is there any alternative to an insurance policy to cover liability for death, injury, etc to third parties?
As an alternative to the insurance, application may be made to the Minister of Transport for a warrant to enable a deposit of £15,000 in cash or securities to be made with the Supreme Court under the provisions of the Motor Vehicles (Third Party Risks Deposits) Regulations 1967.

What is an insurance certificate?
This is a document issued by authorised insurers as proof that a vehicle is insured in accordance with the requirements of the Road Traffic Act 1988.

Under what circumstances can an insurance policy become invalid?
Most policies contain certain conditions which must be observed if the policy is to remain valid, eg policies are usually invalidated if the vehicles insured are not maintained in a safe and roadworthy condition. Cover for liability to third parties is not affected, it is only the policy holder's cover which is invalidated.

Safe Loading of Vehicles

What provisions are there in the construction and use regulations governing the safe loading of vehicles?
The regulations require that "a motor vehicle, every trailer drawn thereby and all parts and accessories of such vehicle and trailer shall at all times be in such condition... and the weight, distribution, packing and adjustment of the load of such vehicle or trailer shall at all times be such that no danger is caused or is likely to be caused to any person in or on the vehicle or trailer or on a road".

In respect of the load the regulations state: "The load carried by a motor vehicle or trailer shall at all times be so secured or be in such a position that danger is not likely to be caused to any person by reason of the load or any part thereof falling from the vehicle or by reason of any other movement of the load or any part thereof in relation to the vehicle".

Are there any specific strength requirements for the load restraint system?
The Code of Practice "Safety of Loads on Vehicles" recommends that the forces to be contained by the load restraint system should be as follows:
- (a) forward — equal to the payload
- (b) rearward — equal to half the payload
- (c) sideways — equal to half the payload.

Specialist Vehicles, etc

What particular requirements are there in respect of special type and specialist vehicles?
Certain vehicles which do not comply in all respects with the construction and use regulations may still be used on the roads, provided they conform with the require-

ments of the Motor Vehicles (Authorisation of Special Types) General Order 1979 as amended.

While this order covers various highly specialised vehicles, such as mobile cranes, the section which is probably most important to hauliers is that concerned with vehicles and trailers used for hauling or carrying abnormal indivisible loads.

The regulations cover such matters as maximum permitted widths, lengths, projection of loads, weight, speed, carriage of attendants, special authorisations, etc and these are dealt with in other chapters, especially Chapter 6.

Are there regulations governing the safe carriage of livestock?

Yes! These have a two-fold purpose. Firstly to minimise the risk of transferring disease and secondly to minimise the distress which most livestock suffer when being transported.

The utmost care and hygiene must be observed when transporting live animals. Vehicles must be thoroughly cleaned, washed out and disinfected as soon as each load of animals has been discharged. An exception to this regulation applies where there are several movements between the same two points on the same day when the vehicle is used for carrying horses. In this case, cleaning and disinfection need only be carried out after the last journey.

There are a number of separate regulations covering different kinds of livestock but basically they are designed to ensure the safety and comfort of the animals covered.

Generally, vehicles must have a roof giving protection from the weather without impeding ventilation. Sides, floor, tailboards and ramps must be designed to minimise the risk of injury to animals and provision made for securing animals (where necessary) to prevent injury.

Arrangements must be made for feeding and watering animals at prescribed intervals on long journeys, eg food and water must be provided for horses at intervals of not more than 12 hours.

What regulations govern the carriage of foodstuffs?

As you would expect the emphasis in the regulations is on hygiene. Special precautions must be taken to observe cleanliness in the handling of food not in containers and articles which could contaminate food must not be carried in a food-carrying vehicle.

Live animals and poultry must not come into contact with meat or fish.

Any stall or delivery vehicle used in a food business must have conspicuously and legibly displayed on it:

(a) the name and address of the person carrying on the business
(b) any other address at which it is kept or garaged unless it bears a fleet number and is kept or garaged at that person's premises and the local authority is notified.

Drivers and mates employed by regular meat carriers must wear clean washable overalls.

Vehicles for the carriage of meat must be kept clean and any wooden floor must be fitted with movable duckboards.

Offal detached from carcasses must be carried in separate impervious containers.

NB For the purpose of inspection and examination of food, any authorised officer of a local council may enter and detain (but not stop) a vehicle.

Hazardous and Dangerous Goods

What are the regulations governing the carriage of hazardous goods?
Because of the potential danger to drivers, handlers, the general public and the environment, these regulations are extensive and detailed and only an indication of the main provisions and matters covered can be given here.

Radioactive Substances
The applicable legislation is contained within the following:
   the Radioactive Substances Act 1948
   the Radioactive Substances (Carriage by Road) (Great Britain) Regulations 1974
   the Ionising Radiations Regulations 1985.

The following Code of Practice has been issued by the Department of Transport:
   Code of Practice for the Carriage of Radioactive Materials by Road.

Because of the potential hazard involved, the movement of radioactive substances is restricted, in the main, to a few nominated organisations who are specialists in this field. Any operator contemplating engaging in this type of activity needs to ensure that he is thoroughly conversant with the legislation and Code of Practice.

Carriage by Road of Dangerous Substances in Road Tankers and Tank Containers
The Dangerous Substances (Conveyance by Road in Road Tankers and Tank Containers) Regulations 1981 extended and updated the then existing legislation on the carrying of dangerous substances by road involving the use of road tankers (of any capacity) and tank containers having a capacity of more than three cubic metres.

To what substances do these regulations apply?
The Health and Safety Commission (HSC) has drawn up a list of substances which may be conveyed in road tankers and tank containers, known briefly as the "Approved List". (Its full title is Approved substance identification numbers, emergency action codes and classification for dangerous substances conveyed in road tankers and tank containers.)

If a substance is not included in the "Approved List" does this mean it is not hazardous?
No! It may mean that it is too hazardous to convey in a tanker or tank container or that it has not yet been approved by the HSC. An operator must always check if asked to convey any substance with which he is not familiar.

Who is the "operator" where these regulations apply?
An operator means, in relation to:
1. a road tanker:
    (a) the holder of an operator's licence
    (b) the keeper of the vehicle (if an "O" licence is not required)

2. a tank container:
   (a) the owner or his agent, if the owner:
      (i) has a place of business in Great Britain
      (ii) is identified as the owner or agent either by the container displaying the information or on a document carried on the vehicle
   (b) the operator of the vehicle on which the container is carried if 2(a) is not satisfied.

The person to whom a tank container is leased is regarded as the owner of that container for the purposes of these regulations.

What regulations apply to the vehicles and containers themselves?

There are very detailed technical regulations covering the construction of vehicles and tank containers — far too detailed to include here (or to be included in examination questions).

In general, any vehicle or tank container used for carrying dangerous goods must be:
   (a) of adequate strength and constructed from sound and suitable materials
   (b) suitable for the purposes for which it is being used having regard to the nature and circumstances of the journey and the type or types of substance being carried
   (c) constructed and maintained so that no contents can escape (except by a suitable safety valve) and that substances carried will not react on the tanker body or cause other substances to form which could be a safety or health hazard.

How can an operator ensure that a tanker or tank container complies with the regulations?

Tanks must be tested and certified by a competent person before they can be used for carrying dangerous substances.

Periodic examinations of all tanks and, where appropriate, testing of the tank and its fittings must be carried out to ensure that they are properly maintained. This work must be done by a competent person and a report issued by him giving details of the results of the examination, the dates of the next examination and/or tests, the suitability of the tank for the purposes specified and, where the tank is a pressure vessel, the maximum working pressure to which it may be subject, which must not be exceeded.

Who is responsible for supplying information on the type of substance to be carried?

An operator may not carry a dangerous substance unless he has obtained information from the consignor enabling him to comply with the regulations and is made aware of the risks involved in relation to the health and safety of any person.

It is the duty of the consignor to ensure that the information is accurate and sufficient for the operator to comply with the regulations.

In turn, the operator must ensure that the vehicle or vehicles to be used for the conveyance of the dangerous substance are appropriate for that purpose and that the quantities carried do not exceed the maximum permitted concentrations.

Additionally, the operator must ensure that the required information is passed on to the driver.

What information must be given to the driver of a vehicle carrying dangerous goods?
He must be provided with full written information on the identity of the substance and the danger which could arise from it, together with the emergency action to be taken.

What is the driver required to do with this written information?
He must keep this information in the cab for the duration of the journey and until the substance has been discharged or unloaded when it should be either destroyed, removed from the vehicle, or placed in a securely closed container clearly marked to the effect that it is no longer applicable.

Is there a standard method of conveying this information?
The TREMCARD (Transport Emergency Card [Road]) meets all the requirements and is acceptable nationally and internationally, having been drawn up by CEFIC (Conseil European des Federations de l'Industrie Chemique — European Council of Chemical Manufacturers' Federations).

What other precautions must be taken by drivers and operators?
Fire and explosion — all necessary precautions must be taken against the possibility of fire and explosion. This applies also to those involved in loading and unloading.

Overfilling — operators/drivers must ensure that tanks are not overfilled.

Parking, etc — where the hazard warning panel is displaying an emergency code ending with the letter "E" or where the numbers 1270 or 1268 are displayed the driver must ensure that when the vehicle is not being driven it is either:

(a) parked in a safe place, or
(b) being supervised at all times by himself or some other competent person over the age of 18.

These requirements do not apply when the driver can show that the substances to which the markings refer have been discharged and the tanks are empty.

What are hazard warning panels?
These are panels which must be affixed to road tankers conveying one or more dangerous substances, giving information concerning the substance carried.

Three such panels must be displayed, one at the rear and one on each side of the vehicle. When multi-loads are carried, two appropriate compartment labels must also be attached as close as possible to the mid-way point, one on each side of each compartment or tank.

All panels and labels must be weather resistant and indelibly marked on one side only, be rigid or fixed so that they are rigid and in a substantially vertical plane. They must be kept clean and free from obstruction except that a rear panel may be fixed behind a ladder of light construction which does not obscure the information from being easily read.

What information must be shown on the hazard warning panels?
Each panel must contain:
(a) the emergency action code

(b) the substance identification number
(c) specialist advice (usually a telephone number from which specialist advice may be obtained)
(d) the symbol indicating the general nature of the substance
(e) if necessary, the manufacturer's or owner's name and/or symbol.

When should hazard warning panels be removed?

When a road tanker or tank container has been emptied and cleaned or purged so that no health or hazard risk remains the panels and compartment labels should be either:

(a) completely removed or covered, or
(b) covered so that only the telephone number in the lowest section of the panel remains visible.

If only one tank or compartment of a multi-load has been emptied and cleaned or purged, that particular compartment label should be removed or covered and the hazard warning panels changed appropriately.

What are the symbols shown on the hazard warning panels?

These are symbols contained in a diamond shaped sign that give an easily recognised indication of the hazard involved, eg the sign which denotes that a vehicle is carrying inflammable liquids consists of a black flame symbol on a red background and the words "INFLAMMABLE LIQUID".

Who is responsible for ensuring the instruction and training of drivers of vehicles carrying dangerous goods?

The operator of tanker vehicles, etc carrying dangerous goods is responsible for ensuring that his drivers are adequately instructed and trained in understanding the dangers attached to the substances being carried and the action to be taken in an emergency and that they understand their duties under the regulations.

The operator must keep a record of the instruction and training given to the driver while in his employment and make a copy available to him.

Who is responsible for enforcing these regulations?

Responsibility rests with the Health and Safety Executive (HSE) or the local authority, as appropriate, to enforce the regulations.

Is there any defence in prosecutions for contravening these regulations?

Where prosecutions are brought it is a defence for any person to prove that all reasonable steps were taken and due diligence exercised to avoid committing an offence.

Are there any regulations covering dangerous goods in packages?

As their title implies the Classification, Packaging and Labelling of Dangerous Substances Regulations 1984 cover the packing and labelling of dangerous goods which are conveyed in package form by road. Under these regulations duties are placed on suppliers and consignors of dangerous substances to ensure that they are properly packed and labelled so that the carrier is aware of the nature of the goods he is conveying.

A further set of regulations entitled The Road Traffic (Carriage of Dangerous Substances in Packages, etc) Regulations 1986 details the requirements and responsibilities of the carrier.

All these regulations are administered by the HSE.

What information must be provided concerning the hazardous substance?

The consignor has a legal duty to supply the operator with information concerning the substance, which the operator must pass on to the driver in writing.

This information must include:
- (a) the identity of the substance
- (b) the nature of the hazards involved
- (c) the emergency action to be taken
- (d) the name, address and telephone number from which specialist advice can be obtained.

Are there regulations governing the marking of vehicles carrying dangerous substances in packages?

If a vehicle carries 500kg or more of dangerous substances it must be fitted with two rectangular orange reflectorised plates — one at the front and the other at the rear. They must be removed when the vehicle has been unloaded.

Are there any requirements for the training of drivers in the handling and conveyance of dangerous substances?

Operators are required to ensure that their drivers receive adequate instructions and training. The operator must keep records of training where total loads of 3000kg or more are carried.

What provision is there for the supervision of parked vehicles?

The driver must ensure that vehicles carrying dangerous substances totalling 3000kg or more are parked in a safe place or supervised at all times either by himself or some other competent person over the age of 18.

Are there any other requirements of which an operator should be aware?

All vehicles carrying dangerous goods, whether in tankers or in packaged form, must carry at least one fire extinguisher capable of dealing with a fire in the engine. It is also advisable to have an extinguisher able to deal, preliminarily, with a fire in the load but expert advice must be obtained as to the correct type for this purpose.

NB The Health and Safety Executive (HSE) has issued an "Approved Code of Practice" (available from HMSO) which gives practical advice on how operators should comply with the law.

CHAPTER 6
(Module B)
Technical Standards and Aspects of Operation

Some readers may be fortunate and find that they are already familiar with the subject of this chapter and the next. For others it will simply mean a hard slog, learning by heart a host of weights, dimensions, etc and a number of definitions relating to goods vehicles.

How is a goods vehicle defined?
It depends upon the context. For the purpose of:
  (a) *"O" licensing* — a goods vehicle is defined as a vehicle used for the carriage of goods in connection with a trade or business and which exceeds 3.5 tonnes gross plated weight or, if unplated, 1525kg unladen weight
  (b) *Driver licensing* — goods vehicles are divided into a number of classes:
    (i) *small goods vehicle*, ie constructed or adapted to carry or haul goods and not exceeding 3.5 tonnes permissible maximum weight (including the weight of any trailer drawn)
    (ii) *medium sized goods vehicle*, ie constructed or adapted to carry or haul goods and exceeding 3.5 tonnes but not exceeding 7.5 tonnes permissible maximum weight (including the weight of any trailer drawn)
    (iii) *heavy goods vehicle*, ie an articulated vehicle or a large goods vehicle, ie a motor vehicle (not being an articulated vehicle) constructed or adapted to carry or haul goods and having a permissible maximum weight (including the weight of any trailer drawn) exceeding 7.5 tonnes.

NB For the purpose of HGV driver licensing, an HGV licence is not required for an articulated vehicle which has a permissible weight not exceeding 7.5 tonnes, or the tractive unit of which does not exceed 2 tons unladen weight.

Are there any other vehicle definitions used in connection with the use of vehicles?
The following apply for the purposes of the construction and use regulations:
  (a) *Motor car* — a vehicle with an unladen weight not exceeding 3050kg
  (b) *Heavy motor car* — a vehicle with an unladen weight exceeding 2540kg
  (c) *Motor tractor* — a vehicle not constructed to carry a load, having an unladen weight not exceeding 7370kg
  (d) *Light locomotive* — a vehicle not constructed to carry a load, having an unladen weight exceeding 7370kg, but not exceeding 11,690kg
  (e) *Heavy locomotive* — a vehicle not constructed to carry a load having an unladen weight exceeding 11,690kg
  (f) *Articulated vehicle* — a motor car or heavy motor car with a trailer so attached that 20% of its load, when uniformly distributed, is borne by the drawing vehicle
  (g) *Dual-purpose vehicle* — a vehicle constructed or adapted for the carriage both of passengers and of goods or burden of any description, with an unladen weight not exceeding 2040kg

(h) *Composite trailer* — a combination of a convertor dolly and a semi-trailer
(i) *Convertor dolly* — a trailer with two or more wheels which allows a semi-trailer to move without any of its weight being superimposed on the drawing vehicle and which itself is not part of either the semi-trailer or the drawing vehicle.

Vehicle Weights

What do the abbreviations ULW, GLW, etc mean?

1. *Unladen weight (ULW)* — the total weight of an unladen vehicle with body, ready for operation on the road but exclusive of water, fuel, spare wheel, tools and loose equipment.
2. *Gross vehicle weight (GVW)* — the total maximum weight of a rigid vehicle as driven, ie with body, payload, fuel, oil and water. This is a figure laid down by the vehicle manufacturer and appearing on his plate. It is essentially a design weight.
3. *Gross combination weight (GCW)* — as for rigid but applied to an articulated vehicle with its loaded semi-trailer.
4. *Gross laden weight (GLW)* — the total weight transmitted to the road by a laden vehicle.
5. *Gross train weight (GTW)* — the total maximum all-up weight of a rigid vehicle together with its loaded drawbar trailer.
6. *Gross plated weight (GPW)* — the weight shown on the DTp plate after the vehicle has been tested and plated. It may be less than the GVW shown on the manufacturer's plate. The DTp plate overrules the manufacturer's plate.
7. *Kerbside weight (KW)* — the total weight of an unladen vehicle with body ready for operation on the road and inclusive of fuel, water, tools and any towing bracket.

What are the maximum permitted gross weights of different types of goods vehicles?

The maximum permitted gross weights depend on the wheelbase, the number of axles and axle spread. All goods vehicles (and trailers over one tonne unladen weight) are fitted with a plate showing the permissible axle weights and total weight, or combined weight of trailer and tractive unit in the case of articulated vehicles.

The *maximum* weights of rigid goods vehicles are:

Vehicle with two axles 17,000kg
Vehicle with three axles 24,390kg
Vehicle with four or more axles. 30,490kg

The *maximum* weight of a drawbar trailer with two axles is 18,000kg.

The *maximum* weight of a drawbar combination, ie vehicle and trailer (not articulated) not fitted with power assisted brakes is 24,390kg
The *maximum* weight of a drawbar combination, ie vehicle and trailer (not articulated) fitted with power assisted brakes is 32,520kg

The *maximum* weights of articulated vehicles are:

Tractive unit and semi-trailer with total of three axles. 24,390kg
Tractive unit and semi-trailer with total of four axles. 32,520kg
Tractive unit and semi-trailer with total of five or more axles. 38,000kg

Note: these are the maximum weights; variations in axle spreads, etc will produce lower maxima which are reflected in the manufacturers' or DTp plated particulars.

NB For rigid vehicles the axle spread is measured by reference to the distance between the centres of the wheels on the front and rearmost axles, for articulated vehicles it is the distance between the centres of the rearmost axle of the tractive unit and the rearmost axle of the trailer.

Types of articulated vehicle

	Maximum weight (kg)
Motor vehicle and semi-trailer having a total of three axles	24,390
Motor vehicle and semi-trailer having a total of four axles or motor vehicle first used before April 1, 1973 and semi-trailer having a total of five or more axles	32,520
Motor vehicle first used on or after April 1, 1973 and semi-trailer having a total of five or more axles	38,000

Is it possible for an axle to be overloaded even though the maximum weight for the vehicle has not been exceeded?
Yes! It depends on how the weight of the load is distributed.

How can a driver tell what weight is imposed on each axle?
The load on the front axle can be calculated by using the following formula:

$$\frac{\text{Payload} \times \text{Distance of centre of load to rear axle}}{\text{Wheelbase}} = \text{Front axle load}$$

and is often simply expressed as $\frac{P \times D}{W}$ = Front axle load.

By deducting the front axle weight from the total weight, the rear axle load can be obtained.

NB You are advised to make a careful note of this formula as it frequently appears in examination questions.

Is it possible to remove part of the load of a vehicle which was previously loaded within its permitted limits (both maximum load and axle loads) and cause it to be overloaded?
Yes! If part of the load is positioned to the rear of the rear axle it has a counterbalancing effect on that part of the load which is forward of the rear axle and if removed has the effect of causing more weight to be transmitted to the forward axle, possibly causing an overload of that axle.

Maximum Dimensions of Vehicles
What are the permitted maximum lengths of goods vehicles?
Rigid vehicles 12m
Articulated vehicles 15.5m*
* This has been increased to 16.5m subject to certain criteria.

NB an articulated vehicle designed to carry indivisible loads of exceptional length is not restricted in length.

Semi-trailers (manufactured from May 1, 1983) 12.2m
NB The maximum length of a semi-trailer excludes the thickness of any front or rear wall or any part which does not increase the vehicle's load-carrying space. In the case of a trailer it excludes any part designed primarily for attaching the trailer to another vehicle.

Trailers
1. With four or more wheels and having a maximum gross weight exceeding 3500kg 12m
2. All other trailers 7m

Road Trains
1. Vehicle and one trailer 18m
2. Vehicle and two trailers 25.9m

NB Where a broken-down vehicle is being towed by a motor vehicle the overall length of the combination may exceed 18m. The registration number of the towing vehicle must be displayed at the rear of the towed vehicle.

A goods vehicle is limited to the towing of one trailer. But where an articulated vehicle (ie tractor unit and semi-trailer) has broken down and has to be towed, it is treated as a single trailer provided the semi-trailer is unloaded.

What are the regulations regarding lengths of tow-ropes, chains and towbars?

Where a motor vehicle is drawing a trailer by means of a tow-rope or chain the distance between the nearest points must not exceed **4.5m**.

The tow-rope or chain must be made clearly visible from both sides when the distance between their nearest points exceeds **1.5m**.

There are no limits of length stated for rigid towbars.

What is meant by the overall length of the vehicle?

The overall length of the vehicle is the distance between the front and rear extremities.

What is the maximum permitted overhang?

For goods vehicles the overhang must not exceed 60% of the wheelbase. For motor tractors, it must not exceed 1.83m.

How is overhang measured?

In the case of four-wheeled vehicles it is measured from the centre line through the rear axle to the rearmost point of the vehicle; in the case of vehicles with six or more wheels, from 110mm to the rear of the centre line between the two rear axles and the rearmost point of the vehicle.

NB A more precise formula for measuring overhang is provided in *Croner's Road Transport Operation*

What are the permitted maximum widths of goods vehicles?

Goods and dual-purpose vehicles.. 2.5m
Refrigerated vehicles (provided side walls, including insulation, are at least 45mm thick)... 2.60m
Trailers (except as below) 2.3m
Trailers drawn by a motor vehicle, having a plated maximum weight exceeding 3500kg... 2.5m
Motor tractors 2.5m
Locomotives 2.75m

What are the maximum heights of goods vehicles?
There are no maximum heights specified for goods vehicles in the United Kingdom except the following: *semi-trailers* having a plated gross weight exceeding 26,000kg and the total laden weight of the semi-trailer and the tractive unit when driven on the road exceeds 32,520kg, are subject to a height limit of 4.2m.
NB This height limit includes any structure attached to the vehicle for containing the load, ie container, but does not include any load which is not a detachable structure or any sheeting or other flexible means of covering or securing the load.

Overloading

What is the procedure if a vehicle is suspected of being overloaded?
The Road Traffic Act 1988, s.78 enables an authorised officer, ie DTp examiner, a specially authorised Trading Standards Officer or a specially authorised police constable, to require a motor vehicle or trailer drawn to be weighed and can instruct the person in charge of the vehicle to proceed to a weighbridge.

Can the person in charge refuse to drive the vehicle to a weighbridge?
It is an offence to refuse or neglect to carry out the officer's instruction to drive the vehicle to a weighbridge or to refuse to comply with any other reasonable instruction, or to obstruct the officer in any way from exercising his duties.

If the vehicle is found to be overloaded, what action is taken?
A GV160 will be issued and the vehicle must be off-loaded to the required limits before it can continue its journey.

Can a vehicle which appears to be overloaded be subjected to several weight checks during its journey?
Where a vehicle suspected of being overweight has been the subject of an inspection and found to be within the permitted limits, a Certificate of Weight will be issued which will enable the vehicle to complete its journey without further checks.

Are there any special provisions for vehicles carrying inflammable or corrosive loads?
In the case of a vehicle carrying an inflammable or corrosive load, the driver may be allowed to take the vehicle to the nearest point where off-loading can be carried out safely.

Long and Wide Loads

What are the regulations concerning long and wide loads?
The regulations govern the maximum length and width of standard vehicles and their loads and also projecting loads. There are also regulations dealing with "Special Type" vehicles for the carriage of abnormal indivisible loads and wide loads.

The action to be taken depends very much on length, width and weight and ranges from a simple indication of the projecting load (a piece of rag tied to the end), through the attachment of marker boards, to notifying the police and to obtaining a special order from the Secretary of State for Transport.

Long Loads

Length		Action Required
If overall length of articulated vehicle, (specially constructed for abnormally long loads) and load plus trailer exceeds	18.3m	2 days' notice to police
If overall length of a combination of vehicles and loads including projections, exceeds	25.9m	2 days' notice to police
If combined length of trailer and load, excluding towing vehicle, exceeds	27.4m	2 days' notice to police and special order issued by Secretary of State for Transport is required.

Wide loads

Loads may not project more than 305mm on either side of the vehicle or trailer. The overall width of the vehicle and load must not exceed 2.9m.

Indivisible wide loads

Loads exceeding 2.9m may be transported if two days' notice is given to the police. Wide loads, carried on "special type" vehicles, must carry an attendant if over 3.5m wide and if over 5m a special order issued by the Secretary of State for Transport is required.

Forward Projecting Loads

Projection		Marker Boards	Attendant	Police Notice
Exceeding but not exceeding	2m 3.05m	End and side boards required	Yes	No
Exceeding	3.05m	End and side boards required	Yes	Yes
Exceeding	4.5m	End and side boards required Additional side boards within 2.5m of normal boards	Yes	Yes

Rearward Projecting Loads

Projection		Marker Boards	Attendant	Police Notice
Exceeding but not exceeding	1m 2m	Not required, but projection must be made clearly visible	No	No
Exceeding but not exceeding	2m 3.05m	End boards required	No	No
Exceeding but not exceeding	3.05m 5m	End and side boards required	Yes	Yes
Exceeding	5m	End and side boards required. Additional side boards within 3.5m of normal boards.	Yes	Yes

Projection Markers

Diagram of end projection surface

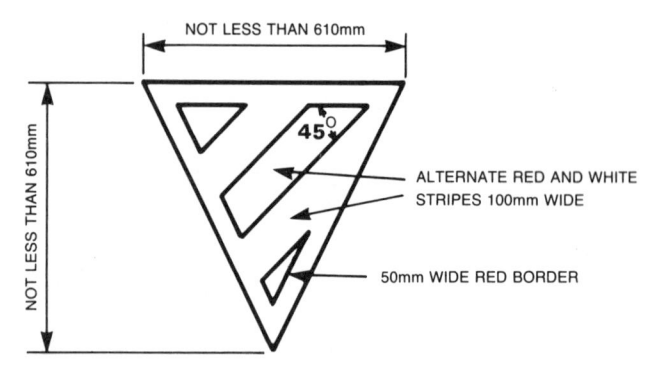

NOT LESS THAN 610mm
NOT LESS THAN 610mm
45°
ALTERNATE RED AND WHITE STRIPES 100mm WIDE
50mm WIDE RED BORDER

Diagram of side projection surface

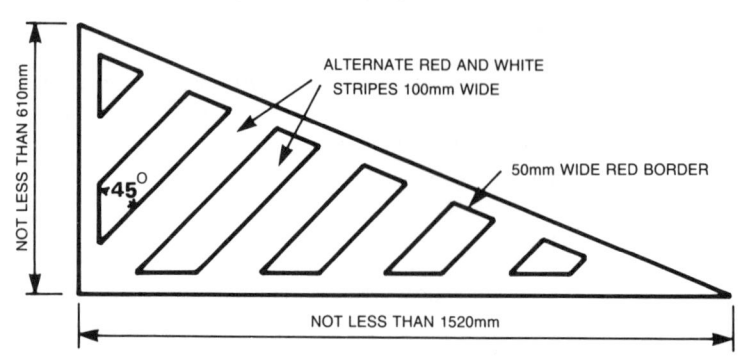

NOT LESS THAN 610mm
ALTERNATE RED AND WHITE STRIPES 100mm WIDE
50mm WIDE RED BORDER
45°
NOT LESS THAN 1520mm

Are there any special requirements concerning lighting on long or projecting loads?

Long loads
Unless illuminated side marker boards are carried all vehicles which (including the load) exceed **18.3m** overall, must carry side marker lights within **9.15m** of the front of the vehicle and **3.05m** of the rear and at intervals of not more than **3.05m** along the sides.
All marker boards must be adequately illuminated at night.
In addition:

Rearward projections
Projections of more than (a) **1m** beyond the rear of the vehicle or (b) **2m** if an agricultural vehicle or vehicle carrying a fire escape, an additional red rear light must be fitted to the vehicle within **1m** of the rearmost part of the vehicle in case (a) or within **2m** in case (b). If the load obscures existing rear lights and reflectors, additional lights and reflectors must be fixed to the load, or the obligatory lamps, reflectors, rear markings transferred to the end of the load.

Side projections
1. If a trailer, not fitted with front position lamps, is wider on any side than the preceding vehicle to the extent that the outermost part of the illuminated area of the obligatory front position lamp fitted to any preceding vehicle is more than **400mm**, a lamp showing a white light to the front must be fitted to the trailer with the outermost illuminated area of the light being not more than **400mm** from the outermost edge of the trailer.
2. If a trailer carries a load which is wider than the trailer and the preceding vehicle and the circumstances are similar to 1. above, a lamp showing a white light to the front must be fitted to the trailer, or load, or equipment so that the outermost part of the illuminating area of the lamp is not more than **400mm** from the outermost edge of the load or equipment, etc.
3. If a vehicle carries a load which is wider on any side of the vehicle so that the distance from the edge of the load or equipment to the outermost edge of the illuminated area of the obligatory front or rear position lamp on that side exceeds **400mm**, either (a) the front or rear position lamp must be transferred to the load, etc to which must also be attached a white front or red rear reflecting device, or (b) an additional front or rear position lamp and a white front or a red rear reflecting device must be fitted to the vehicle, load or equipment.

Abnormal Indivisible Loads and Special Type Vehicles

How is an abnormal indivisible load defined?
An "abnormal indivisible load" means a load which:
   (a) cannot, without undue expense or risk of damage, be divided into two or more loads for the purpose of carriage on roads and
   (b) which:
      (i) owing to its dimensions, cannot be carried by a heavy motor car or trailer complying in all respects with the requirements of the construction and use regulations, or

(ii) owing to its weight cannot be carried by a heavy motor car or trailer having a total laden weight of not more than **38,000kg** and complying in all respects with the requirements of the construction and use regulations.

What are "Special Type" vehicles and trailers?

These are vehicles and trailers which do not comply in all respects with the construction and use regulations and have been designed and constructed for the carriage of abnormal indivisible loads.

Are there any size limits in respect of Special Types?

The overall width of a vehicle must not exceed **2.9m** except where the vehicle is being used with a load which can only be carried safely on a wider vehicle or trailer, the maximum permitted width under any circumstances for a vehicle or trailer or load being **6.1m**.

The maximum permitted length of a vehicle and load is **27.4m** and where the load is carried on a combination of vehicle(s) and trailer(s) including an articulated unit the length of the load and trailer must not exceed **27.4m**.

Are there any maximum weights stipulated?

Maximum permitted weights depend upon the category of the vehicle.
Category 1 — a vehicle or vehicle combination with a total weight up to 46,000kg.
Category 2 — a vehicle or vehicle combination with a total weight up to 80,000kg.
Category 3 — a vehicle or vehicle combination with a total weight up to 150,000kg.

Detailed regulations concerning the number of axles, axle spacings and maximum axle weights determine the category into which the vehicle falls.

Do special speed limits apply to these vehicles and loads?

Speed limits are laid down for (a) Special Types and (b) other vehicles carrying wide loads (see page 29).

Attendants

When are attendants required?

An attendant is required under any of the following conditions:
    (a) where the overall width of a vehicle or its load exceeds **3.5m**
    (b) the overall length of the vehicle including any forward or rearward projections of the load exceeds **18.3m**
    (c) an articulated vehicle or a vehicle and trailer(s) where the length of the trailer and any projection to the front or rear of the load exceeds **18.3m**
    (d) a vehicle drawing a trailer or trailers and the overall length of the combination together with any overhang of the load exceeds **25.9m**
    (e) any vehicle carrying a load or equipment with a forward overhang exceeding **1.83m** or a rearward projection exceeding **3.05m**.

Where attendants are required on special type vehicles and more than three vehicles are involved, travelling in convoy, attendants need only be carried in the first and last vehicles of that convoy.

When is the approval of the Secretary of State for Transport required for the movement of wide loads?
Written notice has to be given to the Secretary of State for Transport when loads exceeding **5m** in width are carried on the road.

The vehicle may only be used for journeys between specified places, times, dates and route as stated in the Secretary's written notice or as the Chief Officer of Police may have designated for the vehicle in each police area.

When must notice be given to the police?
Two clear days' notice (excluding Sundays and Bank Holidays, Christmas Day or Good Friday) are required by the Chief Officer of Police for each area the vehicle is to be operated in. The notice must contain details of the vehicle and the proposed dates, times and route in each area.

The notice applies to vehicles:
- (a) which exceed **2.9m** in width
- (b) where the vehicle and any projections of load exceed **18.3m** in length
- (c) where the load is carried on a trailer or trailers or articulated combination and the length of the trailer and any load projections exceeds **18.3m**
- (d) where the combination of load, vehicles and trailers exceeds **25.9m**
- (e) where any forward or rearward projection of load or equipment exceeds **3.05m**
- (f) where the gross weight exceeds **80,000kg**.

When is it necessary to give notice to highway and bridge authorities or their authorised agents?
Notice to the above authorities is required in the following cases:
- (a) where the gross weight of a vehicle or any combination of vehicles or trailers exceeds **80,000kg** gross or
- (b) where any vehicle or combination of vehicles or trailers exceeds the requirements of the construction and use regulations in respect of the weight transmitted to the road by all or any of the wheels.

What period of notice is required?
Five clear days' notice is required in respect of (a) above, and two clear days in respect of (b).

NB Saturdays, Sundays and public holidays, etc do not count.

Vehicle Selection

What must an operator consider when making his choice of vehicles?
Selection of vehicles and equipment to satisfy the transport operator's requirements is of the utmost importance. Many factors must be taken into account when deciding on the type of vehicle to suit particular operating conditions. The "cheapest" is not always the best but, in so many cases, operators have to give due consideration to initial cost and therefore price sometimes becomes the deciding factor.

What other factors affect his choice?
The operator must first of all be quite definite in deciding what he expects from a vehicle in relation to his operational needs, the decision being based on:
- (a) loads to be carried (light, heavy or bulk)
- (b) degree of operation:
    - (i) annual mileages
    - (ii) distance work, short haul or combination of both
- (c) replacement policy and authorisation.

Considerations under (c) above are of importance in relation to cost and maintenance as some operators prefer to purchase the less expensive type of vehicle and replace at short intervals. This allows for a vehicle being kept in good condition mechanically (minimising repair work and vehicle "down" time) and provides maximum vehicle utilisation. This particularly applies to tipper vehicles, medium trucks and tractors on concentrated work or high mileage.

Conversely, the more expensive type of vehicle may be selected where a longer replacement period and spread of depreciation can be applied.

With a full appreciation of these facts the choice of vehicle should be made with due consideration of the following:
- (a) type of vehicle:
    - (i) articulated — "an articulated vehicle is a motor car or heavy motor car with a trailer so attached that when the trailer is uniformly loaded at least 20% of the weight of the load is imposed on the drawing vehicle"
    - (ii) rigid vehicle — "one which is not constructed or adapted to form part of an articulated vehicle"
- (b) type of body (box, platform or special)
- (c) design and construction:
    - (i) stabilisation and weight distribution
    - (ii) adequate engine power
    - (iii) gearbox and axle ratios
    - (iv) brakes
    - (v) axle loadings
    - (vi) suspension
    - (vii) type equipment
- (d) mechanical handling equipment:
    - (i) hydraulic tail lifts
    - (ii) autocranes
    - (iii) swop bodies and containers.

Mechanical Conditions

What is the purpose of the Motor Vehicles (Construction and Use) Regulations 1986 (SI 1986 No. 1078)?
These regulations govern the construction and use of motor vehicles. The principal purpose of the regulations is to contribute towards safety on the roads by ensuring that the vehicles themselves are safe.

What is the purpose of the Motor Vehicles (Type Approval) Regulations 1980 (SI 1980 No. 1182)?
These regulations provide exemption from the construction and use regulations for vehicles which conform with a number of EC directives and have been issued with a type approval certificate.

What is a certificate of conformity?
When a type approval certificate has been issued to a manufacturer for a vehicle (or component) certifying that it meets the construction requirements of a member country, the manufacturer may issue, for each subsequent vehicle built, a certificate of conformity, ie confirming that it is identical with that vehicle for which the type approval certificate was issued. This certificate of conformity will ensure the acceptance of the vehicle for use in any EC country without question.

What are the requirements concerning the equipment of vehicles?
Brakes
Every goods vehicle must be equipped with either an efficient braking system with two means of operation or two efficient braking systems having separate means of operation. But no account is to be taken of multi-pull means of brake operation unless at the first application it provides a braking efficiency of not less than 25% in respect of heavy motor cars or motor cars registered on or after January 1, 1968.

Parking Brake
Every motor vehicle must have a braking system to prevent at least two wheels (one if a three-wheeler) revolving when the vehicle is not being driven. All vehicles registered on or after January 1, 1968 must have an independent parking brake.

Braking efficiency
Goods vehicles having at least four wheels and required to have two means of operating brakes must have total braking efficiencies as follows:
  If registered on or after January 1, 1968: First means 50%
                                              Second means 25%
The parking brake must be capable, by direct mechanised action, of holding a vehicle stationary on a gradient of at least 16%, ie 1 in 6.25.

Brakes (Trailers)
Trailers manufactured before January 1, 1968 which exceed 750kg gross weight must have efficient brakes which can be applied by the driver or some other person on the vehicle or trailer while the trailer is being drawn, except when the trailer is fitted with overrun brakes.

Trailer brakes must apply to at least two wheels of a vehicle having not more than four wheels or to at least four wheels if there are more than four wheels.

Trailers exceeding 750kg gross weight, manufactured from January 1, 1968, must have an efficient braking system which can be applied by the driver to all the trailer wheels and having the highest braking efficiency of any brakes of the towing vehicle except when the trailer is fitted with overrun brakes. Emergency brakes must act on at least two trailer wheels.

When a trailer is stationary the parking brake must apply to at least two wheels, be capable of holding the trailer on a gradient of at least 16% (1 in 6.25) without the assistance of stored energy and be capable of being operated by a person standing on the ground.

Safety Glass
Goods vehicles must have safety glass fitted to the windscreen and windows on either side of the driver's seat.

Windscreen Wipers and Washers
At least one efficient automatic windscreen wiper or wipers must be fitted to every vehicle from which an adequate view to the front cannot be obtained other than through the windscreen. Wipers must be capable of ensuring that the driver has an adequate view of the road to the front and the front of the near and offsides. Such vehicles must also be fitted with a windscreen washer which, in conjunction with the wiper, can keep the screen clear of mud, etc.

Mirrors
All goods and dual-purpose vehicles must have at least two rear-view mirrors, one fitted externally on the offside and the other either internally, or externally on the nearside, to show traffic to the rear and both sides rearwards.

Tractive units of articulated vehicles must be fitted with an external rear-view mirror on the offside and an internal mirror (if the rear of the unit offers the driver a view to the rear when not carrying a load, ie a container) and an external mirror on the nearside when carrying a load that does not allow him a view to the rear through the internal mirror.

Goods vehicles exceeding 12,000kg maximum gross weight must be fitted with nearside and close proximity wide angle rearview mirrors.

Horns
Every motor vehicle must be fitted with an instrument capable of giving audible and sufficient warning of its approach or position. Only a vehicle used by official emergency services may be fitted with a gong, bell, siren, two-tone horn or instrument capable of emitting a similar sound.

Vehicles first used on or after August 1, 1973 must not be fitted with musical or multi-tone horns.

Motor vehicles used for the conveyance of goods for sale from the vehicle may be fitted with an instrument other than a two-tone horn to announce that goods are for sale. But such an instrument must be in addition to the standard horn.

Horns may not be sounded when the vehicle is stationary on a road nor when it is in motion on a restricted road at night between the hours of 23.30 and 07.00 except in an emergency.

Reversing Alarms
These may be fitted to goods vehicles having a maximum gross weight of 2 tonnes or more. They may not be sounded on a restricted road between 23.30 hours and 07.00 hours.

Petrol Tanks
Motor vehicle petrol tanks must be so maintained that they are reasonably secure against being damaged and are free from leakages. Motor vehicles first used on July 1, 1973 must be equipped with metal petrol tanks reasonably secured against damage and free from leakages.

NB The law does **not** require diesel tanks, as opposed to petrol tanks, to be constructed of metal.

Silencers and Noise
Every vehicle fitted with an internal combustion engine must be fitted with a silencer or similar device to reduce, "as far as may be reasonable", the noise caused by the exhaust.

No motor vehicle or trailer which causes excessive noise may be used on a road, nor may it be used in a manner to cause excessive noise.
Specific noise levels and ways of measuring them are laid down.
Vehicles are subject to spot checks on the road to ensure that they do not make more noise than the standards allow.
All new vehicles registered after April 1, 1970 must meet stringent limits on noise.
References to noise emitted by a vehicle also include noise attributable to any load, burden or goods carried and to the manner in which the vehicle is loaded or fitted. The regulations also include noise made by any trailer being drawn by a motor vehicle.

Smoke
Every motor vehicle must be constructed so that no avoidable smoke or visible vapour is emitted. Excess fuel devices must not be used on diesel-engined vehicles whilst in action. Diesel engines of more than two cylinders built after October 1, 1972 and fitted to vehicles first used on or after April 1, 1973 must have an engine of a type for which a BS AU 141a: 1971 certificate has been issued in respect of exhaust smoke.

Exhaust Controls
Petrol driven motor vehicles not exceeding 3,500kg laden or unladen, first registered on or after November 10, 1973 must be fitted with equipment that reduces the level of carbon monoxide and hydrocarbons escaping into the atmosphere and the vehicle must bear the designated type approval mark for this equipment. This does not apply to vehicles manufactured before September 10, 1973.

When, as a result of an accident, a vehicle has a slightly damaged exhaust, it is not an offence to use the vehicle on the road in order to complete the journey.

Tyres
Goods vehicles and trailers must be fitted with pneumatic tyres, with specialised exceptions. Re-cut tyres may be fitted only to goods vehicles weighing 2,540kg unladen or more and a wheel diameter of 405mm or over and any electrically propelled goods vehicle.

No vehicle or trailer may be used on the roads when fitted with a pneumatic tyre if:
  (a) the tyre is unsuitable for the use to which the vehicle or trailer is being put or to the types of tyres fitted to the other wheels
  (b) the tyre is not properly inflated to make it fit for the use to which the vehicle or trailer is being put
  (c) the tyre has a cut in excess of 25mm or 10% of the section width of the tyre, whichever is the greater, measured in any direction on the outside of the tyre and deep enough to reach the ply or cord

(d) the tyre has any lump, bulge or tear caused by separation or partial failure of its structure
(e) the tyre has any portion of the ply or cord exposed or
(f) the base of any groove which showed in the original tread pattern of the tyre is not clearly visible
(g) either (i) the grooves of the tread pattern do not have a depth of at least 1mm throughout a continuous band measuring at least three-quarters of the breadth of tread and round the entire outer circumference of the tyre, or (ii) where the original tread pattern did not extend beyond ¾ of the breadth of the tread, the base of any groove which showed in the tyre's original tread pattern does not have a depth of at least 1mm.

"Breadth of tread" means the breadth of that part of the tyre which is in contact with the road under normal conditions of use measured at 90° to the peripheral line of the tread.

Paragraphs (c), (d) and (e) above do not apply where the tyre and wheel to which it is fitted are so constructed that when running deflated the tyre will operate safely and its outside wall bears an identifying mark to that effect.

These regulations do not apply to, among others, a broken-down vehicle or a vehicle being taken to a place to be broken up where in either case it is being towed by a vehicle at a speed not exceeding 20 mph.

Recut pneumatic tyres must not be used if the ply or cord has been cut or exposed by the recutting process or it has been wholly or partially recut in a different pattern to that of the manufacturer's recut tread pattern.

The regulations prohibit the fitting to motor vehicles having only two axles and equipped with one or two single wheels, tyres of different types, ie cross-ply, radial or bias-belted, in the following manner:
(a) diagonal-ply tyres or bias-belted tyres on the rear axle and radial ply tyres on the front axle
(b) diagonal-ply tyres on the rear axle and bias-belted tyres on the front axle.

This, however, does not apply if wide tyres are fitted, provided they are not of the type specially constructed for use on engineering plant or fitted to a vehicle which is incapable of exceeding 30 mph on the level under its own power.

Also prohibited is the fitting of tyres of different structures to vehicles with (a) more than one steerable axle, or (b) more than one driven axle not being a steerable axle.

"Axle" means (i) two or more stub axles fitted on opposite sides of the longitudinal axis of the vehicle to form a pair in the case of two stub axles and pairs in the case of more than two stub axles and (ii) a single stub not being one of a pair.

Wide Tyre
This is a tyre having an area of contact with the road of not less than 300mm in width when measured at right angles to the longitudinal axis of the vehicle.

Tyre Standards
It is illegal to supply car tyres (with certain exceptions) unless they are "E" marked to show that they comply with Economic Commission for Europe (ECE) Regulation 30 covering load and speed requirements.

Retreaded tyres must comply with British Standard Specification BS AU 144b: 1977 and be marked "BS AU 144b".

Rear Underrun Protection
Goods vehicles exceeding 3500kg maximum gross weight, manufactured from October 1, 1983 and first used on or after April 1, 1984 and goods carrying trailers and semi-trailers exceeding 1020kg unladen weight, manufactured from May 1, 1983, must be fitted with rear underrun protection devices. Where a vehicle has a tail lift or the bodywork prevents the device from being fitted, one or more such devices must be fitted which are (a) not more than 50cm apart, (b) the outermost end of the device is not more than 30cm from the outermost part of the vehicle, (c) the devices comply with the requirements of EC directives 70/221/EEC as amended by 79/490/EEC.

There are many exemptions from these requirements including the tractive units of articulated vehicles.

Every device fitted to a vehicle must be maintained free from any obvious defect which would be likely to affect its performance in the event of an impact.

Sideguards
Sideguards must be fitted to goods vehicles and trailers, etc (with certain exceptions):
(a) before use for:
   (i) semi-trailers manufactured prior to May 1, 1983 having a plated gross weight exceeding 26,000kg and the distance between the centre of the first axle and the centre of the king pin (the rearmost one if more than one) exceeding 4.5m and the tractive unit having a plated train weight exceeding 32,520kg
     (**NB** There is no requirement for sideguards to be fitted to the aforementioned semi-trailers where the plated *train* weight of the tractive unit and semi-trailer does not exceed 32,520kg.)
   (ii) trailers and semi-trailers manufactured from May 1, 1983 exceeding 1020kg unladen weight and where, in the case of a trailer, the distance between the centres of any two consecutive axles exceeds 3m, and for a semi-trailer the distance between the centre of its first axle and the centre of the king pin (the rearmost king pin, if more than one) exceeds 4.5m
(b) goods vehicles exceeding 3500kg maximum gross weight first used on and from April 1, 1984 and where the distance between the centres of any two consecutive axles exceeds 3m.

Certain vehicles are exempt from these requirements.

Extendable trailers and vehicles constructed to carry demountable bodies must be fitted with sideguards but the fitting requirements are modified for these types of vehicles. Tanker vehicles and vehicles fitted with stabilisers (for loading and unloading) must also be fitted with sideguards providing this is practicable.

Every sideguard must be maintained free from any obvious defect which would be likely to affect its performance in the event of an impact.

Spray Suppression Equipment
Approved spray suppression equipment conforming to BSS BS AU 200: 1986 must be fitted to the wheels of each axle of vehicles and trailers as follows:
   (a) motor vehicles exceeding 12 tonnes maximum gross weight first used from April 1, 1986
   (b) trailers exceeding 3.5 tonnes maximum gross weight manufactured from May 1, 1985

(c) trailers exceeding 16 tonnes maximum gross weight having two or more axles manufactured before May 1, 1985.

Spray suppression equipment fitted to vehicles before January 1, 1985 will be considered acceptable provided it conforms substantially with the British Standard.

Certain vehicles are exempt from these requirements.

Towing

A locomotive may draw up to three trailers.

A motor tractor may draw one laden **or** two unladen trailers.

A motor car or heavy motor car may draw one trailer.

A motor car or heavy motor car may draw two trailers if one of them is a towing implement (ie a dolly) and the other is a vehicle that rests on, or is suspended from, the towing implement.

When an articulated vehicle (ie tractive unit and semi-trailer) has broken down and has to be towed, it is treated as a single trailer provided the semi-trailer is unloaded.

Where a motor vehicle is drawing a trailer, the distance between their nearest points must not exceed 4.5m. If the distance exceeds 1.5m the bar or towing chain must be made clearly visible from either side to other road users by a coloured rag or luminous material.

CHAPTER 7
(Module B)
Plating and Testing, Checks and Prohibitions

What is the purpose of plating vehicles?
It is to indicate by means of an official plate attached to the vehicle or trailer the particulars of that vehicle or trailer, especially those relating to the maximum axle and gross weights, beyond which they cannot be operated. (See also under "Type Approval" page 71.)

Which legislation provides for plating and testing?
The appropriate legislation is the Goods Vehicles (Plating and Testing) Regulations 1982 (SI 1982 No. 1478) and subsequent amendments.

To which vehicles do the regulations apply?
Subject to certain exemptions, the regulations apply to all goods vehicles over 1525kg unladen weight, articulated vehicles and drawbar trailers over 1020kg unladen weight and trailers being converter dollies.

When is a DTp plate issued for the vehicle?
Vehicles first used from April 1, 1983 to which the type approval regulations apply, will be covered either by a Minister's Approval Certificate (MAC) or a Type Approval Certificate (TAC). The MAC or TAC is sent to the DVLC, Swansea, at the time of registration and a plating certificate, showing gross and unladen weights at which the vehicle may operate, is sent to the operator with the plate for display in the vehicle cab.

NB 1. Type approval does not extend to trailers/semi-trailers and the plating certificate is issued at the time of their *first* test.
NB 2. Information on type approval is given later in this chapter.

When are vehicles first required to be tested?
All goods vehicles first registered or trailers first sold to which the regulations apply are required to be tested before the end of the **first anniversary month of their date of registration,** or in the case of trailers, sale, and yearly thereafter not later than the anniversary date shown in the test certificate.

Vehicles which are being imported for the first time are exempted whilst being driven from their place of arrival to where they will be kept until the first examination can be arranged.

Where a vehicle has been off the road and is tested more than 10 months but less than one year after the date it was originally due for its periodical test then the test certificate will be valid for up to 14 months from the date on which it was tested.

Are any vehicles exempt from plating and testing?
There is a long list of exempted vehicles but questions of this nature are not usually set in the examination.

What happens if exceptional circumstances prevent plating and testing?
A certificate of temporary exemption may be issued when exceptional circumstances prevent the plating and testing of a vehicle by the due date. The maximum validity of such a certificate is three months.

What is the procedure for applying for tests?
Applications for first tests must be made on the appropriate forms (VTG1L for vehicles and VTG2L for trailers and semi-trailers) and thereafter on form VTG40L ("L" stands for Local) and sent, accompanied by the correct fee, to the Department of Transport, Goods Vehicle Centre, Swansea. The Centre will retain the fee and pass the application form to the testing station nominated by the operator, who will book the test and notify the operator of the date and time on the tear-off appointment letter contained in the application form.

Forms are available from Traffic Area Offices, Money Order Post Offices and the Goods Vehicle Centre, Swansea.

Should the operator carry out any pre-test procedures?
Before submitting a vehicle for test the operator should ensure that it is clean and in good condition. The driver must remain in attendance during the examination and drive the vehicle or operate the controls as required by the examiner.

Can minor faults be rectified at the testing station?
Operators should send either a driver with mechanical knowledge and tools, or a mechanic with the driver, as it may be possible for the examiner to allow minor faults to be rectified (without delaying the test) before the test is complete. The examiner can refuse to carry out the test for a variety of reasons including: late arrival; non-production of the appointment card and the registration document (or other means of proving the vehicle's registration); where a vehicle stated in the application form to be used in drawing a trailer is not accompanied by a trailer; or if the vehicle is fitted with recut pneumatic tyres (except (a) on goods vehicles of 2550kg or more unladen weight and the rim diameter of the wheel is 40cm or more and (b) electrically propelled goods vehicles).

Who is responsible for ensuring that the vehicle conforms to the regulations?
Responsibility for compliance with the law rests with the user or hirer of the vehicle as well as with the driver and operator and all can be liable for infringements.

Compliance with permitted axle weights needs particular care, especially as individual axle loadings can vary as load decreases, or as a result of "load movement" during transit.

The regulations do not recognise any distinctions between gross and axle overloadings and the latter carry the same penalty as the former. Axle weight infringements can easily arise when the full load is within the permitted gross weight limit, eg when part of a load is removed this may result in the overloading of an axle that was not formerly overloaded.

What procedure must be followed if the vehicle is modified after plating?
Modifications to plated vehicles which:

(a) alter the carrying capacity of the vehicle
(b) adversely affect the braking system
(c) render the vehicle unsafe to travel on the road at plated weight

must be notified to the Department of Transport, Goods Vehicle Centre, Swansea before the altered vehicle is used on the road.

In certain cases the vehicles will have to be submitted for re-examination by the Department of Transport and this will be obligatory where replating is involved.

Type Approval

Is there any compulsory scheme for vehicle type approval?
Yes! The Motor Vehicles (Type Approval for Goods Vehicles) (Great Britain) Regulations 1982 (SI 1982 No. 1271) apply to most goods vehicles manufactured on or after October 1, 1982 and first used on or after April 1, 1983.

What is the effect of this legislation?
Vehicles coming within the scope of the regulations require either:
   (a) a Type Approval Certificate (TAC) for vehicles manufactured within the EC, or
   (b) a Minister's Approval Certificate (MAC) for vehicles manufactured outside the EC, before first registration.

Manufacturers within the EC may also apply for MACs, but manufacturers outside the EC may not apply for TACs.

How does the manufacturer obtain vehicle type approval?
Before he can obtain approval for the whole vehicle, he must first obtain individual system approvals for power to weight ratio, noise and silencers, exhaust emissions, radio interference and brakes. Then, at the time of granting vehicle type approval, the Department of Transport will determine the maximum weights at which the vehicle can be used on the roads in Great Britain in accordance with the construction and use regulations.

What is a Certificate of Conformity?
This is another name for a Type Approval Certificate (TAC). In the case of a whole vehicle this lists all the individual systems that must have their own type approval. The vehicle must also conform to those requirements of the construction and use or lighting regulations which are not included on the certificate.

How does the type approval legislation affect operators?
It is an offence to sell or use on the roads a goods vehicle exceeding 1525kg unladen weight, or forming part of an articulated vehicle, unless it is covered by a valid certificate.

How does the operator obtain the certificate?
Every vehicle will be supplied with two copies of a TAC or MAC, one of which must bear a statement by the manufacturer on whether or not the vehicle is exempt from

the plating and testing regulations and, if any alteration requiring notification has been carried out, whether any action resulting from the notification has been satisfactorily completed.

What kind of alterations must be notified?
Before the first registration certain alterations to vehicles for which certificates of conformity have been issued must be notified to the Department of Transport.
  These alterations fall into two categories:
  (a) *Prescribed alterations* — changes in the number or nominal diameter of the wheels or tyres, are known as prescribed alterations and the Vehicle Approval Division of the Department of Transport has to be informed.
  (b) *Notifiable alterations* — modifications to plated vehicles which:
    (i) alter the carrying capacity or towing capacity of the vehicle
    (ii) alter or affect any part of the braking or steering systems or
    (iii) render the vehicle unsafe to travel on the road at its plated weight
    must be notified to the Department of Transport, Goods Vehicle Centre, Swansea.

Can alterations be made to the vehicle after its first registration?
After first registration an operator can modify his vehicle in any way he wishes, provided that it still complies with the requirements of the construction and use regulations. If, however, any such alteration or modification comes within the notifiable alterations as detailed above, the Goods Vehicle Centre, Swansea, must be notified before the vehicle is again used on the road.

Vehicle Marking Regulations

Is it obligatory to display the name and address of the owner on all commercial vehicles?
No! Only the following categories of vehicle need display names and addresses of the operating companies:
  (a) every kind of vehicle from which milk is sold or offered for sale
  (b) every dealer in ice-cream who in a public place in England and Wales sells ice-cream from a vehicle
  (c) vehicles, stalls and mobile shops from which any food is sold or carried and from which business is conducted
  (d) milk tankers which must display the name and address of the consignor.

Must the unladen weight, etc be shown on the vehicle?
The unladen weight of the vehicle must be painted or plainly marked in some conspicuous place on the left or nearside of locomotives, tractors, and heavy motor cars. However, this is not required when a Ministry plate has been issued for a vehicle which shows its *unladen* weight.
  Vehicles covered by the plating and testing regulations must carry a plate showing the vehicle's plated particulars. These particulars may be painted on the chassis for the convenience of weighbridge attendants.

What are the regulations governing marker boards?

Marker boards or projection marker boards with red and white stripes painted diagonally (see diagram on page 58) must be fitted to some vehicles and equipment.

Where a projecting load is carried, or a projecting special appliance is permanently fitted to a vehicle, marker boards must be fitted as follows:

Forward projecting

Projection exceeding **2m** but not exceeding **3.05m**: end and side marker boards must be fitted and an attendant carried.

Projection exceeding **3.05m**: end and side marker boards must be fitted, an attendant carried and two days' notice given to the police.

Rearward projecting

Projection exceeding **1m** but not exceeding **2m:** steps must be taken to make the projection clearly visible.

Projection exceeding **2m** but not exceeding **3.05m**: an end marker board must be fitted (but see below).

Projection exceeding **3.05m**: end and side marker boards must be fitted, an attendant carried and two days' notice given to the police.

Additional side marker boards are required for any forward projection exceeding **4.5m**, or any rearward projection exceeding **5m**. In these circumstances the marker boards must be fitted within **2.5m** and **3.5m** respectively of the normal marker boards.

All marker boards must be adequately illuminated at night.

A *rear marking* must be fitted to the end projection surface of loads projecting to the rear if the load obscures the vehicle's rear markings.

What are the regulations governing number plates?

The index mark and registration number must be clearly exhibited at the front and rear of every motor vehicle (except works trucks, unless these are required for use on the road between factories). The description and size must conform to the official specification and all number plates must be fixed in a vertical position at front and rear and the rear plate must be illuminated at night.

In the case of a trailer (including a broken-down vehicle being towed) the registration number of the towing vehicle must appear on the rear of the vehicle on tow.

Vehicles first registered from January 1, 1973, including trailers attached to such vehicles, **not** exceeding 3050kg unladen weight, must be fitted with reflex-reflecting number plates. The background of the plate only must be of reflex-reflecting material and must be **white** for the front plate and **yellow** for the rear with letters and figures in black on both plates. Each plate must bear the BSS No. BS AU 145a: 1971.

For vehicles first registered prior to January 1, 1973 not exceeding 3050kg unladen weight, heavy motor vehicles whenever registered, agricultural machines and works trucks the number plates may comprise white, silver or light grey letters and figures indelibly inscribed upon, or attached to, a black surface on a flat rectangular plate or on a flat rectangular unbroken surface forming part of the vehicle.

NB the tractive unit of an articulated vehicle should be fitted with reflex-reflective number plates if it is used on the road without a semi-trailer attached.

Are there special markings for heavy and long vehicles?

In the interests of road safety, heavy motor vehicles are required to be fitted with rear markings which are conspicuous in the light of headlamps and show up well in poor weather conditions as follows:
- (a) motor vehicles exceeding 7.5 tonnes gross weight and trailers over 3.5 tonnes gross weight up to **13m** long must be fitted with rear markings of diagonal stripes of red fluorescent and yellow reflective material as shown in diagram 1 or 2 on page 75. Where the construction of the vehicle or trailer makes the fitting of markings in diagram 1 or 2 impractical the markings shown in diagram 3 on page 75 may be fitted
- (b) vehicles more than **13m** long must be fitted with a rear marking having the words LONG VEHICLE in black lettering on a yellow reflective background with a red fluorescent border as shown in diagram 4 or 5 on page 75
- (c) trailer combinations over **11m** but not over **13m** may fit either type of marking.

Rear markings must comply with BS AU 152: 1970.

Positioning

Markings must be securely fixed to the vehicle, must not project beyond the sides of the vehicle and must be kept clean and in good order. The lower edge of each marking must be horizontal and not more than **1700mm** nor less than **400mm** from the ground. Where divided markings are used (Nos. 2, 3 and 5), the lower edges of each half must be level; each half must be the same distance from the centre and as near to the outermost edge of the vehicle as possible.

Markings Nos. 1 and 4 must be placed so that the centre of the markings is on the centre line of the vehicle.

Rear markings may be fitted to the projecting load when the rear markings on the vehicle are likely to be obscured by the load.

Are any vehicles exempt from these marking requirements?

The following vehicles are exempt:
- (a) a passenger vehicle
- (b) a trailer being a living van, the unladen weight not exceeding 2 tons
- (c) land tractors, implements, conveyors, agricultural trailers or industrial tractors
- (d) a works truck or trailer
- (e) a vehicle partly completed and being moved to or from store or display for sale
- (f) a motor vehicle constructed or adapted for the purpose of forming part of an articulated vehicle
- (g) a broken-down vehicle, engineering plant, a service vehicle for controlling aircraft or a vehicle used for the transportation of two or more vehicles or vehicle bodies or two or more boats
- (h) a foreign vehicle or trailer temporarily imported into Great Britain having previously been imported within the preceding 12 months
- (i) a vehicle in the service of a visiting force and a motor vehicle proceeding to a place for export and a vehicle used for fire-fighting and salvage purposes
- (j) vehicles used as tar boilers or asphalt mixers
- (k) United Kingdom military vehicles.

Size and Type of Rear Markings

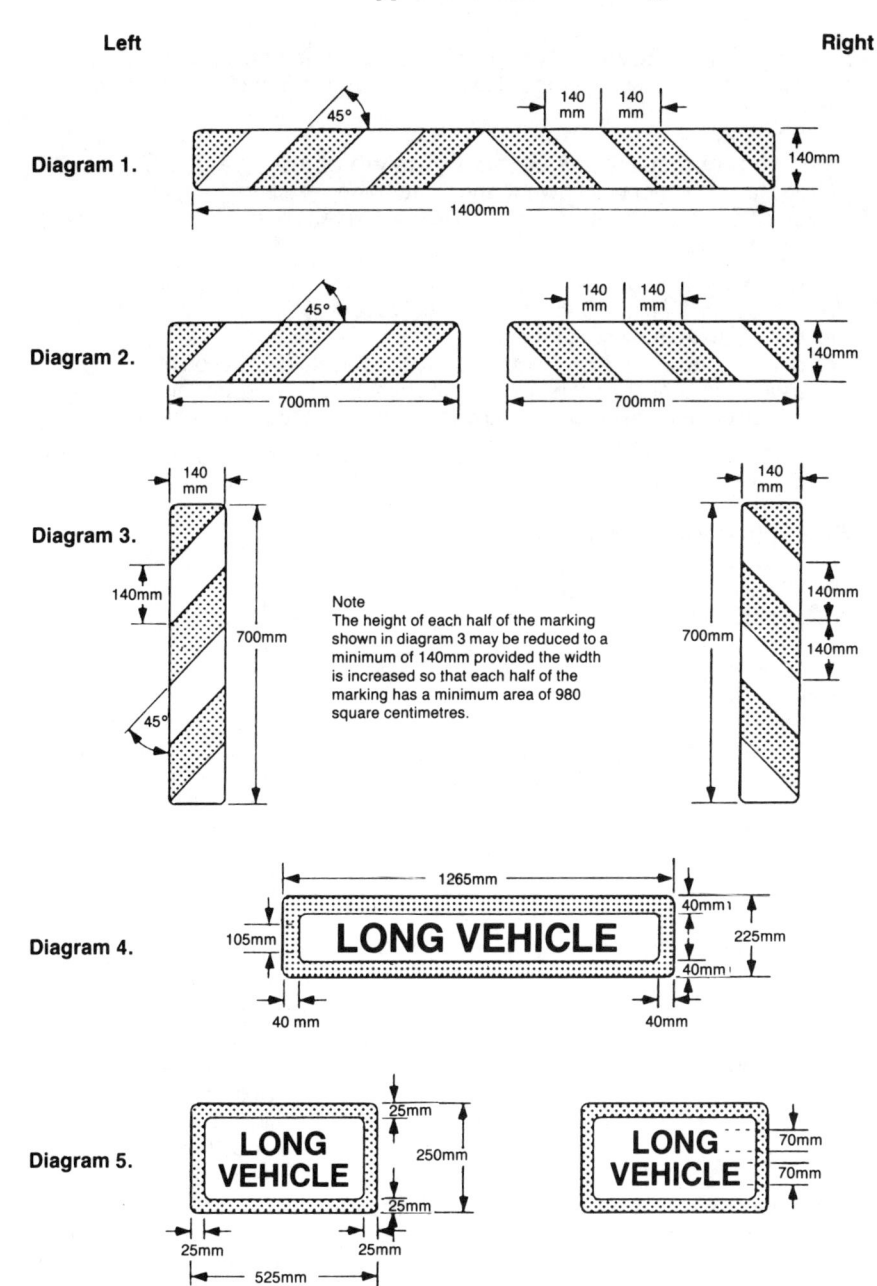

Left   **Right**

Diagram 1. — 1400mm wide, 140mm high, 45° stripes, 140mm stripe widths.

Diagram 2. — Two panels of 700mm wide, 140mm high, 45° stripes, 140mm stripe widths.

Diagram 3. — 140mm wide, 700mm high, 45° stripes, 140mm stripe heights.

Note
The height of each half of the marking shown in diagram 3 may be reduced to a minimum of 140mm provided the width is increased so that each half of the marking has a minimum area of 980 square centimetres.

Diagram 4. — "LONG VEHICLE" sign, 1265mm wide, 225mm high, 105mm lettering, 40mm borders.

Diagram 5. — "LONG VEHICLE" signs; left: 525mm × 250mm, 25mm borders; right: 70mm lettering with 70mm spacing.

Vehicle Lighting

What legislation governs the lighting of vehicles and trailers?
The legislation is contained in the Road Traffic Act 1988 and the Road Vehicles Lighting Regulations 1989.

Are there any restrictions on the lights which may be used?
1. A red light must not be shown to the front of the vehicle.
2. A white light must not be shown to the rear of the vehicle, except in the following circumstances:
    - (a) for the purpose of reversing
    - (b) in order to illuminate the interior of the vehicle
    - (c) to illuminate the rear number plate
    - (d) to illuminate a taxi-meter or public service vehicle destination board
    - (e) a work lamp, but only when used to illuminate a working area or the scene of an accident, breakdown or roadworks in the vicinity of the vehicle.

Special provisions do, of course, apply to fire, police, ambulance and other special vehicles where the use of blue, amber and green lights is permitted.

What lights, etc are obligatory?
The basic requirements call for:

Front position lamps (formerly called sidelamps)	— two
Headlamps (dipped beam/main beam)	— two
Red rear position lamps	— two
Red stop lamps	— two
Rear retro reflectors	— two
Direction indicators	— at least two pairs
Red rear fog lamps	— one or two (obligatory for vehicles first used from April 1980)
Rear registration plate lamp	— one at least
Dim-dip lighting device or running lamps	— obligatory for vehicles first used from April 1, 1987
Hazard warning lights	— obligatory for vehicles first used from April 1, 1986 which must be fitted with direction indicator
End-outline marker lamps	— 2 front and 2 rear. Obligatory for vehicles first used from 1.4.91 and trailers manufactured from 1.10.90.

What are the requirements for headlamps?
Motor vehicles which have three or more wheels are required to be fitted with at least two headlamps (forming a pair), one on each side, which can emit main and dipped beams. In addition main beam headlamps may be fitted.

Headlamps must be fitted so that the outermost surface of the illuminated area of the lamp is not more than **400mm** from the side of the vehicle on the relevant side. They must not be more than **1200mm** nor less than **500mm** from the ground, measured from the highest or lowest surface of the illuminated areas of the lamp.

Headlamps may emit only white or yellow light and each headlamp forming a pair must emit the same colour light.

All headlamps must be securely and permanently fixed to the vehicle and each lamp in the pair must be at the same height from the ground and have the same area and shape when illuminated.

The minimum wattage of a bulb or sealed beam unit must not be less than 30 watts.

What regulations apply to front position lamps (sidelights)?

Two lamps must be fitted showing a white light (or yellow if incorporated in headlamps emitting a yellow light) through frosted glass or other diffusing material.

The maximum wattage of lamps must not exceed 7 watts.

What rear position lamps (rear lights) must be fitted?

At least two red rear position lamps must be fitted to vehicles and trailers. Their positioning depends on when the vehicle is first used, or, in the case of trailers, when manufactured.

Are there any special regulations concerning stop lamps?

Vehicles first used and trailers manufactured from January 1, 1971 must have at least two stop lamps which form a pair. They must show a red light which must be diffused and non-flashing.

Stop lamps on both vehicles and trailers must be operated by the application of the braking system.

What are the requirements for rear retro reflectors?

Motor vehicles and trailers must be fitted with two rear retro reflectors. Motor vehicles having three or more wheels but which have a maximum speed not exceeding 25 mph together with trailers must have four reflectors (two pairs). There are certain specific exceptions to this latter rule where structural difficulties make it impossible for four reflectors to be fitted.

Triangular shaped rear reflectors may not be fitted to any vehicle other than a trailer.

Must flashing direction indicators be fitted?

Only vehicles first registered before September 1965 are permitted to use semaphore type indicators, all vehicles manufactured since that date must be fitted with flashing type indicators.

Motor vehicles having three or more wheels first used from April 1, 1986 must be fitted on each side with:

(a) a single front indicator
(b) one, but not more than two, rear indicators
(c) at least one side repeater indicator.

Trailers manufactured from October 1, 1985 and drawn by motor vehicles must be fitted with one but not more than two rear indicators. Side indicators may also be fitted.

Existing motor vehicles and trailers manufactured before October 1, 1985 must have one front indicator and not more than two rear indicators fitted on each side (additional side indicators may be fitted) which must be plainly visible to the rear in the case of a trailer and to the front in the case of any other vehicle.

General requirements for vehicles of any age
Indicators must emit an amber coloured light. If fitted to a motor vehicle first used before September 1965 they must be:
(a) white or amber if they show only to the front
(b) red or amber if they show only to the rear
(c) amber only if they show to both front and rear.

All indicators on one side of a vehicle (and any trailer being towed) must flash in phase.

A tell-tale indicator must be fitted in the driver's cab so that he is aware when the indicators are working.

The periodicity of the constant flashing light must not be less than 60 nor more than 120 flashes per minute.

Every indicator must perform efficiently regardless of the speed of the vehicle.

Are rear fog lamps obligatory?
Rear fog lamps must be fitted to vehicles and trailers first used from April 1, 1980.

Vehicles to which the regulations apply may be fitted with either one or two rear fog lamps, which must bear the appropriate approval mark.

A rear fog lamp must be fitted at least **100mm** away from a stop lamp.

The electrical connections must be such that a rear fog lamp cannot be illuminated by the application of the brakes.

Every rear fog lamp when lit must show a steady red light to the rear. Such lamps must not cause undue dazzle or inconvenience to other road users and may only be used in conditions where visibility is seriously reduced.

What lamps are required to illuminate rear number plates?
At least one lamp must be fitted so that it illuminates the rear number (registration) plate, which must be distinguishable to a person standing within a square extending 60 feet from the rear of the vehicle. The lamp must be lit when the front position lamps and the red rear position lamps are switched on.

Are there any special provisions in respect of front fog lamps?
Front fog lamps may be fitted to motor vehicles in addition to the obligatory front headlamps but must not be more than **1200mm** above the ground.

Fog lamps may emit either a white or yellow light and must be positioned so that they do not cause dazzle or discomfort to other road users and may only be used in conditions where visibility is seriously reduced.

NB A pair of fog lamps may only be used in place of dipped beam headlamps in poor conditions where they are fitted so that the outermost illuminated area of each lamp is not more than **400mm** from the side of the vehicle.

Are projecting loads subject to special lighting requirements?
Trailers forming part of a combination of vehicles which are wider than any preceding vehicle and loads being carried on any vehicles which are wider than the vehicle are obliged to carry lamps and reflectors outlining their width at night and during periods of seriously reduced visibility.

When rearward projecting loads are carried, an additional red lamp must be fitted within **1m** of the rearmost part of the load when the projection exceeds **1m**. (Within **2m** in the case of agricultural vehicles and vehicles carrying fire escapes, when the projection exceeds **2m**.)

If the projection obscures any obligatory lamp, reflector or rear marking, steps must be taken to either (a) transfer the obligatory lamp, etc to the load or (b) attach an additional lamp, etc to the vehicle or load.

What are the requirements governing side marker lamps and side retro reflectors?

Side marker lamps must be fitted to vehicles or combinations of vehicles when the overall length exceeds **18.3m** in the following positions:

(a) one lamp, not more than **9.15m** from the front of the vehicle or vehicles
(b) one lamp, not more than **3.05m** from the rear of the vehicle or vehicles
(c) other lamps as required so that the distance between lamps is not more than **3.05m**.

Additional side markers must be fitted where a combination of vehicles with an overall length of more than **12.2m** but not more than **18.3m** is carrying a load supported by any two of the vehicles and for other vehicles and combinations exceeding **18.3m** (including load). The lamps must show a white light to the front and a red light to the rear.

Side retro reflectors must be fitted to motor vehicles and trailers as follows:

Motor vehicles first used before April 1, 1986 and trailers manufactured before October 1, 1985 having an overall length exceeding **8m** must be fitted with two reflectors on each side, one fitted not more than **1m** from the rear of the vehicle and the other towards the centre of the vehicle.

Motor vehicles first used from April 1, 1986 and trailers manufactured from October 1, 1985 having an overall length exceeding **6m** must be fitted with at least two reflectors and more, if required, to satisfy the longitudinal requirements below, on each side.

Maximum distances:
(a) from the front of the vehicle, including any drawbar, of the foremost reflector on each side — **3m**
(b) from the rear of the vehicle of the rearmost reflector on each side — **1m**
(c) between reflecting areas of adjacent reflectors on the same side — **3m**

Do any regulations apply to hazard warning lights?

Hazard warning lights may be used *only* when the vehicle is stationary on a road for the purpose of warning other road users that the vehicle is temporarily causing an obstruction or on a motorway or unrestricted dual-carriageway to warn following drivers to slow down because of an obstruction ahead.

Are there regulations governing other non-obligatory lights?

The undermentioned lights are not compulsory but where fitted they must be maintained in working order and comply with certain requirements.

Reversing Lights

These lights must be *white* lights of not more than 24 watts, and so fitted that dazzle is not possible from eye-level at reasonable distance. Vehicles may be fitted with one or two lights. Reversing lights must be fitted for application by separate hand switch or by selection of the vehicle's reverse gear. Where the switch method is used there must be a tell-tale device to warn the driver while in the driving position when the reversing light is on. Such lights must be kept in good working order.

Emergency Service Vehicles
Distinctive lamps emitting blue or amber flashing lights are permitted on certain vehicles carrying out emergency services: ambulances, fire engines, police vehicles, blood transfusion service vehicles, etc are permitted to carry one or more *blue* lamps.

Vehicles used for road clearance and repair, vehicle breakdown and snow clearance, etc are permitted to carry one or more *amber* lamps.

All such lights must be fitted so that the centre of the lamp is at least **1200mm** above the ground and must be visible from any point at a reasonable distance from the vehicle.

Amber lights on breakdown vehicles may only be illuminated when the vehicle is being used in connection with or near to an accident or breakdown or towing a disabled vehicle. Such vehicles are permitted an additional *white* lamp for illuminating the area of an accident or breakdown. The white light must be directed so as not to dazzle or inconvenience other road users.

The periodicity of the amber lights must not be less than 60 nor more than 240 equal times per minute.

Road clearance vehicles are also permitted to carry an amber reflecting surface facing to the rear of the vehicle.

When are lights required to be switched on?
Vehicles travelling on a road during daylight hours where visibility is seriously reduced must have obligatory lamps switched on, ie side lights/rear lights including rear fog lamps *and* either headlamps and a pair of front fog lamps or a matched fog and spot lamp.

It is the driver's responsibility to decide when lights are required, bearing in mind the need "to see and be seen".

Obligatory side lights/rear lights must be switched on when a vehicle is used on the road between sunset and sunrise. Headlamps must also be used when street lamps are more than 200 yards apart.

Rear fog lamps must only be used when visibility is seriously reduced and be switched off as soon as conditions improve.

Vehicle Checks and Prohibitions
In addition to the annual tests, Department of Transport certifying officers, vehicle examiners and police officers in uniform are empowered to carry out tests and inspections on the road or at operators' premises for the purpose of ensuring that goods-carrying vehicles are maintained in a "fit and serviceable condition".

Which goods vehicles are subject to annual tests?
The Motor Vehicles (Tests) Regulations 1981 apply to goods vehicles not exceeding **1525kg** unladen weight, dual-purpose vehicles, living vans not exceeding **1525kg** unladen weight, motor caravans and private cars. Tests apply to these vehicles on an annual basis when three years of age and over. (For vehicles above these weights return to Chapter 5.)

What does the test cover?
Requirements cover the testing of brakes, steering, lights, stop lamps, tyres, seat

belts (condition, correct fitting and anchorage points), direction indicators, windscreen wipers and washers, exhaust systems, audible warning instruments, bodywork and suspension (in relation to braking and steering).

What evidence is required that a vehicle has passed the test?
A vehicle passing the test will be issued with a test certificate.

What are the provisions relating to spot checks and checks on premises?
Under ss.67 and 68 of the Road Traffic Act 1988 an examiner or certifying officer, on production of his authority, may examine a vehicle on the road or enter premises at any reasonable time to inspect vehicles.

Under Regulation 74 of the Road Vehicles (Construction and Use) Regulations 1986 an examiner, certifying officer, or police officer in uniform may inspect vehicles on premises at any reasonable time providing the consent of the owner of the vehicle and/or premises is obtained, or 48 hours' notice is given of intended inspection (72 hours if notice is given by recorded post). The 48 hours' notice does not apply on the case of a vehicle which has been reported in an accident. A person who obstructs an examiner in the performance of his duty is liable to summary conviction.

Examiners and certifying officers usually operate under s.67 of the Act as the powers given to them are much wider than those under the Construction and Use regulations.

What items is the certifying officer, etc likely to examine?
Under the Road Vehicles (Construction and Use) Regulations the certifying officer can examine and test brakes, direction indicators, excess fuel devices, lighting equipment, rear markings, seat belts (correct fitting, anchorage and BSI kite-mark), side-facing reflectors, steering, tyres, windscreen washers, vehicle noise and, on trailers, landing legs. Minor items such as those affecting the security of the body, cab and wings (to ensure maximum safety) may also be subject to report on prohibition notices.

What is meant by "the system of prohibition notices"?
The system of prohibition notices (PGs) is also covered by s.67 of the Road Traffic Act 1988.

Seven forms are used in the system.

1. *Form GV3* — Direction to proceed to a Specified Place for the purpose of inspection.
2. *Form PG9* — Prohibition of Driving a Vehicle on the Road.
3. *Form PG9A* — Variation in the Terms of a Prohibition on Driving a Vehicle on the Road.
4. *Form PG9B* — Exemption from a Prohibition on the Driving of a Vehicle on the Road.
5. *Form PG9C* — Refusal to Remove a Prohibition on Driving a Vehicle on the Road.
6. *Form PG10* — Removal of Prohibition on Driving a Vehicle on the Road.
7. *Form GV219* — Defect Notice.

Serious consequences can result both from the imposition of a PG9 and from using a vehicle in contravention of a prohibition or outside the scope of any variation or exemption. Operators should therefore clearly explain the requirements to their drivers, supervisors and inspectors.

Because of the importance of these notices, we will examine each one in detail

GV3
When an examiner wishes to examine a vehicle, the site may not be suitable and in these circumstances he will issue a form GV3 directing that the vehicle be taken to a place of inspection not more than five miles distant.

PG9 — Immediate or delayed prohibition
The examiner can issue an immediate prohibition notice if he considers that a vehicle is, or is likely to be, unfit for service. He can issue a delayed prohibition notice which will take effect from a specified date, not later than 10 days from the date of the inspection. Form PG9 is used for both these purposes.

The prohibition notice will be given to the person in charge of the vehicle at the time of the inspection who, as soon as possible, must bring it to the attention of the vehicle owner.

The prohibition extends to both laden and unladen vehicles and to towing, as well as moving the vehicle under its own power. A prohibition continues in force until removed by an examiner (but see PG9A and PG9B). The driver's copy of a prohibition notice must be carried on the vehicle at all times whilst the notice is in force and must be presented when the vehicle is submitted for re-examination (see PG9C and PG10).

It is an offence to drive, or cause or permit to be driven, a vehicle whilst a prohibition is in force.

When the vehicle is fit for service it may, despite the prohibition:
(a) proceed to a place (testing station) where the vehicle is to be reinspected, providing an appointment has been made, or
(b) be road-tested within three miles of where it is being repaired.

A Licensing Authority may take action in relation to an operator's licence as a result of prohibitions imposed on his vehicles.

PG9A — Varying the terms of an existing prohibition
This will be used when an examiner considers that the terms of a prohibition may or should be varied, which can be done in one of three ways:
(a) by suspending it, until a given time or date, if it has already come into force
(b) by deferring the date on which it comes into force if it has not already done so
(c) by altering the list of defects which gave rise to the prohibition.

The use of this procedure will be to alter an *immediate* prohibition to a *delayed* one, whereby immediate danger defects are immediately rectified at the inspection site, or to alter a *delayed* prohibition to an *immediate* one when the condition has become one which gives rise to *immediate* danger, or to alter the list of defects.

It is intended that not more than one variation will be made to one prohibition.

The driver's copy of this notice must be attached to his copy of the original PG9 and must be carried on the vehicle at all times whilst it is in force.

PG9B — Permitting movement of prohibited vehicle
Where a vehicle is examined at the roadside and an immediate GV9 is issued, it may be necessary for the vehicle to be moved to a place of repair. This may be permitted by the issue of form GV9B (PG9B) if the examiner is satisfied that one or more of the following conditions are met:
   (a) the vehicle is unladen
   (b) it does not exceed the specified speed limit
   (c) it does not tow a trailer
   (d) it is towed by a rigid towbar
   (e) it is towed by suspended tow
   (f) it is not on the road after lighting-up time
   (g) the vehicle proceeds from the place of inspection to the nearest specified garage.

The notice must be carried on the vehicle and must be handed over to the examiner when the prohibition notice is removed.
The issue of a GV9B (PG9B) does not provide immunity from a prosecution under the construction and use regulations.

PG9C — Refusal to remove a prohibition
When a prohibited vehicle is fit for service and the operator wishes the prohibition to be removed, he should notify the nearest Department of Transport vehicle examiner, testing station or traffic office. If the examiner or certifying officer who re-examines the vehicle is not satisfied that it is fit for service, a GV9C (PG9C) will be issued.
If the form is signed by a vehicle examiner, an operator who wishes to contest this decision can apply to any Licensing Authority to have the vehicle inspected by a certifying officer. Within seven days of this further inspection the certifying officer must notify the owner of the vehicle, in writing, whether or not the prohibition is to be removed.

PG10 — Removal of prohibition
When a vehicle is presented for clearance and it is found to be fit for service, the examiner will issue a form GV10 notifying removal of the prohibition.

GV219 — Defect notice
The defect notice is used to notify an operator of minor defects which are discovered on an inspection but do not warrant the issuing of a prohibition notice.
Copies of defect notices are sent to the appropriate Licensing Authority but action cannot be taken against an operator's licence solely on the strength of defect notices.
The defects should be rectified immediately but there is no need to advise the Licensing Authority that this has been done.

Can an operator appeal against a prohibition?
There is no formal appeal against a prohibition, only against refusal to remove it. Where an operator considers that the issue of a prohibition notice is not justified, full details of the circumstances should be submitted in writing to the appropriate Department of Transport Area Mechanical Engineer.
If an operator's complaint is found to be justified, the Area Mechanical Engineer may recommend to the Licensing Authority that the prohibition should not be taken into account in any licence considerations.

There is no appeal against refusal by an examiner to issue a variation.

An appeal against a refusal of a certifying officer to remove a prohibition must be made to the Secretary of State for Transport, in writing, within 14 days of the notification of the refusal.

An appeal should be delivered or posted to any traffic area office and this should be done on form VT19 obtainable from Department of Transport area offices. Appeals should be lodged within 14 days of the refusal.

What is a GV160?
This is a notice issued when a vehicle has been found to be overloaded and, when issued, it is obligatory for the vehicle to be off-loaded to the required limits before it can continue its journey.

How can a driver avoid further checks once his vehicle has been weighed and found to be within the legal limits?
He should obtain a certificate which will exempt him from further checks before the end of the journey with the same load.

Vehicle Maintenance

Why is so much importance placed on vehicle maintenance?
There are three very good reasons: (a) the statutory requirement that vehicles are kept in good mechanical condition; (b) the maintenance requirements implicit in operator licensing; (c) operational economics.

- (a) *Statutory requirement* — The construction and use regulations state: "A motor vehicle, every trailer drawn thereby and all parts and accessories of such vehicle and trailer shall *at all times be in such condition and the number of* passengers carried by such vehicle or trailer, the manner in which any passengers are carried in or on such vehicle or trailer and the weight, distribution, packing and adjustment of the load of such vehicle or trailer shall at all times be such that no danger is *caused or is likely to be caused* to any person in or on the vehicle or trailer or on a road".
- (b) *Operator licensing requirements* — The operator is required to give a statement of intent in respect of the inspection and maintenance of vehicles (*see Chapter 8*).
- (c) *Economic operation* — Maintenance costs money but failure to ensure that vehicles are adequately maintained can be much more expensive. Defects which are allowed to go unremedied may prove far more costly when breakdown finally occurs: fuel consumption can increase alarmingly, down-time can increase considerably, to say nothing of fines that may be incurred and the possibility of licences being placed in jeopardy. The best possible insurance against such possibilities is a system of regular inspection and planned maintenance.

What arrangements should be made for inspection and maintenance?
It must be emphasised that daily running checks should be carried out by the driver

on such items as engine oil, tyre pressures, etc but that these do not constitute defect inspections.

A defect inspection will cover components such as wheels, tyres, brakes, steering, chassis and lighting, etc which contribute to the safe operation of the vehicle.

It is essential that these inspections are carried out by staff who are aware of the significance of any defects which they may find and have authority to put any remedial work in hand, or withdraw the vehicle from service if potentially dangerous defects are found.

What records should be kept of inspections?
Written records must be kept of:
  (a) when and by whom the inspections were carried out
  (b) the results of the inspection
  (c) when and by whom any remedial work was done and details of such work.

These records must be kept on suitable forms and retained for a minimum period of 15 months.

Need an operator keep records if his inspection and maintenance is done under contract?
The operator must still keep these records, even if his inspections and repairs are done by outside contractors, since the operator is legally the "user". He should therefore ensure that his maintenance contractor keeps the required records and that he is supplied with copies of those records.

How can an operator be sure that his standard of maintenance measures up to that required?
Arrangements can be made with independent bodies such as the Freight Transport Association for an inspection to be carried out to ensure that the vehicles are being kept up to the required standard.

How often should inspection and servicing be carried out?
The vehicle must be examined at intervals of either mileage or time. This may or may not coincide with the manufacturers' recommended intervals for servicing. It is left to the operator to decide upon the frequency of his inspections, since this will depend largely upon the nature of his work, eg tippers may need monthly inspections, whereas a removal vehicle will not normally need inspecting more than once every six weeks and servicing every three months. Thus a service and inspection could be done on one occasion, with an inspection midway between each service, ie four services and eight inspections per year.

How can an operator ensure that inspections and services are carried out at the appropriate intervals?
Like any other system which requires work to be done at regular intervals of time, a diary or wall chart will be necessary to show when the vehicles will be required and in this way the operator can plan ahead, rather than waiting until a vehicle breaks down before it is repaired. Furthermore, parts can be made available in good time and the need to take vehicles off the road for some considerable time to get them through the annual test should be avoided, thus showing a cost saving.

What exactly is the meaning and purpose of planned maintenance?
Planned maintenance is maintenance which is carried out with forethought and organisation control and records. Its object is to maintain the vehicle in a high standard of repair and roadworthiness and it should cover the entire mechanical, electrical, pneumatic and hydraulic equipment of the vehicle. The main interest of any operator is to obtain maximum availability of his vehicles. In a fleet it is up to the fleet engineer to ensure that maximum availability is obtained, taking into account the need for vehicles to be in good condition, to be safe and to be able to give optimum performance and economy, and the maintenance programme must be planned around this requirement.

What level of availability should be aimed for?
Availability of 93-94% should be aimed for, ie 6-7% down-time. Whether or not this is achieved will depend to a large extent on the age of the vehicles and is a factor that must be given prominence in the formulation of a replacement policy and in the selection of vehicles.

What are the broad requirements for a planned maintenance scheme?
To make the maintenance scheme work, separate records must be kept for each vehicle, ie computerised records, card index system, etc. This can give all the essential technical and cost data for the vehicle. In addition, a record of all the work carried out on the vehicle, to show labour and materials, as well as the inspection sheets, is necessary. These records must be filled in regularly.

Stores of fast moving spares such as filters, hoses and drive belts, must be available whenever a vehicle comes in for servicing.

A programme must be prepared in order to:
(a) plan the amount of labour needed during the week
(b) smooth out the work over the week
(c) fit in with the needs of the workshop or transport commitments
(d) allow different specialists to work concurrently on special problems.

What instructions are given to the maintenance staff?
In the maintenance schedules there will be a list of standard routine maintenance jobs that require attention at regular intervals. These jobs consist of
(a) "adjustment" type work
(b) replacement of known parts which require frequent renewals, such as fuel and oil filters
(c) inspection work.

When a vehicle becomes available for specific maintenance to be carried out these are the types of job which the fitter will be instructed to do.

In addition, these standard repeating jobs will be augmented by minor faults, reports from the driver and inspection staff and the necessity to carry out work noted on previous inspections and held over.

Thus, before undertaking planned maintenance on a given vehicle, the fitter should be given a work card which gives the following data:
(a) registration number or fleet number
(b) details of standard jobs which are due
(c) details of special jobs which have been notified

(d) date and time by which work must be completed
(e) an instruction to visually check for any other obvious faults on the vehicle.

Reference should be made to any drawings, workshop manuals, manufacturers' service sheets, special tools or test gear which may be required, also the spares which may have been ordered as a result of past inspections.

The instructions must be clear and concise. It is obviously vital to have confirmation that any work to be carried out has been done and also to provide space for the fitter to report on any faults noted, unscheduled adjustments made, etc.

Leaving a column on the fitter's instruction card to be ticked off provides a feedback system which requires a minimum of writing on the fitter's part.

What is the manager's responsibility in relation to maintenance records and standards?

The operator is ultimately responsible for ensuring that vehicles are not driven on the road in an unsound condition and the Licensing Authority requires proof that a high standard of vehicle maintenance will be provided by the applicant on the granting of an operator's licence.

The whole system of operator licensing is based on safety, which means:
(a) systematic and thorough inspections
(b) regular and effective maintenance
(c) a system of records as proof that (a) and (b) have been properly carried out.

Where the manager is named as the person holding the Certificate of Professional Competence and therefore responsible for the effective running and control of the fleet he will be held responsible if the appropriate standards of maintenance and relevant records are not maintained. In serious cases the operator could lose his licence and the transport manager his Certificate of Competence.

CHAPTER 8
(Module B)
Licensing Requirements for Goods Vehicle Operations
(You should reread Chapter 1 in conjunction with this chapter.)

Existing Legislation

What legislation controls entry to the profession of road haulier?
The Transport Act 1968 made radical changes to the system of licensing road haulage operators. It also laid down the basic procedures for controlling the profession: establishing the procedures to be followed to obtain licences; the requirement to keep records; and limiting drivers' hours of work, etc.

Subsequently the Road Traffic Acts 1972 (now repealed by the 1988 Act) and 1974 (parts of which are now included in the 1988 Act) amended certain sections and added other sections to the 1988 Act. In addition, the Transport Act 1982 introduced the question of the "environment" in connection with the siting of an operator's premises.

Operator Licensing

Who must hold an operator's licence?
Subject to certain exemptions, operator licensing applies to all goods vehicles and vehicle combinations used for the carriage of goods in connection with a trade or business (this includes Local Authorities who are deemed to be carrying on a business) and which exceed *3.5 tonnes gross plated weight* or, if unplated, 1525kg unladen weight, ie it applies to both "hire or reward" and own account activities.

How does one apply for an operator's licence?
An application must be made to the Licensing Authority for each traffic area in which vehicles are based on the appropriate form — GV79.

In addition, 21 days before an application is submitted, or within 21 days of submission, a notice (see page 93) must be inserted in a local newspaper or newspapers circulating in the vicinity of the proposed operating centre to allow any person owning or occupying land in the vicinity to decide whether representations against the grant of or variation to a licence should be made on environmental grounds.

When should one apply for the licence?
The application must reach the Licensing Authority at least nine weeks before it is to take effect. At its discretion the LA may deal with applications at shorter notice.

What information does the Licensing Authority need?
The Licensing Authority must satisfy itself that the applicant:
    (a) is of good repute
    (b) has adequate financial resources

(c) in the case of "hire or reward" operators, is professionally competent, or will at all times during the currency of the licence have in his employment a transport manager who is of good repute and is professionally competent, or, if the applicant has more than one operating centre and the Licensing Authority requires him to have more than one transport manager, such number of transport managers who are of good repute and are professionally competent as are so required and that

(d) following the receipt of objections from planning authorities and/or representations from any person who owns or occupies land in the vicinity of the operating centre, the granting of the licence would not have adverse environmental effects due to the location and operation of the centre or the parking of vehicles in the vicinity.

How is good repute established?

The applicant is required to give details of any convictions incurred by himself, his partners, nominated transport managers or by the company (when it is a company application) during the preceding five years, which are relevant to the application.

What offences are relevant?

The relevant offences are those relating to the roadworthiness of vehicles, speed limits, loading/overloading, drivers' hours and records, driver licensing, vehicle plating and testing, international road haulage permits, forgery, unlawful use of rebated fuel oil and contravention of parking restrictions and prohibitions, etc.

What is the significance of adequate financial resources?

The Licensing Authority has to be satisfied that the applicant has adequate financial resources to keep the vehicles fit and serviceable and has a suitable operating centre. In the case of an application for a new standard licence the LA has to be satisfied that, in addition, the applicant has sufficient financial resources to start up and run the road haulage business properly. He must be satisfied that as well as assets (such as vehicles and premises) there is enough working capital to cover all expenses that are likely to arise before money is earned to meet them.

What is meant by the statement of intent?

The application form (GV79) contains the following statement which the applicant must sign.

"I will make proper arrangements so that:
- the rules on drivers' hours are observed and proper records kept
- vehicles are not overloaded
- vehicles are kept fit and serviceable
- drivers will report safety faults in vehicles as soon as possible
- records are kept (for 15 months) of all safety inspections, routine maintenance and repairs to vehicles, and are made available on request.

I will
- have adequate financial resources to maintain the vehicles covered by the licence
- tell the Licensing Authority of any changes or convictions which affect the licence
- maintain adequate financial resources for the administration of the business (applies to standard licence applicants only)."

Do the convictions referred to in the statement of intent apply only to drivers employed by the applicant?
No! It requires the holder of the operator's licence to report **any** convictions relating to the operation of the road haulage business, or himself (or the company holding the licence), directors or nominated transport managers.

How is professional competence established?
A person will be considered professionally competent if he:
    (a) holds a certificate issued by a body approved by the Secretary of State for Transport, ie the certificate obtained by passing an examination for the Certificate of Professional Competence conducted by the Royal Society of Arts
    (b) holds any other certificate of competence, diploma or other qualification recognised by the Secretary of State.

Who can object to the grant of a licence?
The following persons or bodies are entitled to object:
    (a) a chief officer of police
    (b) a local authority
    (c) a planning authority
    (d) a prescribed trade union or an association whose members consist of or include:
        (i) persons holding operators' licences or
        (ii) employees of such persons.

Who are these prescribed trade unions and associations?
The bodies recognised are:
    The British Association of Removers
    The Freight Transport Association
    The Road Haulage Association
    The General and Municipal Workers' Union
    The National Union of Railwaymen
    The Transport and General Workers' Union
    The Union of Shop, Distributive and Allied Workers
    The United Road Transport Union

On what grounds may they object?
Objections can only be made against the applicant on the grounds that any of the requirements mentioned in s.64(2) of the 1968 Act are not satisfied, that is to say, the applicant is not of good repute, or of adequate financial standing, or that he is unlikely or unable to fulfil the requirements of the "statements of intention", eg he does not have suitable facilities for off-street parking and maintenance.

May anyone object on any other grounds?
Yes! Persons owning or occupying land in the vicinity of an operating centre may make representations on environmental grounds.

What is the procedure for making objections?
All Traffic Area Offices publish weekly or fortnightly notices of "Applications and Decisions", giving details of applications for new "O" licences and variations or

renewals of existing ones, together with licences granted and public enquiries to be held.

Potential objectors, learning of an application by a person or company against whom they may wish to object, must send their objection to the Licensing Authority **and at the same time** send a copy of the objection to the applicant.

Is there any time limit for objections?

Objections and representations must be made in writing and must reach the Licensing Authority not later than 21 days after notice of the application has been published in "Applications and Decisions" in the case of objections, and 21 days after publication in a local newspaper in the case of representations on environmental grounds. The objector must also send a copy of his objections to the applicant within this time.

What happens next?

When an objection is made the Licensing Authority holds a public enquiry at which the applicant and the objector have an opportunity to present their cases. The Licensing Authority will then decide whether to grant or refuse the application.

Can the applicant appeal if his application is refused?

If an application is refused the applicant can appeal to the Transport Tribunal. Objectors also have the right to appeal if a licence is granted against what they consider is a valid objection but this right does not apply to objectors on environmental grounds.

Is there any restriction on the number of vehicles for which an operator can apply?

There is no theoretical limit, but when an operator first applies for a licence, or wishes to increase the number of vehicles authorised when applying for a licence to be renewed, the LA will want to satisfy itself that the number applied for is realistic. Depending on its assessment of the situation he may grant the application in full, or for a lesser number of vehicles.

Must the vehicles be in the operator's possession before he applies for them to be authorised?

No! He can state on his application vehicles "in possession now" and "to be acquired".

Can any provision be made for additional vehicles to be bought or hired to cope with increased business or fluctuations in traffic?

By including "to be acquired" vehicles in his application the operator can acquire a margin to cover expected growth or peaks in demand.

What action must be taken when the new vehicles are acquired?

The LA must be notified within one month of the vehicles being put into service. If vehicles are hired without drivers for periods of less than one month (assuming that they are covered by a margin) the operator need not inform the LA. For periods exceeding one month, details must be sent to the LA and an "O" licence disc obtained for each vehicle.

What is the purpose of "O" licence discs?

"O" licence discs, which must be displayed on the windscreen adjacent to the

Excise Licence, are issued for each specified vehicle following the granting of an operator's licence. Discs are not issued for vehicles which are authorised but not specified, eg those on hire for less than a month.

The colour of the disc denotes the type of operation for which it is specified:

Restricted licence	— orange
Standard national licence	— blue
Standard national/international	— green
Interim	— yellow

What should be done if a disc is lost, destroyed or defaced?

The LA should be notified immediately by letter explaining the circumstances so that a copy can be issued free of charge.

What is the procedure if additional vehicles are required which were not foreseen on the original application?

The operator must apply for a variation of his licence, on form GV81, repeating the statement of intent. He will probably need to satisfy the LA of the need for the extra vehicles.

The application will be published in the fortnightly "Applications and Decisions" and objections may be lodged in the same way as for original licence applications or renewals.

Can vehicles be substituted for those specified on the licence?

Where a vehicle is acquired to replace an existing vehicle which has been sold or scrapped, or is temporarily off the road, a letter should be sent to the LA explaining the circumstances, together with the old disc, to enable a new one to be issued.

Can a vehicle be transferred from a depot in one traffic area to a depot in another traffic area?

This is permitted for periods of up to three months, without notification to the LA. For longer periods the LA must be informed by letter and the vehicle removed from the original licence and specified in the licence for the new area.

If the operator does not hold an "O" licence for the new area, or if his existing licence for that area does not have a margin to cover the transferred vehicle, an application for a licence or a variation must be made to the LA in the new area.

NB This type of situation also requires an advert to be placed in the local newspaper — see page 93.

Are there any other circumstances requiring notification to the LA?

There are several other situations where the LA must be notified by letter:
- (a) if a specified vehicle is no longer used, the LA must be notified within three weeks and the disc returned
- (b) where a reduction in the fleet size is intended, the spare discs must be returned
- (c) if there are any changes in the licence conditions imposed by the LA
- (d) if there are any changes in the licence conditions which the operator wishes to be made
- (e) if there is a change of business name or address the LA must be notified within three weeks

(f) following the death, bankruptcy or liquidation of the original licence holder, any person carrying on the business must advise the LA within two months. The person will be considered to be the holder of the licence provided an application is made for a new licence within:
(i) one month in the case of a restricted licence, or
(ii) four months in the case of a standard licence
of such notice being given, always provided that the licence is not due for renewal during that period
(g) if there are any changes in the structure of the business, ie changes in management, ownership, etc which may affect control of the business.

Can anyone require an operator to produce his O-licence?
The holder of an O-licence must produce it for examination if required to do so by a police officer, certifying officer or examiner, or by any person authorised by the licensing authority.

Is there a time limit for the production of the O-licence?
He must produce it within **14 days** either at an operating centre covered by his licence or at his head or principal place of business within the traffic area, at his option, or if required by the police, at a police station of his choosing.

What powers do Licensing Authorities have in connection with existing licences?
Under s.69 of the 1968 Act, the Licensing Authority may revoke, suspend, or curtail licences for a wide range of acts or omissions.

Revocation means that the licence is taken away. When this occurs the LA may order the holder to be disqualified from holding or obtaining a licence for a limited period, or indefinitely.

Suspension means that, although the licence has not been revoked, it is inoperative for a specified period, or perhaps until some specified happening occurs, eg until certain alterations are made in respect of provision for maintenance.

Curtailment means that the duration of the licence is reduced, or that the number of vehicles authorised on the licence is reduced for a stated period or for the remainder of the currency of the licence.

Trade Licences

What are trade licences?
These are licences issued to motor traders, ie manufacturers, repairers and dealers in motor vehicles and vehicle testers to permit the use on the roads of vehicles which have not been licensed individually. They may not be used for parking on a road when the vehicle is not in use.

Who issues trade licences?
Applications for a trade licence should be made to the Vehicle Registration Office (formerly Local Vehicle Licensing Office) in the area in which the trader's premises are situated. A set of two number plates (trade plates) will be issued to each holder of a trade licence.

Is there any appeal against refusal to issue a trade licence?
An applicant who is refused a trade licence may appeal to the Secretary of State for Transport within 28 days.

What is the duration of a trade licence?
Trade licences are issued on January 1st and July 1st each year and are valid for either 6 months or 1 year.

Can goods be carried on a vehicle operating under trade plates?
This is not permitted unless the goods are:
- (a) a load needed for demonstration or test purposes and is returned to the place of loading after the demonstration or test, except when the load consists of water, fertiliser or refuse
- (b) built-in equipment
- (c) parts designed to be fitted to the vehicle and tools for fitting them
- (d) a trailer

Recovery Vehicle Licences

What is a Recovery Vehicle Licence?
A recovery vehicle is defined as "a vehicle which is either constructed or permanently adapted primarily for the purpose of lifting, towing and transporting a disabled vehicle or for any one or more of these purposes". They were formerly licensed under Trade Licences but since 1988 have been placed in a category of their own.

Are there any restrictions on the use of vehicles under this licence?
Their use is restricted to the following:
- (a) the recovery of a broken down vehicle
- (b) the removal of a broken down vehicle from the place where it broke down to premises for repair or scrapping
- (c) removing a broken down vehicle from premises to which it had been taken for repair to other premises for repair or scrapping, and
- (d) for carrying only fuel and other liquid required for the propulsion, and tools and other articles required in connection with the lift, tow, etc.

Can passengers or goods be carried in the recovery vehicle?
Only if they were being carried in the broken down vehicle immediately prior to its breaking down in circumstances as at (a) and (b) above.

Can a recovery vehicle be used for any other purpose?
Also, in circumstances under items (a) and (b) above it may be used:
- (i) for the repair of a broken down vehicle either at the site of the breakdown or at the place to which it had been moved in the interests of safety, or
- (ii) for towing or carrying one trailer which had previously been towed or carried by the vehicle immediately prior to its breaking down.

A vehicle ceases to be classed as a recovery vehicle if it is used for any purposes other than those described above.

CHAPTER 9
(Module A)
Company Law, Business and Financial Management
Business Units

There is an enormous variation in the size of businesses. Does the law divide them into different categories?
The law recognises three main categories, which are further sub-divided. These are (1) sole trader (2) partnerships and (3) limited companies but size is not the criterion on which distinction is made.

How is the distinction made?
Basically it depends on two things: (a) how is the business owned; (b) who is responsible for its debts?

Is the procedure for starting a business the same in all cases?
The procedure is different in each category and the legal requirements differ. The following brief summaries of the requirements and legal liabilities of the different types of business unit will explain the main points.

The sole trader
The sole trader is sometimes called a one-man business. This does not necessarily mean that he is the only person engaged in the business, he may have others to assist him, but he is the sole owner. The business was started with his capital (or capital that he borrowed) and he alone is responsible for the debts of the business to the full extent of his private wealth.

If a sole trader trades under his own name there are no formal requirements to setting up in business. If however he trades under some other name, the name and address of the owner must be shown on all business communications, letters, orders, invoices etc and displayed prominently in any premises where the business is carried on.

Partnerships
Partnerships are governed by the Partnership Act of 1890 which codified (brought together under one single Act) the vast amount of case law which had accumulated in preceding centuries. The partnership agreement need not be written (though this is advisable) and, like the sole trader, the partnership need not be registered if trading under the names of the partners but must disclose the name and addresses of the partners, in the same way as a sole trader, if trading under any other name.

Limited companies
The principle of limited liability is that the shareholder (a part owner of the business) has no liability for the debts of the company beyond the amount of capital that he has contributed.

There are two types of limited company: (a) the private limited company and (b) the public limited company.

Private limited company
Unlike the public limited company its shares are not quoted on the stock exchange. Both shares and debentures may only be sold by private negotiation and the sale or transfer must have the consent of the other shareholders. A private limited company must have a minimum of two shareholders and a maximum of 50 (excluding employees); its name must end in Limited or Ltd.

Public limited company
The shares of a public limited company are freely transferable. It must have a minimum of two shareholders but there is no limit to the maximum number. It must have a minimum capital of £50,000 and a name ending in plc.

What is the procedure for forming a company and starting operations?

Before a company can legally begin operations, the following procedure must be followed:
1. The minimum number of shareholders must be obtained and they must sign the
2. Memorandum of Association. This document states:
    (a) the name of the company ending with the word Limited (in the case of a private company, or plc in the case of a public company)
    (b) the address of its registered office
    (c) the objects of the company, ie what the company was formed to do
    (d) a statement that the liability of shareholders is limited
    (e) the amount of share capital to be issued and the types of share
    (f) an undertaking by the signatories that they do desire to be formed into a company registered under the Acts and to undertake to purchase the number of shares against their names
    (g) the names and addresses of the first director or directors and the first secretary or joint secretaries of the company, together with the consent of the director(s), secretary(s).
3. Draw up the Articles of Association, ie the rules governing the internal working of the company.
4. Register the company with the Registrar of Companies. This involves presenting the Memorandum of Association, the Articles of Association, a statement of the nominal capital, a list of directors and their written consents and promises to take up shares and a statutory declaration that the Companies Acts have been complied with.

If all this is in order the Registrar of Companies will issue a:

5. Certificate of Incorporation which means that the company now has a legal personality and can do anything which an individual can do except that it cannot yet begin trading. Before this can be done it must
6. Obtain the capital it needs. In the case of a private company this will be provided by the founders; a public company will obtain it through the issue of shares. To persuade the public to invest in its shares the directors will issue a
7. Prospectus. This is a full and frank history of the company, including any information that a prospective investor would need to know concerning the company and its intentions. The directors are liable for the truth of the statements contained in the prospectus. Before the public are invited to subscribe for shares, the prospectus must be registered with the Registrar of Companies.

8. A Certificate of Trading must be obtained before the company can begin trading. This is obtained from the Registrar by lodging with him:
   (a) a statement that the minimum capital (mentioned in the Memorandum of Association) has been obtained
   (b) a statement that the directors have paid for their shares
   (c) a statutory declaration that the Companies Acts have been complied with.

What is meant by the liquidation of a company?

Liquidation or winding-up means realising the assets of a company in preparation for closing it down. The assets will be used to satisfy the claims of creditors, any sum remaining to be distributed among the shareholders.

How is the process of liquidation initiated?

If the company is *solvent* the shareholders may pass a resolution at a general meeting to wind up the company and the directors may appoint a liquidator. This is called a Voluntary Liquidation.

If the company is *insolvent* then the creditors may appoint the liquidator or the Official Receiver may act on their behalf. In this case it is known as a Compulsory Liquidation.

Financial Management

The main sources of funds available to a businessman can be divided into two classes: long term and short term.

Long term

1. Founders capital — the money which the original proprietor invested in the business.
2. Share capital — money invested in the business by shareholders.
3. Debentures — a form of loan bearing a fixed rate of interest. They are attractive to many investors because of their security. Debentures are usually:
   (a) a charge against specific assets, or the assets of a company generally
   (b) have high priority of payment in the event of liquidation
   (c) may be redeemed by the company either:
      (i) at the end of the specified period, or
      (ii) at any time within the specified period, or
      (iii) are irredeemable, except in the event of the winding up of the company.
4. Long term loans — banks prefer not to lend money over long periods, unless the borrower is a very secure risk.
5. Mortgages — loans given against the pledge of a secure asset, eg land and/or buildings, the documents of title being lodged with the mortgagor during the currency of the loan.

Short term

1. Bank loans — interest is payable on the whole amount borrowed.
2. Overdraft — the customer is allowed to overdraw to the extent of the overdraft facility granted. Although the rate of interest charged is usually higher than for a loan, it is charged only on the amount actually overdrawn, ie you do not pay for what you do not need, or for a longer period than is needed.

3. Tax reserves — money set aside to meet future tax liabilities may be used to meet short term needs, provided that it is replaced before the tax becomes due.
4. Creditors — money set aside for the payment of creditors may be used for other more pressing purposes, but this practice should be avoided unless absolutely necessary as it may result in the reputation of a "bad payer" and loss of credit status.

What is the "purpose of trading"?

The purpose of trading is to produce a sufficient surplus of revenue over expenditure so that after allowance for tax and depreciation there is available, for distribution to the owners, a sum which is greater than that which could be obtained by alternative investment of capital.

What is the purpose of the Trading Account?

This is an account into which all revenue from trading, ie selling goods and services (predominantly the latter in the case of road haulage) is gathered and totalled. From this total the total of all the expenses directly incurred in selling those goods and services is deducted. What remains is the gross profit which forms the starting point of the Profit and Loss Account.

What does the Profit and Loss Account reveal?

Whereas the Trading Account was concerned with the revenue and the expenses directly incurred in selling goods and service, this account brings in all those other costs directly incurred in running the business, ie rent, rates, telephone, heating and lighting bills, office salaries, directors fees, etc which are collectively known as overheads. These, when totalled and deducted from the gross profit, reveal the net profit before tax. If, of course, the total costs exceed the total revenue the result will be a net loss.

What is the balance sheet?

This is a statement drawn up at the end of each trading or financial period, setting forth the various assets and liabilities of the concern as at that date.

A company is legally required to produce an annual balance sheet but may produce balance sheets at more frequent intervals to suit its own convenience.

What information is given in the balance sheet?

Among other things, it gives information on the four following important aspects:
(a) the nature and cost of the assets
(b) the nature and extent of the liabilities
(c) whether the firm is solvent, ie able to meet its liabilities
(d) whether the firm is over-trading, ie contracting debts it is unlikely to be able to repay.

What is the difference between debtors and creditors?

Debtors are people or companies who owe the company money.
Creditors are people or companies to whom the company owes money.

What is meant by working capital?

This is the amount left over after the purchase of the fixed assets that is available for working or running the business, eg for the purchase of materials, payment of wages, etc. Although the running costs will eventually be met out of income, unless there is a reserve of capital on which to draw, the business can run into cash flow problems when, due to fluctuations in the level of income received, there is insufficient cash to meet immediate needs.

What exactly is meant by cash flow?
This is the rate at which money flows into and out of the company. At times the income exceeds the expenditure and vice versa; the two are rarely exactly equal. It is necessary to budget as far as possible for maximum spending at times of maximum inflow. Sometimes, when seasonal variations are extreme, overdraft facilities may be useful in bridging the gap. Offering customers a cash discount to encourage them to pay more promptly, is another way of improving cash flow.

What is meant by "factoring debts"?
Under normal trading conditions, a period of credit is allowed before payment of invoices. One method of dealing with a temporary acute shortage of cash is to sell the invoices to a third party at less than face value for immediate cash. The third party will then collect the full amount when payment falls due. This process is known as factoring debts.

Why are long term debtors regarded as a liability?
Although the operator has earned this money, the fact that the debts have been outstanding for a very long time suggests the probability that many of them may never be recovered. They will initially have been included in the total earnings, but to continue to regard them as assets to be realised would distort the actual position. From time to time a proportion of them will have to be written off — a deduction from the gross profit. They therefore represent a probable liability rather than an actual asset.

What is meant by the expression "total capital employed?"
The *capital* of a business is the sum total of its assets. This capital will have been derived from the money invested in the business by its owners — the original proprietor or its shareholders — together with any surplus profits that have been retained in the business.

The *trading capital* of a business is the total of its *fixed assets*, land, buildings, etc, ie those assets acquired for the purpose of earning income, and *current assets*, ie cash, stocks of materials, short term investments, book debts, etc.

Because money is frequently referred to as capital, ordinary loans, mortgages, debentures, etc are often referred to as *loan capital* but this is considered wrong by many accountants as these items are not assets but liabilities.

To the purist, total capital employed will consist of that represented by its fixed and current assets, while others would include loan capital.

What is working capital ratio?
Working capital is the capital available for running a business after the purchase of the fixed assets. At any given time, however, in addition to the *current assets*, the business will have *current liabilities*, eg bills for goods and services received, interest due, wages and salaries earned but not yet paid, taxes, etc so that to find the true, or net, working capital it is necessary to deduct the current liabilities from the current assets, ie:

Current Assets − Current Liabilities = Net Working Capital

For example, Thurrock Haulage Ltd have current assets of £15,700 and current liabilities of £7500, leaving a working capital of £8200 for the business.

The working capital ratio is the ratio of current assets to current liabilities, thus:

$$\frac{\text{Current Assets}}{\text{Current Liabilities}} = \text{Working Capital Ratio}$$

If current assets and current liabilities are equal, there is a 1:1 ratio but this would mean that, if the business was unable to collect all money owed by its debtors, it would need to borrow in order to pay its own creditors. To be safe, something better than a 1:1 ratio is needed.

For example, taking Thurrock Haulage Ltd figures:

$$\frac{15{,}700}{7{,}500} = 2.1 \text{ times} \quad (2.1:1)$$

This is a much more satisfactory situation.

What is the current ratio?

This is another name for working capital ratio. If, of course, the ratio was 4:1 or greater, this would indicate that the working capital was not being fully used and it should be used to acquire new vehicles or equipment (if needed), invested, or used for some other purpose more beneficial to the company.

What is meant by liquidity ratio?

This is a variation on the working capital or current ratio, sometimes also called the "acid test" ratio. If, in a period of economic restriction, it became necessary to convert all the current assets into cash in order to meet current liabilities, this might prove difficult with some assets, eg stocks of raw materials, or work in progress. The value of stocks of diesel cannot be realised until it is needed for operational purposes. A haulage contract to move a large quantity of material might provide for payment on completion of the contract some weeks or months hence. The acid test is how quickly the assets can be realised. In the examples given — not quickly enough — they are not sufficiently "liquid". The liquidity ratio gives the ratio between those assests that can be quickly turned into cash — the liquid assets — and current liabilities.

How does increasing the stock percentage in the current assets affect the liquidity rate?

Its effect would be to lower (worsen) the liquidity ratio, because it would mean that a smaller percentage of the current assets could be readily converted into cash.

Elements of Costing

What is costing?

The term costing is an abbreviation of the term cost accounting. That is, a system of tracing costs to their sources and recording them so that, from the information recorded, the best use can be made of the resources of the business.

How can these records assist in ensuring that the best use is made of resources?
There are many ways. Some common ones are:
  (a) in identifying and isolating areas of high cost. The high cost may be unavoidable but it could indicate inefficiency and the need for some remedial action to be taken, eg where an operator undertakes all his own maintenance it may demonstrate that this is not economic and should be contracted out
  (b) the records form a sound basis for estimating future costs and therefore enable the business to produce a realistic pricing system
  (c) they enable realistic budget forecasts to be prepared, against which the performance of the business can be measured. Where performance does not match the forecast, the situation can be investigated and remedial action taken before the effects become too serious. If performance is better than forecast, again it should be investigated to see if any further advantage can be obtained, eg dropping one particular traffic for another that is more profitable.

Why is costing especially important to the road haulage operator?
Too often road haulage operators have been unaware of their true costs and, in consequence, areas of waste and inefficiency have been allowed to continue unchecked. More particularly, pricing policy has often been based on "What X down the road charges". This is fraught with danger because X's prices may not be realistic. Even if they are, they may relate only to his costs and not to those of other businesses which may differ considerably.

What generally are the advantages to the road haulage operator of a proper costing system?
1. It gives him up-to-date information on profitability for the business as a whole, for individual depots, for individual vehicles and for different types of traffic.
2. Adverse trends can be quickly spotted, enabling management to take the appropriate action.
3. By knowing accurately how profitable specific operations are, rates can be adjusted realistically during times of severe competition, thus preventing jobs being undertaken at a loss.
4. The guesswork is taken out of rate-fixing.
5. A close watch is maintained to ensure that the business is providing an appropriate return on the capital employed.

Is costing a complicated and expensive business?
In a large transport undertaking the costing system may be very detailed and may cost a lot of money but, if designed to meet the needs of a particular undertaking, the money saved should be far greater than the money expended. It does not need to be complicated. Designing the system may require a lot of thought but after that it is more a matter of careful recording.

Can a costing system be equally valuable to a small business?
Provided that it is designed to meet the needs of the business it can be of value. Keeping records and statistics which are never used is clearly wasteful. Care should be taken to ensure that only necessary information is recorded.

Why do cost accountants use so many different names for costs?

By giving different kinds of costs different names the cost accountant is able to define precisely what he is talking about.

It is important to separate the different parts of a business so that costs can be allocated to the particular area or unit that incurred them, enabling profitability, efficiency, etc of that area or unit to be accurately determined.

It is important to distinguish between those costs attributable to a particular unit and those which are incurred by the business as a whole but which must be apportioned fairly between the various units.

It is also important to distinguish between those costs that remain the same, irrespective of the level of business activity and those that vary according to the amount of work undertaken.

It is necessary to examine some of the terms used to obtain a clearer understanding of how a costing system works.

Cost centre
An area of the business, a particular unit or particular activity, against which costs are charged, eg the traffic office, the workshop, individual vehicles or part of the fleet, eg tankers, container vehicles, or general goods vehicles.

Direct costs
Those costs which are directly attributable to a specific cost centre, eg drivers' wages to vehicles, wages of clerical staff to the office, fitters' wages to the workshop, etc.

Indirect costs
Those costs which cannot be directly attributed to a single cost centre but must be apportioned between several cost centres, or over the entire business, eg management expenses must be apportioned over the whole business.

Fixed costs
Those costs that do not vary according to the level of business activity. They may relate to the business as a whole, eg salaries, rent, rates, or to a particular vehicle, eg road licence, insurance, depreciation. In the transport industry it is customary to refer to the costs which relate to administration as establishment charges and fixed costs which relate to the vehicle as standing charges. (The latter is rather appropriate as the costs continue when the vehicle is standing doing nothing.)

Variable costs
Costs referred to as "running costs" in the road transport industry are those which vary directly with the mileage operated, eg fuel, oil and tyres.

Eventually, all charges relating to the non-revenue producing parts of the business (collectively called overheads), must be charged out to vehicles. This is because indirectly they have been incurred for the benefit of the vehicles and must be taken into account in assessing the profitability of those vehicles and in rate calculation.

Total vehicle costs appear like this:

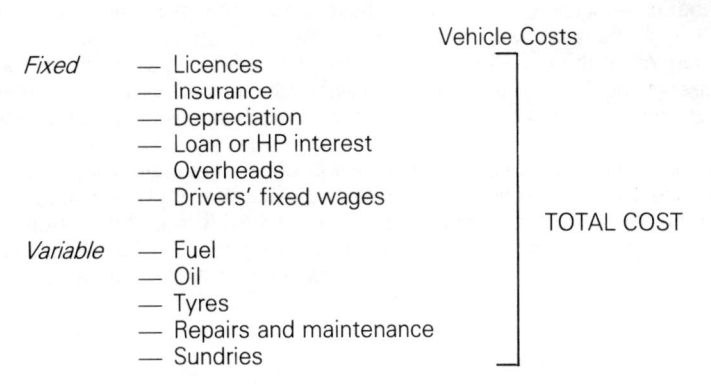

```
                           Vehicle Costs
   Fixed     — Licences          ⎤
             — Insurance         ⎥
             — Depreciation      ⎥
             — Loan or HP interest
             — Overheads         ⎥
             — Drivers' fixed wages
                                 ⎬  TOTAL COST
   Variable  — Fuel              ⎥
             — Oil               ⎥
             — Tyres             ⎥
             — Repairs and maintenance
             — Sundries          ⎦
```

What is depreciation?

Depreciation is the gradual and permanent decrease in the value of an asset, eg a vehicle, from any cause.

Why should it be a charge against the revenue of a business?

Many of the assets of a business gradually wear out and eventually have to be replaced. Vehicles are a very good example of this. Unless provision is made out of revenue for the replacement of assets, when the time comes, there could be no money available, ie the capital of the business which was sunk in its assets has disappeared. (This is called erosion of capital by accountants.)

How is this avoided?

To avoid erosion of capital accountants write off the value of the asset over its estimated life. At the same time a sum of money equal to that written off is set aside to provide funds for the assets' replacement.

The money set aside should be invested in easily realised investments so that it is readily available when required. The interest earned on the investments should, hopefully, be sufficient to cover any increase in price of the new asset. In times of rapid inflation a close watch must be kept to ensure that there will be sufficient money available to meet a much higher replacement cost and, if necessary, additional money must be set aside for this purpose.

How is the amount of depreciation calculated?

There are many methods but the two simpler ones are:
   (a) straight line or fixed instalment method
   (b) diminishing or reducing balance method.

Using a motor vehicle as an example, the following illustrate the methods used.

Straight line method

Large modern vehicles are expected to have a normal working life of four to six years although many operators sell their vehicles before this. A vehicle will have some value left at the end of its working life. The earlier it is sold, the higher the value is likely to be. Even if the vehicle is only fit for scrap, that has a value. This value which remains at the end of its working life with the business is called the residual value.

To calculate depreciation on a straight line basis, deduct the residual value from the purchase price and divide the remainder by the number of years estimated as its working life. The figure obtained is the amount which must be written off as depreciation each year, eg if a vehicle purchased new for £36,000 is to be kept for five years and at the end of that time it is estimated that its residual value will then be £6000:

Purchase price of the vehicle =	£36,000
Less residual value	£ 6,000
	£30,000
Divide by number of years of estimated life	$\dfrac{£30,000}{5}$
Annual depreciation	£6,000

Many people in the road haulage industry, however, would say that trying to estimate the probable resale price of a goods vehicle in five years' time is impossible and residual value should be ignored. This is probably the better view and any money that is realised can be used to compensate for the increased cost of replacement.

Because tyres form part of the running costs of a vehicle and the original set of tyres will have been replaced several times during its working life, many accountants prefer to deduct the cost of the original set of tyres from the purchase price of the vehicle before calculating the annual depreciation.

Diminishing balance method

In this method, instead of deducting a fixed instalment each year, a fixed percentage is deducted from the reducing value of the vehicle until only its residual value remains. It is sometimes claimed that this method has a particular advantage where vehicles are concerned because larger amounts are deducted in the early years when maintenance costs should be lower and smaller amounts in the later years of the vehicle's life when maintenance costs tend to be higher. In view of the relatively short life of vehicles, this advantage may be more theoretical than practical.

A rather complicated formula is available for calculating the rate percent to be deducted, but over the short life of a vehicle absolute precision is not required and a satisfactory percentage can be found by trial and error.

Using a purchase price of £36,000, the following examples illustrate the method over five years and six years using percentage deductions of 33⅓% (⅓) and 25% (¼) respectively.

	£36,000			£36,000
Less ⅓	£12,000	1st year	Less ¼	£9,000
"	£24,000			£27,000
	£8,000	2nd year	"	£6,750
"	£16,000			£20,250
	£5,334 (approx)	3rd year	"	£5,063 (approx)
	£10,666			£15,187
"	£3,556 (approx)	4th year	"	£3,797 (approx)
	£7,110			£11,390
"	£2,370	5th year	"	£2,848 (approx)
Residual value	£4,740			£8,542
		6th year	"	£2,135 (approx)
		Residual value		£6,407

In neither case is the residual value exactly as estimated in the earlier example but as this estimate is largely guesswork, the difference is unimportant. What is important is that a realistic amount in respect of depreciation should be allowed for each year.

What is the best way of calculating a company's level of profitability?

The best way is to calculate the return on capital employed.

When money is invested in a business, either by the original proprietor, or by shareholders, they are looking for a reasonable return on their capital. A business may be showing a profit but if that level of profit is very low, ie well below the level that could be obtained if the money had been invested elsewhere, the investors may regret their decision to put money in the business. It is necessary, therefore, not merely to show a profit but to generate sufficient profit relative to the amount of capital invested in the business, eg:

	Company A	Company B
Capital invested —	£20,000,000	£100,000
Net profit —	£1,000,000	£12,000
Return on Capital	5%	12%

Although the £1 million profit of Company A looks impressive when taken on its own, the performance of the firm is poor compared with that of Company B which has what appears to be a very modest profit.

What level of profit should an operator aim for?

He should aim for a level of profit considerably above that which could be obtained by investing in the money market because he has taken on the risk involved in running a business. If this cannot be obtained, the operator, providing he is able, might be advised to sell out or reinvest his money and live a life of ease, or find some other occupation. Because of the risk involved and also inflation, the operator should aim at a profit level of 25% before taxation.

How can the operator be sure that he will secure the level of profit?

He cannot but at least he should be aware that this is the level of profit he should be aiming for to make his business worthwhile. This means that when he is determining his rates he must add on an amount calculated to produce the desired profit. Of course, during periods of recession and extreme competitiveness this level of profit will almost certainly need to be drastically reduced in order to keep rates competitive and to stay in business. This situation cannot, of course, carry on for too long or the undertaking will fail.

What method should be used to calculate rates?

Having determined all the indirect costs of the business — the overheads — these must be apportioned to the vehicles. If all the vehicles in the fleet have the same payload capacity, there is no problem, the overheads are divided equally among the vehicles. Where the vehicle size varies, overheads must be apportioned on a payload basis. It would, of course, be unrealistic to expect a 7.5 tonne vehicle to carry the same burden of overheads as a 20 tonne vehicle when its revenue earning capacity is so much lower.

These overheads, when added to the other vehicle fixed costs, ie licences, insurance, depreciation, loan or hire-purchase interest charges, produce the annual fixed cost of the vehicle.

Similarly, with profit loading, having calculated the total gross profit that must be earned to give an appropriate return on capital invested, this must also be apportioned to each vehicle on the basis of payload. The annual profit loading for each vehicle is now known.

Once the annual fixed costs and annual profit loading have been determined, rates can be fixed. This can be done on a daily basis, using a calculated number of operating days per year (say 225) with an addition to cover variable (running) costs (oil, tyres, etc) according to the distance to be covered. Alternatively, rates can be calculated entirely on a distance basis working to an estimated number of miles per year. Neither of these methods is entirely satisfactory and a method based on dividing the profit loading between time and distance is preferable. For example, given annual fixed vehicle costs of £21,858 (32.5 tonnes artic), annual profit loading of £8,327.60, variable costs of 49.46 pence per mile and an estimated annual mileage of 40,000 miles, vehicle rates can be established as follows:

Annual fixed costs	£21,858.00
Half annual profit loading	£4,163.80
	£26,021.80
Variable costs per mile	49.46p
Profit loading per mile	10.41p
(£4,163.80 ÷ 40,000)	59.87p

Rate per day £26,021.80 ÷ 225 = £115.65 plus
Rate per mile 59.87p.

To assist operators to obtain a better understanding of costing and financial management, and to enable each operator to set up a costing system to meet his own needs, Croner Publications Ltd, publish *Croner's Operational Costings for Transport Management*. Operators will also find that the tables published by Motor Transport and Commercial Motor will provide useful cost comparisons.

Purchasing and Stock Control

What is the importance of purchasing and stock control?

These are areas in which unnecessary costs can be incurred and profits eroded, unless they are closely watched.

Purchasing control

Remembering what was said about cash flow, it becomes obvious that foreseeable purchases should be scheduled for those periods when the firm is enjoying maximum inflow of revenue, ie when cash is readily available without recourse to increasing the overdraft or loans. Conversely, when cash inflow is low, purchases must be confined to essentials whose purchase cannot be deferred.

While flexibility must be maintained to enable small purchases to be made without constant reference to a central authority, it may be desirable to route all purchases above a certain level through a central department or individual who will have an overall picture of the undertaking's purchases. In this way purchases can be related to cash flow as indicated above, bulk purchases can be arranged where desirable and the most favourable discounts negotiated.

How does stock control tie in with this?

Stock control is important to the business in two major ways:
    (a) to ensure that materials and spares are available when required
    (b) to ensure that capital is not tied up in unnecessarily high levels of stock.

Examining (a) we find that:
    (i) non-availability of materials or spares may cause unnecessary deferment of work and, at worst, result in vehicles being out of commission
    (ii) emergency purchase of stock is likely to involve a higher level of expenditure because advantage cannot be taken of
    (iii) pre-planning of stocks, ie calculation of annual consumption, maintenance of minimum stock levels, etc enables the person or department responsible for purchasing to bulk buy at the most advantageous times and prices. Where smaller items and quantities are concerned the person responsible has time to shop around for the best terms.

What problems arise if stock levels are unnecessarily high?

Raw materials and stores in any excessive quantity tie up a large amount of capital which could be used for other purposes in the business, or reinvested elsewhere. Where a firm is operating on an overdraft the cash released if stocks are maintained at a lower level could be used to reduce the overdraft, with consequent lower interest charges.

A balance must be maintained between the level of stocks required to ensure the unhindered running of the business and the cost of maintaining the stocks, eg it would be ridiculous to hold in stock a spare for every part of every vehicle in case it should be needed. Most parts would never be needed and the cost would be prohibitive.

How can an accurate check be kept on fuel issued from a bulk tank?
When making a physical check, the opening stock (ie the reading at the last check), plus deliveries from the oil company, less the total of issues to vehicles, should equal the current reading. If any serious discrepancy is revealed, this must be investigated with a view to tightening up receiving and issuing procedures.

What kind of spares should be held?
This is largely a matter of experience. Spares which regularly require replacement can be stocked in convenient quantities and replaced on a periodic basis. Unless the fleet is very large and consists of standardised types it is probably better to rely on the replacement services of stockists and manufacturers than to hold extensive stocks of all but the most regularly used items. When there is the likelihood of a long delay in obtaining particular spares, it is a question of weighing up the possible costs of down-time, against the certain costs of stock maintenance.

Should the operator take advantage of special offers for bulk purchases?
There is always a temptation to take advantage of special offers which appear to give the operator an opportunity to reduce costs. In some circumstances these can be profitable, in others there are hidden snares. Before embarking on any large-scale purchase, or taking advantage of a special offer, the following factors should be considered:

(a) for how long will the quantity purchased last?
(b) will the stock purchased deteriorate over that period of time?
(c) will the items purchased become obsolete?
(d) does the saving in price outweigh the interest on capital invested in the stocks?
(e) could the space required for storage be better utilised for other purposes?

Only if favourable answers are obtained to these questions should money be invested in purchases far in excess of those normally made.

CHAPTER 10
(Module A)
The Commercial Conduct of Business

Why does a road haulage operator need to have knowledge of general commercial practice?

Although a road haulier is supplying a service, viz the carriage of goods and will be familiar with the documents used in this aspect of commerce, he is continually in contact with people who supply goods and services other than transport. If he has a knowledge of general commercial practice it will assist him not only in running his own business but also in his dealings with his customers and suppliers.

How are prices determined?

In setting his prices, a businessman must take into account his costs and the level of profit he expects to obtain on his goods and services supplied. As seen earlier, his costs will include direct costs and overheads. Whereas transport is the end product where a road haulier is concerned, it is another cost to a manufacturer. Whether he treats it as an overhead or as a direct cost, will depend on the product concerned.

To a manufacturer of foodstuffs selling under brand names with a countrywide distribution at a recommended retail price, it will be treated as an overhead and distance will not affect the price of individual consignments. To a manufacturer of heavy plant and machinery, costed on an individual basis, it will be treated as a direct cost in respect of each order.

Prices may be established:
(a) on a national basis
(b) on an individual basis.

They may be determined:
  (i) by what the market will bear. This concept of pricing is only really effective where the product or service is unique, or in a monopolistic position. The price is not determined by costs but by how much customers will be prepared to pay to obtain the product or service
  (ii) on a cost plus profit basis. Here the profit margin is likely to be affected by the level of competition from suppliers of similar products or services, or of alternatives, eg the rates charged by other road hauliers, or the rates charged by British Rail.

What is the relationship between wholesale and retail prices?

Many manufacturers do not wish to involve themselves with supplying small quantities to individual retailers and many retailers have neither the space nor the capital to deal with large quantities. Between these two the wholesaler performs a useful service. He takes goods in bulk from manufacturers, warehouses them and breaks down the large quantities into smaller units for distribution to retailers. The wholesaler, by buying in bulk, obtains goods at a low price. To this price he adds a percentage to cover his costs plus profit and sells to the retailer at a price (the wholesale price) which still leaves the retailer with a margin of profit on the price at which he sells to the consumer (the retail price).

What are discounts?
Discounts are reductions from the normal price. There are two principal forms of discount in regular use in business.
1. *Cash discount* — This is given to customers who either settle in cash at the time of purchase or within a specified time of the invoice being rendered (the latter is sometimes called a discount for prompt payment). Although giving a discount means that the trader's profit is smaller, it may be cheaper than allowing debts to accumulate and may be useful in assisting the reduction of overdrafts or improving cash flow.
2. *Trade discount* — This is quite different from a cash discount. It is a reduction in the catalogue price given by the wholesaler or manufacturer to a retailer or tradesman to enable him to make a profit, eg a painter or decorator will be able to obtain his supplies of paint, etc from a builders' merchant at a cheaper rate than a householder doing his own decorating.

What is the difference between cash and credit sales?
In the retail trade, most goods are supplied against the immediate payment of money. These transactions are called cash sales. By agreement, particularly between businessmen, payment is often deferred until a later date. This is called a credit sale. The length of time allowed for payment varies according to the agreement between the parties and the custom of a particular trade. A regular arrangement is that accounts are settled monthly, ie all transactions completed in one month are paid for during the first few days of the following month.

Credit sales to members of the general public are often made to stimulate the sale of items too costly to be met in one payment out of the normal weekly or monthly pay packet, eg consumer durables such as furniture and electrical appliances. The customer is allowed to spread the cost of this purchase over a limited period, paying in instalments (with or without interest) rather than having to resort to more costly hire-purchase arrangements.

What is the significance of the terms "carriage paid" and "carriage forward"?
Carriage paid means that the carriage charges have been, or will be, paid by the consignor (sender), while carriage forward means that the carriage charges will be the responsibility of the consignee (receiver).

Can a carrier protect himself in any way against non-payment of his charges?
A common method is to include a lien in his Conditions of Carriage (see chapter 11).

A lien is a right of retention, ie he is entitled to hold goods against payment of his charges. There are several kinds of lien, the most useful being one which is general and active. This means that the carrier is able to hold any goods belonging to the same consignee against payment of his charges and also enables him to sell them after a reasonable time if his charges are still not paid.

Why does the lien operate against the consignee and not the consignor?
This is because legally, once the goods have been handed by a seller to an independent carrier for carriage to the buyer, those goods become the property of

the buyer, unless the seller has specifically stated that the ownership shall remain with him until some stipulated event occurs, eg until paid for.

What documents are regularly used in commerce?

Each business tends to create documents and records to meet its own particular needs but there are a number of documents which are common to most businesses and whose purpose is universally recognised.

Quotation

This is a statement of the price or prices at which a company is prepared to supply goods or services. Often it is a written confirmation of an initial oral statement. Sometimes it is a more formal document which also sets out the terms and conditions to be observed by both parties to the transaction. It may form the basis of a contract, or be the basis on which a contract is negotiated.

Order

This is a request from a customer to a supplier for the supply of goods or services. It may repeat prices and conditions which have been given in a quotation so that no confusion can arise as to terms agreed. Many firms use an official order form when placing orders, which offers advantages to both the orderer and supplier. Some of the advantages of this practice are:
- (a) the recipient has no doubt as to the genuineness of the order
- (b) the order number is a convenient reference to both supplier and customer
- (c) unauthorised ordering of goods is eliminated
- (d) copies of the order provide a permanent record and may be made an essential part of the book keeping system, stores procedure, etc
- (e) checking the progress of the order is facilitated.

Order forms are frequently issued by suppliers for the use of their customers. This practice may have the following advantages:
- (a) the convenience offered encourages customers to order. This is more apparent in dealing with the general public than with businessmen
- (b) orders are received in a form which fits conveniently into the supplier's system
- (c) where items are in printed list form confusion is avoided
- (d) the supplier can set out his terms and conditions and avoid possible subsequent disputes.

Invoice

A document made out by a seller advising the buyer of the amount due in respect of a particular transaction.
The invoice usually shows:
- (a) the names and addresses of both seller and buyer
- (b) a description of the goods or services supplied
- (c) the date of the sale
- (d) the terms of sale, eg any discounts, periods of credit, etc
- (e) the amount due
- (f) the customer's order number, if one was given.

The invoice sent to the customer is usually the top copy of a set. The number and use of the other copies, which will have different headings, vary from business to business, but the following are commonly in use:

Top copy — Customer's invoice.
2nd copy — Copy invoice or Day Book copy, which forms part of the firm's accounting system.
3rd copy — Stores or Warehouse copy, kept as a record by the stores or warehouse against the issue of goods.
4th copy — Delivery note, given to the driver who presents it to the customer for signature when the goods are delivered.
5th copy — Advice note which is packed with or accompanies the goods and assists the customer in checking the contents of parcels or quantities received.

Credit note
This is issued when it is necessary for a seller to credit a customer with an amount that has previously been invoiced to him. This necessity may arise from three causes:
    (a) to credit a debtor with returns. Returns may occur in the following ways:
        (i) the goods are unsatisfactory, eg wrong size, wrong colour, not to sample, defective, etc
        (ii) empties are returned
        (iii) the customer has changed his mind and the seller has agreed to take back the goods
    (b) to credit the seller with an allowance. This may be given in the following circumstances:
        (i) the customer agrees to accept goods which are not completely satisfactory, provided an allowance is made
        (ii) the goods have suffered minor damage which the buyer agrees to put right, subject to an allowance to cover his costs
        (iii) the cost of returning unsatisfactory low cost goods is not justified, an allowance is made and the customer retains or disposes of the goods
    (c) to credit a debtor with an overcharge caused by:
        (i) an incorrect rate being charged
        (ii) an incorrect quantity being charged
        (iii) an error in calculation or typing.

Debit note
This is a document used to rectify an undercharge. Just as overcharges can occur and are corrected by credit notes, so, when the reverse occurs, it is corrected by a debit note. A debit note can also be used to charge out expenses which were not known at the time the invoice was made out, eg charges for carriage and insurance.

Statement
This is a summary of the invoices sent during the preceding month, or simply a statement of the total indebtedness of the customer to the supplier at the date of the statement. It is a reminder to the customer of the amount that he owes. Where there is regular business between two parties it is often convenient to pay once a month on receipt of the statement, rather than send a continuous stream of cheques to meet individual invoices. This practice has gained widespread acceptance.

Consignment note
This accompanies goods, giving full details of the consignor and consignee, the goods carried and delivery instructions; it frequently provides prima facie evidence

of the contract of carriage. It is not obligatory for national operations but its use is mandatory in connection with contracts for the international carriage of goods by road. The rules of the CMR Convention which are incorporated in the Carriage of Goods by Road Act 1965 stipulate that three copies (at least) of the consignment note must be used and specify the information which must be shown on it.

CMR consignment notes are obtainable in this country (to members only) from the Road Haulage Association or the Freight Transport Association.

The CMR consignment note is made up in quadruplicate with coloured lines on a white background for ease of use, ie:

　　　First copy (for sender) .... Red
　　　Second copy (for consignee) .... Blue
　　　Third copy (for carrier) .... Green
　　　Fourth copy (for file). .... Black

Waybill
This is a document which contains a detailed statement of goods entrusted to a public carrier. In many ways it is similar to a consignment note and the terms are often interchanged. A waybill does not usually contain as much information regarding the contract of carriage as does a consignment note.

Other Services

The Advantages and Scope of Insurance

What is the nature of insurance?
It is the pooling of risks. If we take any large group of people or undertakings, we can be certain that sooner or later one or more of them will suffer a misfortune — a fire, an accident, goods lost or stolen, etc — and depending upon its severity, the misfortune could prove disastrous to that person or undertaking and anyone dependent upon them. We can be equally certain that the same misfortune will not overtake all members of the group at the same time.

Realising the possibility that misfortune could strike one of their number at any time, the members of the group could each agree to contribute a sum of money for the creation of a fund or a pool to be drawn upon by any member of the group suffering a loss from specified causes. This is the principle on which insurance is founded.

Why is it necessary to have insurance companies?
No matter how wide a circle of acquaintances and business contacts a person has, it is very unlikely that one could persuade sufficient people to contribute in order to produce a pool large enough to provide cover against the risks that might be encountered.

This is where the insurance companies come in. They are able to reach a much larger number of potential contributors and the accumulation of hundreds of thousands of individual premiums guarantees cover against the risks provided for, as far as each individual is concerned.

On what basis do insurance companies calculate their charges?
Insurance premiums are based on the risk involved, ie the likelihood of a loss occurring to a specific individual, the length of time they are required to cover against that risk — the longer the time, the greater the possibility — and the sum of money likely to be required as compensation for the loss.

How do they assess the degree of risk?
Statistics kept by individual companies on particular types of risk and those available to the industry as a whole, enable insurers to estimate with considerable accuracy the percentage claims and their likely value in respect of any particular class of insurance they are asked to provide. They will also take into account any particular circumstances applicable to specific requests for insurance, eg any special risks, the past record of the proposer, etc. Where an entirely new class of business arises, the insurer must use his experience, coupled with the statistics of other kinds of risk, to make an appropriate rate.

It is well known that many homes are destroyed by fire each year, yet an individual would consider it very unlucky if it happened to him. The odds against this happening must be very high indeed but the consequences if it should happen could be disastrous without insurance cover. An insurer knows just what those odds are and in fixing his rates he must ensure that they are low enough to attract business, while being sufficient to provide him with a profit when all claims and expenses have been met.

As a haulage operator, what should one insure against?
The risks to be covered can be divided into two categories:
    (a) those that it is a statutory obligation to cover
    (b) those that it is commercially prudent to guard against.

What insurance is required by Statute?
To satisfy the requirements of the Road Traffic Act 1988 (ss.143-158) all users of road vehicles on the road in the United Kingdom must be insured with an authorised insurer who is a member of the Motor Insurer's Bureau against liability at law in respect of death, compensation for injury caused to another person, the cost of any emergency medical treatment resulting from an accident and damage to property. All passengers must be covered and any "own risk" agreements that may be agreed between passengers and the owner or user of the vehicle have no effect.

NB This insurance does not cover employees travelling as passengers; these are specially covered under "Employers' liability insurance" (see page 116).

As an alternative to the insurance policy, The Motor Vehicles (Third Party Risks Deposits) Regulations 1967 (SI 1967 No. 1326) allows application to be made to the Secretary of State for the Department of Transport for a warrant to enable a deposit of £15,000 in cash or securities to be made with the Supreme Court.

Why are insurers who are members of the Motor Insurers' Bureau specifically stipulated?
This is because the Motor Insurers' Bureau has undertaken to pay any unsatisfied judgement debt in respect of death, personal injury, emergency medical treatment and third party damages, ie where a court has awarded damages to the victim of an uninsured driver and that person does not have the means to pay.

Where his vehicles are concerned, what other risks should an operator insure against?

A "Third party" insurance policy provides cover for the statutory requirements. Many policies limit the cover against claims for property damage to £250,000 on any one claim. In view of inflation and the fact that courts have been known to award damages in excess of this amount many insurers are increasing this limit. The operator should periodically check his policies to ensure that his cover is adequate.

The protection mentioned so far does not extend to damage to the user's own vehicle as the result of an accident, or loss resulting from fire or theft. Unless the owner is prepared to accept the very heavy burden that could arise from loss or damage through these causes, he should take steps to increase his cover.

The prudent course is to take out a Comprehensive policy, which will cover not only third party, fire and theft risks but also the cost of repairs to a vehicle following accidental damage.

Will a Comprehensive policy give complete cover?

In spite of its name a Comprehensive policy does not cover every eventuality. Insurance policies invariably contain some exclusion clauses. The following exclusions are common to most Comprehensive polices:

    (a) depreciation, wear, tear, mechanical or electrical breakdown
    (b) damage to tyres by application of brakes or by road punctures, cuts or bursts.

Is it possible to obtain cover against these risks?

By payment of an additional premium, cover can be obtained against losses arising under those excluded headings. It is the responsibility of the insured to decide what additional cover is required.

Should an operator try to find the cheapest insurance available?

He should be wary of cut-price insurance. Usually this is achieved by setting low maximum limits in respect of individual claims, or by increasing the number of risks which are excluded from the cover, or both. Cheap insurance could prove very costly in the long run, when he may find himself faced with a loss which his insurance does not cover. Nevertheless it is worthwhile to make comparisons before committing himself to a particular insurance policy. Some policies may include cover which is not required but for which he must still pay. Others, by eliminating certain risks, may be cheaper yet still satisfy his needs.

How can an operator find the company which offers the best policy for his needs?

This is best done through a good insurance broker. Insurance brokers are not tied to one company but can introduce a wide range of policies offered by many companies. The broker will be able to recommend the most suitable policy.

What other insurance does an operator need?
Apart from the statutory requirements, the most important cover for an operator is insurance against legal liability for loss or damage to goods entrusted to his care, ie "goods in transit" insurance. When effecting this type of insurance he must ensure that the cover fully indemnifies him in accordance with the conditions under which he carries goods. He should, therefore, advise his insurers of his conditions of carriage.

From time to time a client may request wider cover for his goods than that provided for under the operator's conditions of carriage. Before agreeing to carry the goods the operator should check with his insurers and receive their confirmation that they will extend the cover.

Are there likely to be any restrictive clauses in goods in transit policies?
Owing to adverse claims experience in recent years, particularly as a result of theft, many insurers have inserted restrictive clauses. Two usual ones are:
- (a) Immobiliser clause — requires goods vehicles to be fitted with an approved anti-theft device which is put into effective operation when a loaded vehicle is left unattended
- (b) Night risk clause — warrants that vehicles left loaded overnight must not be left unattended unless locked and immobilised in accordance with any such provision under the policy and also that they are either left in a building or yard which is also securely closed or locked, or in an attended official car park.

An operator should take careful note of these and any other restrictive clauses in his policy and make sure that his drivers are fully aware of what is required of them; failure to observe the stated conditions could invalidate the cover.

What is meant by an "excess clause" in a goods in transit policy?
This means that the insurance company will only pay the excess above a minimum amount, ie the insured (the carrier) meets all claims below a set figure. This avoids the insurance company having to pay numerous relatively small sums and, in return, the insured pays a lower premium.

Is there anything else he must consider where goods in transit insurance is concerned?
Even though the operator's vehicles do not leave this country he may find himself involved in a contract for the International Carriage of Goods by Road to which the CMR Convention applies, eg where the operator undertakes one leg of a journey involving a loaded trailer. Should this occur he must ensure that the CMR conditions are adopted and obtain the necessary extension of cover under his goods in transit policy.

What else does he need to cover?
Other items to be covered include:

Employers' liability — He is required by law, under the Employers' Liability (Compulsory Insurance) Act 1969, the Employers' Liability (Compulsory Insurance) General Regulations 1971, and Employers' Liability (Defective Equipment) Act 1969 to ensure against liability for personal injury to his employees, eg a fitter slips and falls into a repair pit which has defective rails and injures himself.

Public Liability — This is designed to protect him against claims from the public arising from his negligence or that of his employees, eg a lorry sheds its load which was not properly secured and injures a passer-by.

It is possible to obtain a policy which combines cover for liability to both employees and public.

Fire insurance — This should include:
  (a) damage to premises, stocks and equipment
  (b) loss of profits should the operation of the business be interrupted by fire.

Where fire insurance does not cover loss of profits (loss of trade), a separate policy against consequential loss will be required.

Personal accident — For a small premium, cashiers can be covered against personal violence when conveying cash to and from a bank. Similar cover can be arranged for drivers who may suffer violence in cases of hijacking, etc.

Cash in transit — Cover should be arranged against robbery when cash is being transferred to and from a bank and wages held on the premises prior to and during pay out should also be covered.

The operator should also consider:

Fidelity insurance — Cover should be arranged against losses arising from the dishonesty of employees.

Loss of partner or vital employee — Where the loss of a partner or a particularly important member of the staff could seriously affect the business it is advisable to take out insurance cover.

Personal liability — This protects the insured and his family as private individuals against liability at law to pay damages arising from accidents away from home.

Wherever a risk can be foreseen it can be insured against. It is up to the individual to decide whether the risk of possible future loss (it could be tomorrow), is sufficiently high to justify paying premiums today.

Banking Services

What are the main services provided by banks to industry?
The function of banks falls into three main areas of activity and within those areas they provide a multitude of services.
1. *The collection and safeguarding of surplus funds* accumulated by industry (and individuals). Think how inconvenient and expensive it would be if each individual and company had to store and protect his or its accumulated wealth. Moreover that wealth would be laying idle, of no use to anyone, until the owner needed it to pay for some purchase or for some service rendered. Meanwhile there would be other companies and individuals hampered in their efforts to begin new business enterprises or expand existing ones because they had no easy way of contacting people with surplus funds. This is where the bank's second function comes in.

2. *The lending of surplus funds, not immediately required* by their present owners and lodged with the banks, to others in need of funds. Again it would be most inconvenient if, to transfer those funds, or in settling the indebtedness of one person to another it was necessary to transfer large amounts of cash. Here the bank's third function comes into operation.
3. *Providing a system whereby funds can be transferred* from one person to another without leaving the bank.

How do these three functions operate?
To become a customer of a bank a person or company opens an account. If he merely wishes the bank to look after his money for him and at the same time for that money to earn interest, he will open either a savings account or a deposit account.

How do these differ?
A savings account is intended for the small saver and enables him to put money away for particular purposes, eg holidays. The rate of interest paid on savings accounts is lower than that paid on deposit accounts but the money saved is available on demand.

A deposit account is used for the deposit of cash resources which the depositer is not likely to require to meet his current needs. The rate of interest earned is usually 2% less than the Bank of England's minimum lending rate. This money can then be loaned out to borrowers usually at 2½% above the minimum lending rate. In this way the bank earns sufficient money to pay interest to the depositors and to make a profit itself. Theoretically, money deposited in a deposit account is not immediately withdrawable and seven days' notice should be given. In practice, unless the sum demanded is very large, the bank waives the nominal seven days' notice and instead charges seven days' interest on the sum withdrawn.

A third kind of account is the current account and this is the one most commonly used. It is through these accounts that the majority of day to day business is transacted.

How does a current account work?
Before a bank agrees to grant current account facilities to a new depositor, it must first be sure that he is reliable. He is usually asked to provide a reference and if this is satisfactory the bank will accept his deposit and issue him with a cheque book. Thereafter he will be able to deposit money, using a paying in slip and withdraw it or pay his debts by means of a cheque.

What are cheques?
Legally, cheques are a form of a bill of exchange but, in simple terms, a cheque is regarded as an order to the bank to pay the sum specified to the person named on the cheque. Theoretically, a cheque can be made out on any piece of paper, but in practice banks issue cheques in standard sizes for the convenience of their customers and to fit their own internal systems.

How does the cheque system work?
Basically cheques are used for two purposes:
    (a) to enable the drawer (the person who makes out the cheque) to withdraw money from his current account
    (b) to instruct the drawer's bank to pay money to another person.

In the first case the drawer simply makes out the cheque, presents it to the cashier at the branch of the bank where his account is kept and obtains cash in return. He may also have an arrangement whereby he can cash cheques at another branch or branches of his bank. When the intention is for money to be paid or credited to a person other than the depositor the procedure varies.

A bearer cheque — an uncrossed cheque, made out "Pay bearer", which enables anyone who presents it to the bank to obtain payment.

An open cheque — an uncrossed cheque that can be cashed at the bank by anyone who presents it claming to be the payee named on the cheque. He must endorse it, ie sign his name on the back, when he presents it.

A crossed cheque — a cheque with two lines across it, sometimes with the words "& Co" between the crossed lines. It will only be cashed across the counter of the bank if the person presenting it is known to the cashier, otherwise it must be cleared into a bank account.

The type of crossing mentioned above is known as a *general crossing*, other types of crossing are:
- (a) *special crossing,* here the name of the banker is written between the crossing lines and normally will only be cleared into the account of the payee at the bank named
- (b) *A/C Payee,* here the person drawing the cheque wishes it to be paid only into the account specified (often at the request of the payee). If it is paid into any other account the bank must enquire whether the payee has authorised payment to that other account, or the bank will be liable to the payee if an unauthorised person should collect the money.

What is a credit transfer?
This is a method of payment directly into a payee's bank account. Using a bank giro credit slip accompanied by a cheque or cash, the payment can be made at any bank and the amount will be transferred to the payee's bank and credited to his account.

How does a standing order (banker's order) work?
A standing order is an instruction from an account holder to pay a specified sum at regular intervals, eg monthly, quarterly or yearly, to a specified bank account.

How does this differ from a direct debit?
A bank will continue to pay the amount specified on a standing order on the due dates until instructed to do otherwise. If the amount needs to be altered then a new standing order will need to be issued.

When periodic payments need to be varied from time to time, eg when changes in interest rates affect mortgage repayments, this would involve frequent changes to standing orders. This problem can be avoided by using a direct debit request which authorises the account holder's bank to pay to a specified creditor such amounts as are requested by that creditor from time to time.

Methods of Operating

What are the advantages and disadvantages of own and hired transport?

This is a subject on which precise, positive answers are hard to come by. Any group of transport men, operators and users are likely to have many different opinions concerning claimed advantages and disadvantages of the two systems. It is possible, however, to state a number of claimed advantages and disadvantages which have gained some measure of acceptance as being widely, though not universally, applicable.

Own transport

Advantages:
1. Complete control over drivers, specification and operation of vehicles.
2. Advertising value of vehicles.

Disadvantages:
1. Return loads are difficult to organise, hence high proportion of light running, particularly if operating on a restricted licence.
2. Garaging and maintenance facilities must be installed, or maintenance contracted out.
3. A fleet big enough to cover peak periods is expensive to provide and usually means that hiring must be done at busy times.
4. Full capital costs, overheads and operating costs are not always debited and a false impression of the cost of carriage results.
5. Danger of misuse — vehicles used without proper costing or planning because they are readily available.

Hired transport — Contract hire

Advantages:
1. Almost complete control over vehicles and drivers.
2. Advertising value of vehicle (if in hirer's livery).
3. No garage or maintenance facilities to provide.
4. Full cost is known.

Disadvantages:
1. Return loads difficult to organise.
2. Hired vehicles must be fully employed for the duration of the contract.
3. More expensive than running own fleet or using public hauliers.

Hired transport — Public hauliers (Spot hire)

Advantages:
1. Can obtain lowest haulage rate for each delivery.
2. Can obtain suitable vehicle for each delivery.
3. Deliveries can be arranged without reference to return loads.
4. Peak times and slack periods can be more easily catered for.

Disadvantages:
1. Less control over drivers.
2. Difficulty may be experienced in catering for urgent loads at times.
3. No advertising values from vehicles.

The decision as to which type of fleet to use will probably be based on the following factors:
   (a) does traffic flow in regular streams?
   (b) can return loads be arranged for a high proportion of journeys?
   (c) is the advertising value of vehicles important?
   (d) can vehicles be garaged and can maintenance facilities be provided without heavy capital cost?

What is a clearing house?
A clearing house is an organisation which undertakes to arrange transport of loads for customers requiring transport. The clearing house acts as contractor and sub-contracts to other hauliers.

What is the role of a sub-contractor and his relationship with the contractor?
A sub-contractor is a haulier who undertakes to perform work on behalf of the original contractor.

The sub-contractor undertakes to perform the work in compliance with the conditions agreed between himself and the contractor. If operating under RHA conditions, the sub-contractor is entitled to the same protection and benefits that the contractor derives from those conditions.

The contractor agrees to pay the rate agreed between himself and the sub-contractor on completion of a job.

Who is liable if a sub-contractor fails to complete a contract?
If a sub-contractor fails to perform a contract made by the original contractor with another party, that other party will claim against the original contractor who will be liable for any loss which has arisen. The original contractor must, in turn, seek to recover his losses from the sub-contractor.

What is the role of the freight forwarder?
A freight forwarder acts as an agent for his principal (the customer) as is indicated by his former title of shipping and forwarding agent.

It is no simple matter to define the role of a freight forwarder (freight forwarders have been trying to do this for a number of years), because it is continually growing.

A freight forwarder, if requested, is usually prepared to perform any of the following services on behalf of his clients:
   (a) arrange transport
   (b) arrange packing of goods
   (c) prepare customs and transport documentation
   (d) arrange clearance of goods through customs
   (e) arrange warehousing of goods
   (f) arrange insurance
   (g) pay all charges in connection with the carriage and render one bill to the customer which includes his own commission for services rendered.

Depending on the size of the freight forwarding firm, some of the services rendered may be performed directly by the freight forwarder and others may be arranged with independent contractors on behalf of his principals.

What is a groupage service?
Groupage is the consolidation of a number of small consignments into a unit load. This is a service that is often offered by freight forwarders.

CHAPTER 11
(Module A)
Structure of the Law

What exactly is "the law" and who is responsible for making it?

The law in this country is not derived from one single source but has developed over the centuries into the complex system that operates today.

The principal sources of law are:
(a) Ancient custom
(b) Common Law
(c) Equity
(d) Statute Law
(e) Delegated or subordinate legislation
(f) Judicial Precedent and Case Law (really a continuation of Common Law)
(g) Aspects of EC Law and International Law which affect the United Kingdom.

How did all these different sources originate and are they all relevant today?

The law has reached its present state as a result of development and adaptation over many centuries. It can best be understood how and to what extent these sources fit into the present system by embarking on a brief survey of those various sources.

Ancient custom

Before the coming of the Normans, Saxon England was ruled by laws based on the democratic nature of Saxon society which permitted each man to express his point of view at tribunal gatherings. From the decisions at these gatherings a body of law based on the customs and practices of the community was established.

These customs and practices obviously varied in different parts of the country, although a few customs were widespread enough to attain the status of Ancient Custom of the Realm.

Common Law

The Normans gradually replaced the system of Law based on local customs by Common Law, ie a uniform system of law common to all the land. The assize system, only finally abandoned in 1971, was the biggest single influence in this change. Assizes involved judges travelling around the country trying cases in the county towns, generally according to local customs.

By a process of supporting good customs and rejecting bad ones a system of common law was established. Since the decisions of other judges had to be followed — a decision by one judge was binding on others (judicial precedent) — this decision became effective throughout the country.

Equity

Equity means fairness and Equity decisions were designed to reverse some of the unfair legal decisions by overruling the Common Law (you may have heard the expression "It may be the law, but it's not justice") in favour of something more just. Equity was first administered by the King's Chancellor and later by a special court called the Chancery Court. It did a great deal to overcome the rigidity and inadequacies of the Common Law. Equity was gradually amalgamated with the

Common Law and today any judge can give a common law remedy if that is appropriate, or an equity remedy if that is fairer.

Statute Law
A statute is an Act of Parliament (before Parliament was established a law was passed by the King). Parliament is the supreme law making body and can make or repeal any law it wishes. Statutory Law overrides Common Law and Equity and is therefore the most important source of law in this country, at least as far as status is concerned.

Delegated or Subordinate legislation
In addition to Acts which specify in detail the law relating to a particular subject, Parliament passes many enabling Acts of Parliament which give Ministers and certain other officials the right to make administrative orders which have the effect of an Act of Parliament since they draw their authority from the Act (the construction and use regulations are a good illustration). It is a very important part of the law making process and operates at various levels, right down to very local levels of administration such as the imposition of movement control orders during outbreaks of foot and mouth disease.

Judicial Precedent and Case Law
Judicial precedent has been a very important feature of English Law since 1066 when Norman Laws began to replace Saxon customs. The idea was that a decision made by a judge would be upheld by other judges, or only overturned for the most serious reasons and after prolonged consideration. Once a judge had heard the facts about a particular case and reached a decision on the matter, that decision would stand for similar cases that arose later.

The actual part of a judge's ruling which decides the case is called the *ratio decidendi* which is Latin for "the reason for the decision". A judge may say many things during the course of the ruling, because it is a judge's function to interpret and declare the law. Things which do not refer to the specific facts of the case but which refer to hypothetical situations used to clarify his decisions are called *obiter dicta* (things said along the way). Only the *ratio decidendi* forms a binding precedent but the *obiter dicta* may assist other judges and are said to be persuasive only.

Not only do the decisions of judges on every case that is heard become precedents for all future cases but even Statutes become subject to judicial interpretation whenever Parliament fails to make itself clear. There are many occasions when Statutes are rushed through Parliament in great haste without proper debate. If such a Statute proves to be unclear, or even enacts a manifest absurdity, the judges must interpret it to make sense of it.

This accumulation of decisions in cases based on Common Law, or the interpretation of Statutes, is referred to as Case Law and is a very important source of law in this country. It ensures that the Common Law is kept up-to-date and continues to grow and make sense of ambiguous Statute Law, even to the extent of drawing Parliament's attention to the need to repeal or amend legislation which is out of date, ambiguous, or unjust.

EC Law and International Law
Since becoming members of the European Community the United Kingdom has become increasingly subject to Community Law, eg the regulations concerning drivers' hours, tachographs, etc. It is, however, important to note that EC directives

(as opposed to regulations) do not become binding in this country until they have been made law by Parliament or through delegated legislation.

Even before joining the EC the United Kingdom was bound by many international agreements, entered into voluntarily by means of International Conventions. The Convention on the International Carriage of Goods by Road (CMR) is a good example of this. These International Conventions ensure that the laws governing particular aspects of life are the same in all countries which adopt a specific Convention. Again, like EC directives, these Conventions do not become law until legislated for by Parliament. The CMR Convention was enacted into United Kingdom law by the Carriage of Goods by Road Act 1965.

Law of Business and Carriage

The law of carriage
Although the *operation* of goods vehicles has been subject to a tremendous volume of legislation over the years, the law governing the contract of carriage has barely been touched and although there are many Acts of Parliament and numerous regulations governing the operation of road transport, the contractual relationship between the carrier and his customer is relatively free from statutory legislation.

Which Acts of Parliament apply to the carriage of goods by road?
The Carriers' Act 1830 which deals with the carriage of valuable goods only applies to common carriers and as they are now probably extinct it need not be of concern. There is also the Carriage of Goods by Road Act 1965 which gives the force of law to the Convention for the International Carriage of Goods by Road, usually abbreviated to CMR and which only concerns carriers engaged in international operations.

What are international operations?
When delivering to or collecting vehicles or trailers from the docks which are going to or have come from outside the United Kingdom, the CMR regulations will apply. These regulations are dealt with in the international section of this book.

If there is no statutory control, presumably Common Law applies?
Yes! The contract between the carrier and his customer is largely governed by the vast body of case law that has been built up in connection with business relationships.

What happens if a contract is not signed?
The fact that a written document has not been signed does not mean that a contract does not exist. This is a common misconception. A contract can be in writing, oral, or implied by the conduct of the parties.

What is a contract?
It is an agreement between two or more people which is intended to be legally enforceable. It does not cover social or domestic agreements.

What does "legally enforceable" mean?
It means that if either party does not honour their part of the agreement, the other party has the right to compensation (damages) if the breach has caused them to

suffer loss and, if the party in breach fails voluntarily to compensate the aggrieved party, the right to compensation can be enforced in court.

Is compensation the only remedy for breach of contract?
No! Where money is not appropriate there are other remedies available, eg:
- (a) *specific performance* — a court could order the party in breach of contract to fulfil the agreement
- (b) *an injunction* — a court could order the party in breach of contract to cease any actions which were contrary to the agreement
- (c) the aggrieved party could, if it suited their purpose, treat the contract as void, ie no longer applicable and refuse to carry out their part of the bargain, without themselves being liable for breach of contract.

How can one tell if a contract exists or not?
There are a number of essential elements in the formation of a valid and enforceable contract. These are:
- (a) there must be offer and acceptance
- (b) there must be consideration
- (c) there must be an intention to create legal relations
- (d) the parties must have capacity to contract
- (e) there must be genuineness of consent by the parties to the terms of the contract
- (f) the contract must be legal and possible.

These terms probably need further explanation.

Offer and acceptance
It is sometimes difficult to decide who has made an offer and who has accepted it.
1. If X says to Y "I will sell you this watch for £10" and Y says "I agree", it is quite clear that X has made an offer which Y has accepted.
2. If Y says "I will give you £10 for the watch" and X says "I agree" then Y has made an offer which X has accepted.
3. If X says "I will sell you this watch for £10" and Y says "I will give you £8 for it", then X replies "I agree", Y has made a counter offer which X has accepted.

Frequently this process of offer and counter offer with first one side then the other making proposals and counter proposals, adding a condition here, conceding a point there, goes on for some time. In the end, for a contract to have been agreed, it must be possible to isolate the situation where one party has made a final offer which the other has accepted.

In contrast, sometimes a contract may be implied by the conduct of the parties, eg when a bus travels along a certain route there is an implied offer to carry passengers at the published fares. When a passenger boards a bus he makes an implied acceptance of the fare.

Can an offer be withdrawn once it has been made?
Yes. An offer can be withdrawn at any time before acceptance provided that the withdrawal has been communicated to the person to whom it was made (the offeree).

Consideration

The most common form of consideration is money but it is not the only form.

It is sometimes said that a contract consists of "a promise for a promise", eg "I promise to carry your goods if you promise to pay me a stated sum of money", but "I promise to give you my old car, if you promise to maintain my new one for me" is equally good consideration, although one would probably say "You can have my old car if you will maintain my new one". Alternatively, it can be said that the principle of consideration is that each person must derive some benefit from the contract.

Intention to create legal relations

If a husband promises to pay his wife £X per week as housekeeping money, she cannot enforce that promise through the courts if he fails to pay her, because this is regarded as a domestic arrangement which is not intended to have legal consequences.

If you are invited to dinner, accept and then fail to turn up, your disappointed host would have no legal redress even though he had incurred considerable expense, for this was a social arrangement.

Sometimes the parties to an arrangement expressly provide that it is not to be legally enforceable. Thus in entering the football pools you agree to abide by the rules which state that the agreement is binding in honour only and not to be subject to legal action.

Capacity to contract

Generally adult citizens have full capacity to enter into any kind of contract but certain groups of persons may not have this full capacity and contracts with them may be unenforceable, eg:

(a) a contact with an enemy alien during time of war is illegal and void
(b) contracts with minors (persons under the age of 18) may be void in some circumstances, unenforceable in others and finally perfectly valid in others. Often the minor is able to sue for a breach of contract against him. Dealings with minors should therefore be treated with circumspection and preferably with an adult acting as guarantor
(c) contracts with persons suffering from mental disorders, or while drunk, may, under certain circumstances, be voided (set aside) at the option of that person.

Genuineness of consent

A contract which in all other respects appears to be perfectly valid may be set aside if there is no real consent to it by one or both of the parties. Consent may be rendered unreal by mistake, fraud, misrepresentation, duress and undue influence.

Legal and possible

Agreements which are illegal are void. This does not necessarily mean an agreement to commit a crime but may refer to an agreement to commit an act which is morally wrong, or which contravenes the provisions of a statute or regulations issued under a statute, eg a haulier has contracted to move some cattle to market. Before this can be done an order is made forbidding the movement of cattle because of an outbreak of Foot and Mouth disease. The contract would be void because it would be impossible to fulfil it without breaking the law.

Impossibility of performance — where, for example, a person offers to sell something which, unknown to the parties, has already been destroyed. Even if the offer is accepted, the buyer could not obtain damages on the grounds that the seller has not honoured his bargain.

How does all this apply to contracts of carriage?
Generally this is concerned with offer, acceptance and consideration. When a carrier is offered a load, he is usually asked to quote his price and if it is acceptable to the customer he gets the job. There are also other factors to be considered. As will be seen later, once the carrier accepts the load he takes on certain obligations and incurs certain liabilities in respect of the goods.

How have these obligations and liabilities arisen?
They arise out of Common Law, the principles of which have been developed and interpreted in thousands of cases over many centuries until we now have a well-developed body of Case Law.

Is there any way one can avoid or minimise these liabilities?
Yes! By including limiting or exclusion clauses in the contract of carriage. Whereas any clause which purports to alter or avoid a statutory requirement is void, in matters governed by Common Law there is almost complete freedom of contract. The parties are usually free to make whatever conditions are mutually acceptable.

In what way is there not complete freedom of contract?
Frequently traders (including carriers) draw up a standard form of contract to which their customers are required to agree whenever they do business with the trader.

This agreement is not necessarily the result of formal negotiations but is implied by the conduct of the parties, eg the trader indicates on his stationery — consignment notes, etc — that all business is conducted in accordance with "XYZ conditions". By signing the consignment note, order form, etc the customer is presumed at law to have assented to those conditions. If subsequently a dispute arises which goes to court, the court could declare void any clause which appears to be "contrary to the fundamental purpose of the contract", or which was so outrageously unjust that "it was contrary to public policy".

Since the passing of the Unfair Contract Terms Act 1977 there is a much greater possibility that terms in standard form contracts will be rejected by the courts.

In connection with a contract of carriage, what do the terms "Carriage Paid" and "Carriage Forward" mean?
Carriage paid means that the carriage charges will be paid by the sender (consignor). Carriage forward means that the carriage charges will be paid by the receiver (consignee).

How can one ensure that any trading conditions adopted are not overruled in this way?
Trading conditions should be drawn up by a legal expert in such matters. Alternatively, the standard conditions of a professional body such as the Road Haulage Association (RHA), which have been drawn up for the benefit of their members, could be adopted.

Are there any precautions which must be taken if standard conditions are adopted?
Yes! There are two things which must be carefully observed.
1. If, for example, the RHA conditions are adopted (but see page 135) no alterations should be made to them. They have been carefully drawn up following the best legal advice and any attempt to try to improve them could have the opposite effect.
2. Whatever conditions an operator decides to adopt he must ensure that they are brought to the notice of his customers. This is best done by including a note on all relevant business documents to the effect that goods are carried only under those conditions. Copies of the conditions should be available to customers on request. This ensures that the "genuineness of consent" requirement is satisfied.

Conditions of carriage refer to agents and servants. What is the function of an agent?
An agency arises when one person (the principal) authorises another person (the agent) to make contracts on his behalf with third parties. One can say, therefore, that an agent's function is to enter into contractual relationships with third parties on behalf of his principal or principals.

How does an agent differ from a servant?
Sometimes there is no difference. If a servant (employee) is given authority to enter into contracts on behalf of his master (employer) he is an agent, eg managers are frequently authorised to enter into contracts for specified goods or services on behalf of their employers.

Whereas an agent always has authority to contract on behalf of his principal, servants are less likely to have that authority.

What are the employer's liabilities in respect of the actions of his agents and employees?
1. Agents
(a) Provided that the agent has acted within the limits of his authority, the principal is bound by any commitment that his agent has entered into on the principal's behalf.
(b) Even when the agent acts beyond the limits of his authority, or if his agency has been terminated, the principal may still be liable for the agent's acts if:
  (i) the third party had no reason to believe that the agent was not authorised and
  (ii) the principal delays too long in repudiating the contract.
(c) The principal is liable for the frauds and misrepresentations of his agents if they were done in furtherance of the principal's business and not merely for the agent's personal gain.
(d) The principal is liable *to* the agent in respect of any commission he has earned and for expenses incurred in the performance of his duties.

2. Employees
It is a long established principle of Common Law that a master is vicariously liable for the acts of his servant committed within the course of his employment, ie he is liable as though he had committed the acts himself.

What exactly does "within the course of his employment" mean?

It means that the act must have been committed during the performance of the duties for which he was employed. It does not matter that the duties were performed in a manner with which the employer disapproves or has even expressly forbidden. What matters is that the employee was employed to do that particular job, eg:

1. Suppose an employee engaged solely for the performance of clerical duties decides to drive a lorry belonging to his employer without his employer's permission, and due to his negligence damages property belonging to a third party. The employer would not be liable because the servant was not acting "within the course of his employment". He was employed as a clerk, not a driver.
2. A driver negligently omits to sheet up a vehicle, though his employer has given express instructions that loads must always be sheeted. In consequence the load is damaged by rain. In this case the employer will be liable to the owner of the goods, because the driver was negligent in performing the duties for which he was employed.

Can an employer avoid this liability in any way?

As far as his customers' property is concerned, he could avoid liability by an exclusion clause in his contract, ie excluding him from liability due to the negligent acts of his servants but this would not be looked upon favourably by his customers.

Where people with whom he has no contractual arrangement are concerned, he cannot avoid liability, he can only protect himself by insurance.

This suggests that an operator can incur liabilities other than those imposed on him by statute, or arising out of contract.

In addition to covering contractual relationships, Common Law recognises other obligations. Even when no contract exists, people have duties towards each other and towards each other's property. If a person fails in those duties the person who suffers through such acts or omissions has a right of redress.

What are these breaches of duty called?

The legal expression is "torts". A tort has been defined as "the breach of duty imposed by law whereby some person acquires the right of action for damages".

What torts is one likely to be affected by?

Probably the best example and the one met most frequently is the duty of care. Each person has a duty to take care to ensure that he does not injure other people or damage their property. If a person fails to take reasonable care he is guilty of the tort of negligence.

How is "reasonable care" defined in law?

It cannot be defined. It is impossible for the law to define "reasonable" because what is reasonable varies according to the circumstances of every case. Nevertheless, people are capable of forming an opinion about what is reasonable and what is not. If a group of individuals is given a set of facts and each is asked to state whether or not a certain course of conduct is reasonable, in most cases a fairly unanimous decision can be reached.

What about those cases where a decision is not unanimous?
This is where the problems concerning "reasonableness" arise. In a dispute where two parties cannot agree on what is reasonable, they may agree to abide by the decision of a third unbiased party (an arbitrator) or leave the decision to be decided in court.

Is the same degree of care required from everybody?
No! A child would not be expected to exercise the same degree of care as an adult and therefore, where children are concerned, greater care is, or should be, exercised by an adult to compensate for this. Extra care is needed where dangers exist which would be obvious to adults but not to small children.

Is this the only difference?
No! The degree of care that is regarded as being reasonable varies according to the status of the person. Generally, if a person is being paid for doing something, he is expected to exercise greater care than if he were upaid. In both cases reasonable care is expected.

What is the justification for this difference?
When a person is being paid to do a job, he is expected to use his professional knowledge and expertise in order to foresee and guard against possible hazards to people and property.

What other torts could one be liable for?
There are many but two of the most common are nuisance and trespass.

What is nuisance?
There are two kinds: (a) public nuisance and (b) private nuisance. Public nuisance is some unlawful act or omission which endangers or interferes with the lives, safety or comfort of the public generally.

How is an operator likely to commit a public nuisance?
The most likely cause would be obstruction. An operator who keeps a vehicle in a street for an unreasonable time for the purpose of loading or unloading can cause an obstruction which may amount to a public nuisance, even though there may be no waiting or loading restrictions in force at that particular place.

A public nuisance is a crime and criminal proceedings may be taken by the police or by the Attorney-General. In addition to this official action, a private individual may sue in tort if he has suffered some particular damage beyond that suffered by the public in general, eg if the obstruction denied him access to his premises or caused him loss of business because the obstruction deterred potential customers.

What is a private nuisance?
A private nuisance is an unjustifiable interference with a man's use of his property, or with his health, comfort or convenience. Many things constitute nuisance, eg noise, vibrations, fumes, smell, smoke and dirt. As far back as 1661 nuisance was defined as "Anything obnoxious to the community or individual by offensiveness of smell or appearance, by causing obstruction, damage, etc."

Some individuals seem to regard the mere existence of heavy goods vehicles as offensive and the slightest noise or smell as obnoxious. What is the operator's position where this sort of complaint is made?

The law recognises that in modern industrial society some nuisance may be inevitable. It does not concern itself with trivialities, neither does it take account of the extra sensitivity of certain individuals.

Generally, the test of whether or not an act or omission constitutes a nuisance is whether or not it is reasonable. What might be acceptable in a busy commercial or industrial part of a town or city might be regarded as unacceptable in a predominantly residential area, or a quiet country town.

Many of the things to which opponents of the heavy lorry object are noise, vibration, weight, fumes, visual intrusion. These are covered by statute and if individuals or sections of the community are unhappy with the standards laid down by Parliament, they must seek to change them through their elected representatives. They are unlikely to obtain satisfaction through the courts.

Does this mean that provided one complies with the statutory regulations one cannot be said to be committing a nuisance?

Not entirely — although vehicles may comply with the regulations and vehicles as such cannot be called nuisances their manner of use may constitute a nuisance, eg continuous use of heavy vehicles on a main road leading to a depot would be perfectly proper and necessary. But if drivers regularly use a quiet residential street as a short cut, this might constitute a nuisance which could give rise to a series of actions, eg:

(a) an injunction to prevent the nuisance from continuing
(b) a claim for damages if vibration had caused damage to property
(c) a claim for damages for loss of value to property if residents attempted to sell.

Can a person do what he likes on his own premises?

Within reason — the basic rule is "Use your own property in such a manner as not to injure that of another" or "Live and let live". Some revving of engines may be necessary when vehicles are being serviced but if this went on throughout the night neighbours would probably have cause for complaint.

What is trespass?

To the man in the street, trespass usually means unauthorised entry on another person's land. In law it has a much wider meaning. There are three types of trespass:
1. Trespass to the person
2. Trespass to goods
3. Trespass to land ("land" includes premises).

1. *Trespass to the person* may be by: (a) assault (b) battery and (c) false imprisonment.
   (a) *Assault* occurs when a person threatens to use unlawful force on another, in such a way that the person threatened is put in fear of violence. Mere words are not enough, they must be accompanied by actions or gestures, eg attempting to strike a person, throwing a missile even though it misses, possibly even seizing a potential weapon.

(b) *Battery* consists of applying unlawful force, however slight, upon another person.
(c) *False imprisonment* means bodily restraining a person without lawful justification, eg locking up a trespasser is unlawful unless he has forcibly effected an entry, or you have reason to suspect he has committed a criminal act. Similarly, using force to eject a trespasser who has not forcibly effected an entry is a trespass against him, unless you have first requested him to leave and he refuses. Even then you must only use reasonable force.
2. *Trespass to goods* is wrongful interference with the possessions or goods of another. It is essentially a tort committed against the goods of a person lawfully entitled to possess them, ie he need not be the owner. In fact the owner cannot maintain an action if he has transferred the right of possession of the goods to another, eg by lending, hiring, handing over for repair or transport. So a haulage operator would be the person to bring an action against someone interfering with goods entrusted into his possession and not the consignor or owner.
3. *Trespass to land* is unjustified interference with it. It may take any one of three forms:
   (a) entry onto the land of another
   (b) remaining on the land of another
   (c) depositing anything on the land of another.

What action can be taken against a trespasser on a person's land?

1. If the owner simply wishes him to leave:
   (a) he can ask him to leave
   (b) give him sufficient time to do so, then
   (c) if he still refuses to leave, sufficient force (but no more) may be used to eject him.
2. If the trespasser has caused damage he may be sued for damages.
3. To prevent a repetition or continuation of the trespass an injunction may be sought against him.
4. If the land is unlawfully occupied, eg a tenant whose lease has expired but who refuses to leave, the owner may bring an action of ejection for the recovery of his land.

Has an occupier any liability towards people who enter his premises?

Yes! This is called Occupier's Liability.

Is Occupier's Liability the same towards all people?

It varies according to their status, eg whether they are visitors or trespassers, adults or children.

Is there any general rule which should be observed?

There is a Common Law duty of care. In this instance it means that the occupier must take such care as is reasonable in the circumstances to see that visitors are safe in using the premises for the purposes for which they are invited or permitted to be there.

How does the difference in degree of care demanded vary between adults and children?

Where children are concerned, they are not so alert to possible dangers as adults and may be less likely to appreciate the importance of warnings. Indeed, where warning notices are concerned, small children may be unable to read or to fully comprehend them. Therefore, where children can be expected, much greater care must be exercised to guard them against potential dangers.

Does the occupier owe a duty of care to trespassers?

He has no active duty of care towards a trespasser. A trespasser enters the occupier's premises at his own risk. At the same time the occupier must not deliberately create hidden dangers, what have been called "hidden snares or pitfalls", designed to trap or injure him.

Does this apply to child trespassers?

Yes! It must be remembered, however, that children are less likely to be able to read and understand warning notices, or if able to do so may not appreciate the gravity of the danger. What would be an ample warning to an adult might be regarded as inadequate where children are concerned. If the danger exists in something that might exercise an attraction for children, then it could be regarded as a "hidden snare or pitfall".

A further most important point concerning children applies where there is recurring trespass. If, for example, it is known that children are in the habit of entering the premises through a hole in the fence and the occupier does nothing about it, they may acquire the status of visitors. Failure to repair the fence could then be regarded as a failure in the duty of care.

Can an occupier restrict or modify his duty of care in any way?

Yes! To a certain extent he is free to contract with a visitor to exempt himself from liability. Then the rule of "*volenti non fit injuria*" (no injury can be done to a willing person) applies. This means that the visitor accepts that a degree of risk exists and that he cannot hold the occupier liable if he suffers injury.

Can an occupier insist on visitors agreeing to such a condition?

Yes! Provided that they have the option of refusing to enter his premises he can insist on such a condition but not if they have no real choice in the matter, for example:

1. Suppose a party from a local college wish to enter the occupier's premises in order to study his operations. He could make the visit conditional upon their absolving him from any liability for injury.
2. A lorry driver has to enter the premises to collect or deliver goods. A notice to the effect that "Visitors enter these premises at their own risk" would almost certainly be ineffectual against risks other than those normally expected in his profession. This is because he has no real choice in the matter, he has to visit the premises in order to do his job.

How can the limitations on the road carrier's power to restrict his legal liability be summarised?

Generally a carrier can restrict his legal liability by means of conditions in his contract of carriage, provided that:

(a) the conditions do not contravene any statute
(b) the conditions do not defeat (or make nonsense of) the purpose of the contract
(c) the conditions are willingly consented to by the other party to the contract.

The RHA conditions of carriage satisfy (a) and (b) above and because of their widespread application are unlikely to be objected to by customers.

Conditions of Carriage, 1982

For many years the RHA has published, for the guidance and use of its members, a set of standard Conditions of Carriage. Since the first edition of this book these have been revised to meet the requirements of the Restrictive Trade Practices Act 1976 and the Unfair Contract Terms Act 1977.

It should be pointed out that these conditions are the copyright of the RHA and should not be used by non-members.

CHAPTER 12
(Module A)
Social Legislation

The syllabus of the examination for the Certificate of Professional Competence calls for a knowledge of around 20 Acts of Parliament and associated Codes of Practice. It would be unrealistic to expect a candidate to have a detailed knowledge of the mass of legislation which would tax professional lawyers. Instead, a knowledge of the main objectives is required.

The legislation is grouped into four sections: Industrial Relations; Social Security; Discrimination; Safety.

Industrial Relations

Trade Union and Labour Relations Act 1974 as amended by the Employment Acts 1980 and 1982 and the Trade Union Act 1984

What are the main objectives of the 1974 Act?
This Act repealed the Industrial Relations Act 1971 but re-enacted certain provisions which related to unfair dismissal and the code of industrial relations practice (subsequently, re-enacted further by later legislation) and identified situations where the organisation of industrial action may be lawful.

The Act defines:
(a) those employees who are included and those who are excluded from the provisions of the Act
(b) trade unions
(c) employers' associations
(d) trade disputes.

What were the effects of the Employment Acts 1980 and 1982 on the 1974 Act?
Measures were introduced to alter the balance between employers and unions and individual employees by:
(a) redefining trade disputes
(b) amending the law on picketing.

Trade disputes
In law, industrial action will only be lawful where it is carried out in connection with a trade dispute. Trade disputes are disputes between employees and employers which relate wholly or mainly to:
(a) terms and conditions of employment, or the physical conditions in which any workers are required to work
(b) engagement or non-engagement, termination or suspension of employment or the duties of employment, of one or more workers
(c) allocation of work or the duties of employment as between workers or groups of workers
(d) matters of discipline

(e) the membership or non-membership of a trade union on the part of a worker
(f) facilities for officials of trade unions
(g) machinery for negotiation or consultation and other procedures relating to any of the foregoing matters, including the recognition by employers or employers' associations of the right of a trade union to represent workers in any such negotiation or consultation or in the carrying out of such procedures.

Picketing
Picketing is only lawful if it is carried on in contemplation or furtherance of a trade dispute; its purpose is only to peacefully obtain or communicate information; or to peacefully persuade any person to work or to abstain from working and if it is carried out by employees at or near their place of work (or in the case of employees dismissed during the course of the dispute, their former place of work) or by trade union officials at or near the place of work of a member of the union whom they are accompanying and representing.

If it is impracticable for a person to picket his own place of work — because he normally works at more than one place, or for some other reason — he may picket the premises of his employer from which he works or from which his work is administered.

Unlawful industrial action
Any industrial action taken outside of these limits is unlawful and its organisers may be sued for damages by those people damaged by the action. If the industrial action was authorised by a trade union there are limits on the amount of damages, depending on the number of union members, as follows:

less than 5000 members	£10,000
5000 to 24,999 members	£50,000
25,000 to 99,999 members	£125,000
100,000 or more members	£250,000

What is a recognised trade union?
A "recognised" trade union is one that is recognised by an employer, or two or more associated employers, for the purpose of collective bargaining.

Disclosure of information
An employer is required to disclose to representatives of a recognised independent trade union, on request, all information in his possession relating to his company without which the representative would be impeded to a material extent in carrying on collective bargaining with the employer, or which he should disclose in accordance with good industrial relations practice for the purposes of collective bargaining.

Redundancies
An employer who proposes to make employees redundant and who recognises an independent trade union for those employees, will be required to consult the trade union as soon as possible and, where at least 10 people are to be made redundant, with the following limits:
(a) when 100 or more employees are to be made redundant within 90 days or less, consultation must begin at least 90 days before the first dismissal
(b) where between 10 and 99 employees are to be made redundant within a period of 30 days or less, consultation must begin at least 30 days before the first dismissal.

Who is responsible for drawing up codes of practice?
Originally codes of practice relating to industrial relations were the responsibility of ACAS (Advisory, Conciliation and Arbitration Service) a statutory institution set up to improve industrial relations (see page 142) but now the Secretary of State for Employment also has the power to produce them, after consultation with ACAS and after consideration of representations from other interested bodies.

What are the real consequences of actions which do not conform to codes of practice?
Codes of practice do not have the force of law but are regarded as setting standards of conduct. The practical effect of failing to observe them is that if any of their provisions are not followed this may be used as evidence in subsequent court or tribunal proceedings.

How many codes of practice have been issued by ACAS?
ACAS has issued three codes of practice, the main parts of which are given below. In addition, the Secretary of State has issued codes of practice on picketing and closed shops (see page 148):

(1) Disciplinary practice and procedures in employment
The purpose of disciplinary procedures is to promote fairness and order in the treatment of individuals and in the conduct of industrial relations.

Employees need to know what standards of conduct are expected of them and the consequences of failing to observe those standards. It is recommended that the rules should be readily available and that management should endeavour to ensure that employees know and understand them. This may be best achieved by giving every employee a copy of the rules and by explaining them orally. In the case of new employees this should form part of the induction programme.

Disciplinary procedures should:
(a) be in writing
(b) specify to whom they apply
(c) provide matters to be dealt with quickly
(d) state the disciplinary actions which may be taken
(e) identify those with authority to take disciplinary action and the extent of that authority
(f) provide for individuals to be informed of complaints against them and to be given the opportunity to state their case before decisions are reached
(g) give the right for an individual to be accompanied by a trade union representative or a fellow employee of his choice
(h) ensure that, except for gross misconduct, no employee is dismissed for a first breach of discipline
(i) ensure that disciplinary action is not taken until the case has been carefully investigated
(j) ensure that individuals are given an explanation for any penalty imposed
(k) provide a right of appeal and specify the procedure to be followed.

The procedure in operation
When a disciplinary matter arises, the following procedure should be observed:
(a) the supervisor or manager should promptly establish the facts

(b) before a decision is made or a penalty imposed, the employee should be advised of his rights, including his right to be accompanied by a representative
(c) for a minor offence, an oral warning should be given
(d) for a repeated minor offence, or a more serious offence, a written warning should be given
(e) further misconduct might warrant a final written warning which should contain a statement that any recurrence would lead to suspension, or dismissal, or some other penalty, as the case may be
(f) the final step might be disciplinary transfer or disciplinary suspension without pay, where these are provided for in the employment contract, or dismissal.

Cases requiring special consideration
1. Trade union officials — disciplinary action against a trade union official might be seen as an attack on the trade union and lead to a serious dispute. Therefore, although normal disciplinary standards should apply, no disciplinary action beyond an oral warning should be taken before the case has been discussed with a senior trade union official.
2. Special arrangements may have to be made to cover disciplinary matters among nightshift workers, or workers in isolated locations where no one is present with the necessary authority to take disciplinary action, or where no trade union representative is immediately available.
3. Where criminal offences are committed outside employment they should not be considered as automatic reasons for dismissal.

Points to note:
1. Only in cases of gross misconduct, eg theft, fighting or gross negligence, may an employee be dismissed without prior warning.
2. When determining the disciplinary action to be taken, the need to satisfy the test of reasonableness must be borne in mind. Account should be taken of the employee's record and other relevant factors.
3. Except in the case of oral warnings, the employee and, if desired, his representative, should be given written details of any disciplinary action and advised of any right of appeal.
4. Careful records should be kept of any disciplinary action and the reason for it. These records should be confidential.
5. After a specified period of satisfactory conduct previous breaches of disciplinary rules should be disregarded.

Grievance procedures
This should be established to enable disputes to be settled fairly, promptly and as near the origin of dispute as possible, to prevent the dispute from developing into something more serious.
  The basis of a grievance procedure should be:
  (a) the employee should discuss his grievance with his immediate superior
  (b) if unresolved, the employee may progress to a higher level of management, accompanied by his representative if he wishes
  (c) if the grievance cannot be satisfactorily resolved within the company, provision may be made for the right of appeal to an external body, eg ACAS.

Review of procedures
Rules and procedures governing disciplinary matters and grievances should be

reviewed periodically and, if necessary, revised in order to ensure their continuing relevance and effectiveness.

The Code is currently under review and a revised draft was issued by ACAS in November 1985 entitled "Disciplinary and Other Procedures in Employment". At the date of going to press this draft had not been approved by Parliament.

(2) Disclosure of information to trade unions for collective bargaining purposes

Employers have a duty under the Employment Protection Act 1975 to disclose at all stages of collective bargaining information requested by representatives of independent recognised trade unions.

The information requested has to be in the employer's possession, or in the possession of any associated employer and must relate to the employer's undertaking.

The information to be disclosed is that without which a trade union representative would be impeded to a material extent in bargaining.

The following are examples of information which could be relevant to collective bargaining situations:

> Pay and benefits
> Conditions of service
> Manpower
> The performance of the company
> Financial — costs, profits, etc.

Employers should aim to be as open and helpful as possible in meeting trade union requests for information.

If a trade union considers that an employer has failed to supply information to which it is entitled, it may complain to the Central Arbitration Committee.

(3) Time off for trade union duties and activities

The general purpose of the Code is to aid and improve the conduct of industrial relations. To further this aim, employers and trade unions should reach agreement on arrangements for handling time off in ways appropriate to their own situations.

Time off for trade union officials

Employees who are lay officials of trade unions may, in addition to their work as employees, have important duties concerned with industrial relations. To perform these duties effectively an official should be permitted to take reasonable paid time off during working hours for such purposes as:

(a) collective bargaining
(b) informing members about consultations and negotiations with management
(c) meetings with other lay officials, or full time officers concerning industrial relations matters connected with the employer
(d) interviews with, or on behalf of, members, on grievance and discipline matters concerning them and their employer
(e) appearing on behalf of members before an outside body such as an industrial tribunal
(f) explaining to new employees the role of the union in the workplace industrial relations structure.

To carry out their duties effectively trade union officials may need training relevant to those duties. Where such training has been approved by the TUC or the official's union, the official should be permitted reasonable time off, with pay, to undergo that training.

Time off for trade union members
To operate effectively and democratically trade unions need the active participation of members in certain union activities. The Code recommends that members should be permitted to take reasonable time off for the purpose of such activities as voting in union elections, meetings of official policy making bodies or representing the union on external bodies. There is no requirement that employees should be paid for such time off.

Industrial action
Management and unions have a responsibility to use agreed procedures to resolve problems constructively and avoid industrial action. Where an official is not taking part in the action but represents members involved, normal arrangements for paid time off should apply. There is, of course, no obligation on employers to permit time off for trade union activities which consist of industrial action.

The Employment Protection Act 1975 (as amended by the Employment Act 1980)

What are the main objectives of this Act?
They are twofold:
(a) to introduce a series of rights for employees and to provide greater job security (these provisions have now been incorporated into the Employment Protection (Consolidation) Act 1978)
(b) to introduce machinery to promote the improvement of industrial relations.

What is this "machinery"?
It involved the setting up of the following organisations:

1. The Advisory, Conciliation and Arbitration Service (ACAS)
The powers and duties of ACAS include:
(a) offering conciliation and other assistance to help settle individual and trade disputes
(b) offering advice to employers, employers' associations, workers and trade unions on industrial relations and employment policies and publishing general advice
(c) issuing codes of practice containing practical guidance for promoting good industrial relations (see below).

2. The Central Arbitration Committee
An independent recognised trade union can complain to the Central Arbitration Committee (CAC) if an employer has failed to disclose information required for the purpose of collective bargaining.

The CAC may pass the complaint on to ACAS for conciliation or it may hold a hearing to determine whether the complaint is well-founded or not.

If it decides in favour of the trade union it will make a declaration specifying the information which must be revealed and the date by which the employer must disclose that information.

3. The Certification Officer
The Certification Officer is an independent statutory authority, appointed by the Secretary of State for Employment. He is responsible, among other things, for certifying the independence of trade unions and for monitoring certain aspects of the ways unions conduct their affairs, eg seeing that proper accounting records are kept and are audited and that annual returns are submitted.

Employment Protection (Consolidation) Act 1978 as amended by the Employment Acts 1980 and 1982

This Act consolidates all the legislation on the individual, as opposed to collective, rights of employees that were formerly contained in the Redundancy Payments Act 1965, the Contracts of Employment Act 1972, the Trade Union and Labour Relations Act 1974 and the Employment Protection Act 1975.

What rights for employees are covered by the Act?
These are extensive and detailed. The following are brief summaries of the main provisions:

Written particulars of terms of employment
All employees on 16 hours or more a week must, not later than 13 weeks after their employment began, be given written details concerning their main terms and conditions of employment. The following information must be included:
 (a) the identity of the parties
 (b) the date when employment began
 (c) the date previous employment began
 (d) the rate of pay, how it is calculated and the pay period (hourly, weekly, etc)
 (e) rules as to hours of work, holiday entitlement and holiday pay
 (f) rules on sickness provisions, pensions and pension schemes
 (g) length of notice the employee is entitled to receive and give
 (h) employee's job title
 (i) disciplinary rules and grievance procedures where these exist.

Itemised pay statement
Employers must give employees, on or before pay day, itemised statements of pay, detailing gross pay, variable and fixed deductions, and net pay.
 A statement of fixed deductions need not be made each time, provided that a standing statement of fixed deductions is made at least once in every 12 months.

Guarantee payments
Provided he has been continuously employed for at least one month, an employee is entitled to be paid for up to five workless days (ie when he is available for work but none is available) in any three month period. He is entitled to £11.30 per day (from April 1, 1988) or the normal pay for the day, whichever is the lesser. (This provision, however, does not give employers the right to lay off workers.)

Medical suspension
An employee who has been continuously employed for at least one month will be entitled to be paid for up to 26 weeks if he is suspended from work on certain specified medical grounds.

Trade union membership and activities
In every contract of trade union membership it will be implied that a member has the right to terminate his membership on giving reasonable notice and complying with any reasonable conditions.

Every employee has the right not to have action taken against him by his employer for the purpose of:
   (a) preventing or deterring him from being or seeking to be a member of an independent trade union
   (b) preventing or deterring him from taking part in the activities of an independent trade union at any appropriate time
   (c) compelling him to become a member of a trade union
   (d) enforcing a requirement that in the event of his failure to become, or his ceasing to become, a member of a trade union, he must make payments to some other body (usually a charity).

Employees also have the right not to be unfairly excluded or expelled from a trade union when a closed shop agreement is in operation.

Time off for trade union duties
Employers must allow employees who are officials of recognised trade unions reasonable time off, with pay, to carry out industrial relations duties and to undergo training in respect of those duties.

Time off for trade union activities
Members of independent trade unions recognised by employers must be given reasonable time off during working hours, without pay, to take part in activities of their union.

Time off for public duties
Employees who are JPs, members of Local Authority Councils, Statutory Tribunal members, Water or Health Authority members, or school or college governors must be allowed reasonable unpaid time off to perform their duties.

Time off to look for work or for retraining
Employees who have been continuously employed for two years or more and who are made redundant must be given reasonable time off, with pay, during their notice period, to seek new employment or to arrange for further training.

Ante-natal care
Where, on medical advice, a woman who is pregnant has made an appointment to receive ante-natal care, she has the right to take time off, with pay, to keep that appointment.

Right to return from maternity leave
Female employees with the necessary two years' qualifying service may take leave at any time after the beginning of the 11th week before the expected week of confinement and the employee has the right to return up to 29 weeks afterwards provided that, where practicable, she gives her employer 21 days' written notice of her intention to leave work and return after maternity leave.

The employee has the right to postpone her return for a further four weeks if a doctor certifies that she is not capable of work after the 29th week. The employer may postpone the date of return for up to four weeks, provided he notifies her of the reason.

If her employer writes at least 49 days after her confinement asking for written confirmation of her intention to return to work, she must reply within 14 days, or lose the right to return.

On her return to work she must be reinstated in her original job or, if this is not possible because of redundancy, in a suitable alternative position. Where alternative employment is offered, her conditions of employment must be no less favourable than she enjoyed before.

Where a company employs five or less people and it is not reasonably practicable for her to return to her former position, or a reasonable alternative, she does not have the right to return to that employment.

Minimum periods of notice

An employer is required to give *minimum* periods of notice to employees who have been continuously employed for at least one month, as follows:
   (a) continuous employment of less than two years — one week's notice
   (b) continuous employment for two but less than 12 years — one week's notice for each year
   (c) continuous employment for 12 or more years — not less than 12 weeks' notice

An employee is required to give his employer one week's notice if he has been continuously employed for one month or more.

Dismissal

Dismissal means the termination of an employee's contract, with or without notice, by an employer.

Summary dismissal, ie without notice or pay in lieu of notice, can only be justified in cases of gross misconduct.

An employer who dismisses an employee, for reasons other than gross misconduct, without the notice required by contract or statute, whichever is the longer, is in breach of contract and the employee is entitled to recover damages in the county court.

Employees' rights during notice

Employees who are entitled to only the statutory minimum period of notice and are:
   (a) ready and willing to work but are given none to do
   (b) incapable of work because of sickness or injury
   (c) absent from work on holiday,

are guaranteed a minimum rate of pay when they have been given notice of dismissal by the employer.

Written statement of reasons for dismissal

An employee with six months' continuous service is entitled to request a written statement of the reasons for his dismissal. The statement must be provided within 14 days of the request.

Unfair dismissal
An employee who has been continuously employed, ie:
- (a) has worked for 16 hours or more per week for two years or more
- (b) has worked for eight hours or more but less than 16 hours per week, for five years or more,

has the right not to be unfairly dismissed and if he is so dismissed can complain to an industrial tribunal.

This provision does not apply to all workers. Categories of workers in the road transport industry who do not have this protection are:
- (a) any employees whose contracts of employment provide for them ordinarily to work outside Great Britain
- (b) employees who, before the date of dismissal, had reached normal retirement age
- (c) employees working under certain fixed term contracts who have agreed in writing to exclude any claim for unfair dismissal if the contract is not renewed at the expiry of its fixed term.

Automatically unfair dismissals
In certain circumstances dismissal will automatically be regarded as unfair where the employee:
- (a) was, or proposed to become, a member of an independent trade union
- (b) had taken part in, or proposed to take part in, at an appropriate time, the activities of an independent trade union
- (c) had refused to belong to a trade union which was not an independent trade union
- (d) in a group of employees equally affected by redundancy, was selected from the group for redundancy either:
  - (i) for one of the trade union reasons outlined above, or
  - (ii) was selected in contravention of an agreed redundancy selection procedure (eg, last in, first out)

Dismissal of a pregnant employee
Dismissal of an employee solely because she is pregnant, or for any other reason connected with her pregnancy, will be treated as unfair dismissal, unless she is incapable of doing her job because of her pregnancy and no other reasonable alternative exists.

Dismissal of a temporary replacement
It is unfair to dismiss an employee temporarily engaged to cover a worker absent because of pregnancy, unless at the time of engagement the replacement worker was told in writing that she would be dismissed and the dismissal is carried out in a fair manner, ie with adequate warning.

Dismissal in connection with industrial action
An industrial tribunal has no jurisdiction over the case when an employee claims that he has been dismissed because of a lock-out, strike, or other industrial action, unless:
- (a) one or more employees who were also taking action were not dismissed
- (b) one or more such employees were offered re-engagement within three months and the complainant was not.

Remedies for unfair dismissal
An employee who is found to be unfairly dismissed can choose one of two remedies: reinstatement or compensation. The tribunal must always first consider reinstatement or re-engagement. Only if this is not practicable, or the employee does not want this, should they award compensation. The aim is to restore the employee as nearly as possible to his position before the dismissal.

Interim awards
Employees who believe that their dismissal was unfair on trade union grounds may make an application to an industrial tribunal, within seven days of the dismissal, for interim relief. If the tribunal accepts there are grounds for believing the dismissal was unfair, it will make an order that the contract of employment remain in force until the claim is determined by a trade union in the normal manner.

Redundancy payments
The right to a redundancy payment stems from legislation formerly contained in the Redundancy Payments Act 1965 which has been absorbed into the Employment Protection (Consolidation) Act 1978. The Act applies to men aged between 18 and 65 and women aged between 18 and 60 who normally work for 16 hours or more per week (or have worked for eight hours or more but less than 16 for at least five years or more) and have done so for at least two years and are dismissed because of redundancy.

Scale of redundancy payments
The Act provides for the following payments:
   1½ week's pay for each year of employment which consists wholly of weeks during which the employee was aged between 41–64 inclusive for men and 41–59 inclusive for women.
   One week's pay for each year of employment which consists wholly of weeks during which the employee was aged 22–40 inclusive.
   Half a week's pay for each year of employment not falling within the above mentioned categories (ie employees aged 18–21 inclusive).

No compensation is payable for a fraction of a year but any excess reckonable service in a higher age group counts towards service in the age group immediately below.

Taxation of redundancy payments
Employees do not have to pay tax on redundancy payments which they receive in accordance with the Act.

Employment Acts 1980 and 1982

In addition to amending the Trade Union and Labour Relations Act 1974, the Employment Protection Act 1975 and the Employment Protection (Consolidation) Act 1978, the Employment Acts of 1980 and 1982 made certain other provisions.

Payment to trade unions
The Certification Officer may make payments to independent trade unions towards expenditure incurred in holding ballots in connection with: strike action; elections;

amendments to rules; amalgamations; acceptance or rejection of employers' proposals relating to contractual terms and conditions of employment; and other matters specified by the Secretary of State.

Use of employer's premises for the purpose of holding ballots

Where a recognised trade union proposes to use an employer's premises to hold a ballot for any of the above purposes, it may complain to a tribunal if permission is refused and may be awarded compensation if the refusal is held to be unreasonable.

Codes of practice

The Secretary of State for Employment may issue such codes of practice as he thinks fit for the purpose of improving industrial relations.

After consulting with ACAS, a draft of the code must be published and any representations made taken into consideration. The codes must be approved by Parliament before taking effect.

The original Industrial Relations Code of Practice, which was first approved under the Industrial Relations Act 1971, remains in force under these provisions. In addition, the Secretary of State has issued a code on picketing, the main points of which are detailed below. Another code of practice on Closed Shop Agreements has been issued but is no longer of significance owing to changes in the law which have effectively made closed shops unenforceable.

Picketing

The Code is intended to provide practical guidance on picketing in trade disputes for those who may be contemplating, organising or taking part in a picket and for those who, as employers or workers or members of the general public, may be affected by it.

There is no legal "right to picket" as such, but peaceful picketing has long been recognised as being lawful. However, the law imposes certain limits on how and where lawful picketing can be undertaken. In particular it should normally only be carried out by people attending at or near their own place of work.

Lawful purposes of picketing

The only lawful purposes of picketing are:

(a) peacefully obtaining and communicating information

(b) peacefully persuading a person to work or not to work.

Pickets may, therefore, seek to explain their case to those entering or leaving the picketed premises and ask them not to enter or leave the premises where the dispute is taking place. They have no powers to stop people or to compel them to listen.

A picket has no right under law to require a vehicle to stop or be stopped. A picket may not physically obstruct a vehicle. On the other hand a driver must exercise due care and attention when approaching or driving past a picket line and may not drive in such a manner as to give rise to a reasonably foreseeable risk of injury.

The criminal law protects the right of every person to go about his lawful daily business free from interference.

A picket may exercise peaceful persuasion but if he goes beyond that he may commit a criminal offence.

Role of the police
It is not the function of the police to take a view on the merits of a particular trade dispute. They have a general duty to uphold the law whether on a picket line or elsewhere. The law gives the police discretion to take reasonable measures in order to ensure that picketing remains peaceful and orderly.

The police have no responsibility for enforcing civil law. An employer cannot require the police to help in identifying the pickets against whom he wishes to seek an order from the civil court. The police may, however, decide to assist an officer of the court if they think there may be a breach of peace.

The police have discretionary powers, in criminal law, to limit the number of pickets at any place where they have reasonable cause to fear disorder. If a picket does not leave the picket line when asked to do so by the police he is liable to be arrested for obstruction, either of the highway, or of a police officer in the execution of his duty, if the obstruction is such as to be likely to cause a breach of peace.

Limiting numbers of pickets
A major cause of violence and disorder on a picket line is excessive numbers of pickets. Wherever large numbers of people with strong feelings are involved there is a danger that the situation will get out of control and that those concerned will run the risk of arrest and prosecution.

This is particularly so whenever people, by sheer weight of numbers, seek to stop others going into work or delivering or collecting goods. This situation, sometimes described as "mass picketing", is not peaceful persuasion but obstruction and sometimes intimidation. It may well result in a breach of the peace, or other criminal offence.

Accordingly, pickets and their organisers should ensure that the number of pickets at any entrance does not exceed six (or fewer if appropriate) and that anyone seeking to demonstrate support for those in dispute is kept well away from the picket line.

An experienced person, preferably a trade union official who represents those picketing, should always be in charge of the picket line. He should have a letter of authority from his union which he can show to police officers or to people who want to cross the picket line. Even when not on the picket line himself he should be available to give the pickets advice if a problem arises.

An organiser of pickets should maintain close contact with the police. Advance consultation is always in the best interests of all concerned. He should seek direction from them on the number of people who should be present and where they should stand in order to avoid obstructing the highway.

Consultation with other trade unions
Where several trade unions are involved in a dispute, they should consult each other about organisation. They should agree how many pickets there should be from each union and who should have overall responsibility for organising them.

Right to cross picket lines
Everyone has the right to decide for himself whether he will cross a picket line. Disciplinary action should not be taken or threatened by a union against a member on the grounds that he has crossed a picket line which it had not authorised or which was not at a member's place of work. Under s.4 of the Employment Act 1980 exclusion or expulsion from a union in a closed shop on such grounds may be held to be unreasonable.

Essential supplies and services
Pickets should take very great care to ensure that their activities do not cause distress, hardship or inconvenience to members of the public who are not involved in the dispute.

Pickets should take particular care to ensure that the movement of essential goods and supplies, the carrying out of essential maintenance of plant and equipment, and the provision of services essential to the life of the community are not impeded, still less prevented. Arrangements to ensure this should be agreed in advance between the unions and employers concerned.

Lawful secondary industrial action
Secondary action — when an employment contract is broken (or is threatened with a breach) or is otherwise interfered with and the employer under the contract is not a party to the dispute — is unlawful and so actionable in the civil courts, unless:
  (a) its principal purpose is to prevent or disrupt the supply of goods or services between the employer in dispute and direct customers or suppliers of the employer or
  (b) its principal purpose is to prevent an associated company of the employer in dispute supplying the customers of that employer with goods and services which would have been supplied by the employer had it not been for the dispute or
  (c) if it is taken during the course of lawful picketing.

The secondary action must also be likely to achieve its purpose and must have been approved in a ballot.

Trade Union Act 1984 as amended by the Employment Act 1988

Ballots
In order to attract immunity from civil actions, industrial disputes must have been approved in a ballot (which must have been held no more than four weeks before the industrial action was endorsed or authorised) by a majority of those voting in the ballot.

The following requirements must be satisfied in relation to the ballot.
1. Entitlement to vote must be accorded to those members of the union who it is reasonable for the union to believe will be called upon to take industrial action and to no others.
2. Voters must be asked whether they are prepared to take part in a strike or action short of a strike, whichever of the two is relevant. In cases where both types of action are contemplated, voters must be asked whether they are prepared to take part in each. For industrial action to be regarded as having been approved in a ballot, the majority of those voting must answer "yes" to the appropriate question.
3. Ballot papers must contain the following (unqualified) statement: "If you take part in a strike or other industrial action, you may be in breach of your contract of employment".

4. All people entitled to vote must be allowed to do so without interference and without incurring direct costs, and the ballot must be conducted so that, as far as is reasonably practicable, those voting can do so in secret and the votes given are counted fairly and accurately.
5. All people with voting rights must:
    (a) be supplied with a voting paper, or have one made available to them at their place of work — or at a more convenient place — immediately before, immediately after or during working hours; and
    (b) be given an opportunity to vote by post and/or to vote immediately before, after, or during working hours at the workplace or at a more convenient place.
6. There must be a separate ballot for each place of work and before action is taken at any particular workplace, a majority at that workplace must vote in favour of action. However, one aggregated ballot covering different workplaces will be permissible in situations where all those who are entitled to vote have a factor in common which relates to terms and conditions of employment or occupational description.

As soon as is reasonably practicable after the ballot, the union must take such steps as are reasonably necessary to inform those people entitled to vote of:
(a) the number of votes cast
(b) the number of "Yes" votes and
(c) the number of "No" votes and
(d) the number of spoiled voting papers.

Check-off agreements
Where an employer collects union dues from employees, a trade union member may certify in writing to his employer that he is exempt from the obligation to contribute to the union's political fund, or that he has notified the union in writing of his objection to contributing to it. On receipt of such certificate, the employer is required to ensure, as soon as it is reasonably practical to comply, that no amount is deducted from the employee's pay in respect of this fund (unless or until the certificate is withdrawn).

Employment Act 1988

Right to be balloted before industrial action
Where a trade union authorises or endorses industrial action without holding a proper ballot, individual trade union members have the right to seek a court order requiring the union to withdraw that authorisation and to ensure that its members are not induced to take part in industrial action

Right not to be unjustifiably disciplined
Trade union members have the right not to be unjustifiably disciplined by their unions for certain specified actions, such as failing to participate in or support a strike or other industrial action, or alleging that the union or one of its representatives has broken union rules or acted unlawfully. Discipline includes: expulsion from the union, fines and the withholding of benefits normally provided by the union. Union members who believe they have been unjustifiably disciplined may claim compensation from a tribunal.

Right to stop check-off
Where employees certify to their employer that their union membership has terminated or is to do so, the employer must stop deduction of union dues from pay. Where an employer continues to deduct subscriptions, an employee may claim compensation from an industrial tribunal.

Closed shop agreements
Closed shop agreements are now effectively unenforceable. Dismissal of an employee for non-membership of a trade union is now unfair even where a closed shop operates and, in addition, any industrial action taken to enforce a closed shop will be open to legal action.

Industrial Training Act 1982 (as amended)

Industrial Training Boards
Under the Industrial Training Act 1982 (as amended) the Secretary of State for Employment after consultation with the Training Commission is empowered to set up Industrial Training Boards (ITBs) for individual industries.

What are ITBs?
The purpose of ITBs is to make better provision for and encourage the adequate training of people over compulsory school age for employment in the activities of industry and commerce.
   They are empowered to:
   (a) provide courses themselves
   (b) arrange for others to provide courses
   (c) approve courses and facilities provided by others
   (d) conduct research into the nature and length of training required and the methods and standards to be adopted
   (e) assist others in carrying on such research
   (f) provide advice on training and assist people in finding facilities for training
   (g) apply or make arrangements for the application of selection tests, etc for ascertaining the attainment of any standards recommended by the board and may award certificates for such attainment.

Can the ITB's make grants towards training?
An ITB can provide financial assistance in a variety of ways, by:
   (a) paying maintenance and travelling allowances to people attending approved courses
   (b) making grants or loans to people providing courses and facilities
   (c) paying fees to persons providing further education for employees who receive further education in association with their training in approved courses
   (d) granting payments to people who make arrangements for themselves or their employees to make use of approved courses or facilities.

How is this all financed?
To pay for the cost of training, an ITB may impose a levy on employers in the industry, generally not exceeding 1% of the employer's payroll.

Do small employers have to pay this levy?
Small firms are exempt from paying the levy. Currently in the road transport industry this means employers with a payroll of £24,500 or less (although in certain cases the threshold is either higher or lower than this).

How does the Act seek to ensure a fair distribution of the cost of training?
This is done through a system of exemptions and grants.
1. Companies who provide training at their own establishments which meet criteria laid down by the ITB may be granted exemption from the levy.
2. Grants are given to people who make arrangements for themselves or their employees to make use of approved courses or facilities.

In this way those firms which provide their own training are exempted from the levy, those that send employees on approved courses are able to recover a large part of the levy (proportionate to the amount of training they sponsor) and those that do neither, pay the whole of the levy and so contribute to the provision of courses and the training of personnel who they may one day recruit.

Social Security

Social Security Pensions Act 1975 and the Social Security Act 1986

The Social Security Pensions Act 1975 (as amended) introduced a new State earnings-related pension scheme — SERPS. It also gave employers the option of replacing part of the State scheme with their own by "contracting-out". Further changes took place as a result of the Social Security Act 1986. Notably, the Act made it possible for individual employees to contract-out of SERPS by having their own appropriate "personal" pensions.

How does SERPS differ from the flat-rate national insurance retirement pension?
The scheme is in two parts, providing for:
- (a) a "basic pension" which is equivalent to the flat-rate national insurance pension
- (b) an "additional pension" which is paid on an earnings-related basis.

Are there any rules governing "contracting out"?
Yes. Employers may contract-out of SERPS with either a salary-related or a money purchase scheme. Salary-related schemes have to satisfy a minimum benefit test to ensure that they provide members with benefits which are at least as good as those provided by the State scheme. Money-purchase schemes must satisfy a minimum contribution test instead. Contracting-out by either method is strictly governed by legislation with regard to scheme content and the procedures which must be followed.

Does a member of a contracted out scheme lose his rights to a State pension?
The contracting out arrangements are only in respect of the "additional pension", employees will still be entitled to the "basic pension".

How much is paid under SERPS?
The basic flat-rate element corresponds to the basic flat-rate national insurance pension. Entitlement to the full rate depends on the claimant having qualifying years of contributions for about 9/10ths of his working life.

The additional earnings related part of the pension consists of 1.25% of a person's average earnings since 1978 taking account only of those earnings on which employees' national insurance contributions have been made. Earnings figures are revalued in line with the rise in national average earnings.

Do women get the same pension?
Women who pay standard rate contributions to the scheme qualify for the same amount of pension as men but from age 60.

Social Security Acts 1975 to 1988

The Social Security Acts 1975 to 1988 provide a large range of benefits in appropriate circumstances:
- (a) Unemployment Benefit
- (b) Sickness Benefit
- (c) Invalidity Benefit
- (d) Severe Disablement Allowance
- (e) Maternity Allowance
- (f) Widow's Payment, Widowed Mother's Allowance, Widow's Pension
- (g) Guardian's Allowance
- (h) Retirement Pensions
- (i) Attendance Allowance
- (j) Invalid Care Allowance
- (k) Mobility Allowance.

How is the scheme paid for?
By obligatory contributions from employees, employers, self-employed persons, and by voluntary contributions from non-employed or otherwise exempt persons who wish to be covered by the scheme.

Is anyone living in this country entitled (or required) to belong to the scheme?
Regulations define the conditions of residence in Great Britain which must ordinarily be complied with before a person can become insured under the Act. These regulations also deal with payment of contributions and entitlement to benefits arising out of former residence abroad.

What is the situation of a person temporarily working or resident abroad?
Reciprocal arrangements have been made between Great Britain and many other countries who operate schemes on a similar basis by which contributions paid in

one country, or in some cases residence in one country, will provide entitlement to benefit in the other country.

Where EC countries are concerned, EC regulations provide for equality of treatment and protection of benefit rights for employed workers, pensioners and dependants of those people who move between the countries of the EC.

Self-employed persons, etc are covered by reciprocal agreements.

To whom does a United Kingdom citizen working in another EC country, pay his contributions?
A United Kingdom national who goes to work in another EC country for 12 months for a United Kingdom employer will still be subject to the United Kingdom national insurance requirements, ie the United Kingdom employer will continue to pay United Kingdom contributions.

The reverse situation applies when an EC national comes to work for an EC employer in the United Kingdom for 12 months, ie the employer will not be liable for United Kingdom contributions.

Social Security and House Benefits Act 1982

This Act introduced the statutory sick pay scheme whereby employers are required to take over responsibility for the payment of sick pay to employees. The rules of the scheme are complex with an employee's entitlement being contingent upon specific rules regarding the length of any period of incapacity for work, periods of entitlement, qualifying days and notification of absence.

For how long must an employer pay statutory sick pay (SSP)?
Statutory sick pay is payable for up to 28 weeks in any period of incapacity for work. If the employee returns to work for more than eight weeks the next period of illness will start a new entitlement to SSP.

How much SSP is payable?
Weekly rates of SSP are set each year by the government. The rate payable is related to the employee's average weekly earnings.

Can the employer recover the cost of SSP?
Yes, the full amount paid together with a sum representing national insurance contributions payable on SSP is recoverable from the Government.

Social Security Act 1986

This Act introduced the statutory maternity pay scheme whereby employers must pay maternity pay to female employees who take maternity leave or leave employment because of pregnancy or confinement. Entitlement to statutory maternity pay (SMP) depends on a number of qualifying conditions regarding, for example, length of continuous employment, date of expected week of confinement, average weekly earnings and notification of absence.

For how long must an employer pay SMP?
SMP is payable for a period of up to 18 weeks. This period may be shorter if the employee continues to work beyond a certain point in her pregnancy.

How much SMP is payable?
There are two levels of SMP — a higher and a lower rate. Which of these an employee receives depends on her length of employment. The higher rate is 9/10ths of an employee's average weekly earnings. The lower rate is set each year by the Government.

Can the employer recover the cost of SMP?
Yes, the full amount paid together with a sum representing national insurance contributions payable on SMP is recoverable from the Government.

Discrimination

Equal Pay Act 1970
(As amended by the Equal Pay (Amendment) Regulations 1983)

The main objective of this Act is to eliminate discrimination between men and women as regards pay and conditions of employment when they are employed on the *same or broadly similar work,* or work which though different has been judged as equal under a job evaluation scheme, or work of equal value.

Does the right to equal pay and conditions work both ways?
Yes! A man doing the same, or broadly similar, work to that which a woman does under more favourable pay conditions, is entitled to equal treatment just as much as if the positions were reversed.

Does the right to equal pay apply in all cases?
No, where a man and a woman are paid differently because of a genuine material difference (not based on sex) between their cases, the equal pay rules do not apply. A genuine material difference might include, for example, length of service or work performance.

Are there any other exceptions?
In some instances special provisions are made for women, eg:
  (a) where the law regulating the employment of women makes special provisions for the terms and conditions of that employment
  (b) in connection with pregnancy and maternity
  (c) in relation to pension scheme benefits.

What is job evaluation?
This means an investigation and evaluation of a job in order to establish its position relative to other jobs in a business or group of businesses, having regard to the effort, skill and decision making required.

How are disputes resolved?
If a claim for equal treatment cannot be settled between the employee and employer, the matter can be referred to an industrial tribunal which can, if the complaint is upheld, award arrears of pay, or damages, in respect of unequal conditions for up to two years.

Does a woman's contract have to include an equality clause?
If no equality clause is incorporated in a woman's contract it shall be deemed to be incorporated.

Sex Discrimination Act 1975 as amended by the Sex Discrimination Act 1986

How does this Act differ from the Equal Pay Act 1970?
Whereas the Equal Pay Act is concerned with pay and conditions of employment, the Sex Discrimination Act makes it unlawful to discriminate against a person on the grounds of sex (or marital status) in many other areas.

Does the Act apply equally to discrimination against men and women?
Although most cases of discrimination have been and are likely to be against women, it is equally unlawful to discriminate against a man (or a married person) unless it can be shown that there are special reasons which justify the discrimination.

What kind of things would justify discrimination in employment?
A genuine occupational qualification, eg:
- (a) where the essential nature of a job calls for a man, eg a male part in a play (or vice versa a female part)
- (b) to preserve decency or privacy, eg where men are in a state of undress or using sanitary facilities.

What sort of discrimination is unlawful in employment?
In addition to pay and conditions of service covered by the Equal Pay Act, it is unlawful to discriminate on the grounds of sex in respect of offers of employment, opportunity for promotion, transfer or training, dismissal, access to any other benefits, facilities and services open to members of the opposite sex.

What discrimination is unlawful before employment?
The pattern is generally the same, eg unless there are specific reasons why the matter should apply to one sex only, discrimination is unlawful. Probably the most important example is in respect of advertisements, where it is unlawful to publish an advertisement which might reasonably be understood to indicate an intention to commit an unlawful discriminatory act, eg to employ persons of one sex to the exclusion of others.

How is the Act enforced?
Individuals can claim compensation from an industrial tribunal. In addition, the Equal Opportunities Commission can issue a non-discrimination notice requiring the employer not to discriminate.

Code of practice
The Commission has issued a code of practice on the elimination of sex and marital discrimination in employment and the promotion of equal opportunities at work.

Race Relations Act 1976

The Act and those that preceded it, ie the Race Relation Acts of 1965 and 1968, were designed to eliminate discrimination on racial grounds. The Act applies to a wide range of activities but is particularly important in the field of employment. The provisions of the Act cover: recruitment, terms and conditions of employment, access to training schemes, benefits, facilities, services and promotion.

Does the Act apply to any particular nationalities?
The Act makes it unlawful to discriminate in respect of employment in Great Britain against a person of any particular racial group on the grounds of his colour, race, nationality, or ethnic or national origins.

What is racial discrimination?
Discrimination occurs when:
  (a) a person is treated less favourably, on racial grounds alone, than are persons of a different racial group, or
  (b) only a relatively small number of people within a racial group are able to comply with a particular, apparently non-discriminatory, condition and
    (i) the requirement or condition cannot be justified as being necessary for the job, and
    (ii) not being able to comply puts the person at a disadvantage.

Is racial discrimination ever permitted?
There are three main circumstances when discrimination is permissible:
  (a) where membership of a particular racial group is a genuine occupational requirement for the job, eg work in ethnic restaurants, or certain kinds of community social work
  (b) where a job is given to provide training in skills which will be used outside Great Britain or where a job will be done wholly or mainly outside Great Britain
  (c) where special training arrangements are made to meet the needs of a special racial group which is under-represented in a particular occupation.

What provisions are there for enforcing the Act?
Complaints against employers can be brought before an industrial tribunal and if justified can result in the award of compensation. The tribunal may instead or, in

addition, make a recommendation as to what action the employer should take to stop the discrimination complained of.

Can only complainants bring up questions of racial discrimination?
The Commission for Racial Equality (CRE) (which took over from the Commission for Community Relations and the Race Relations Board) has included in its powers and duties the right to investigate companies where discrimination appears to be persistent and to take action in connection with discriminatory advertising.

Where the Commission finds, following investigation, that discrimination is taking place it may issue a non-discrimination notice requiring the offender not to commit such acts.

Code of Practice
The Commission for Racial Equality has published a Code of Practice for the elimination of racial discrimination and the promotion of equality of opportunity in employment. The Code gives guidance to help employers, trade unions, employment agencies and employees understand the provisions of the Race Relations Act and shows how they can implement policies to eliminate racial discrimination and enhance equality of opportunity.

Disabled Persons (Employment) Acts 1944 and 1958

These Acts are intended to make provisions for persons handicapped by disablement to secure employment or work on their own account.

How is a "disabled person" defined
The Act defines a disabled person as one who "on account of injury, disease or congenital deformity, is substantially handicapped in obtaining or keeping employment or in undertaking work on his own account of a kind which, apart from that injury, disease or deformity, would be suited to his age, experience and qualifications".

How does the Act seek to assist disabled persons?
The Act assists by requiring the Employment Service to establish and maintain a register of disabled persons, and by requiring employers of 20 or more persons to employ a quota of registered disabled persons.

What size is the quota?
The standard quota is 3%, but this may be increased or decreased according to whether the employment, trade or industry is particulary suitable or unsuitable for disabled persons.

Are any jobs reserved for disabled persons?
Certain classes of employment which are regarded as particularly suitable are designated for the purpose of appropriating them, as vacancies occur, for registered disabled persons. These positions are excluded from the quota calculations.

Safety

The Health and Safety at Work, etc Act 1974

The main purpose of this Act is to make work safer and healthier for all workers and members of the public who may be affected by activities at work.

How does it seek to do this?
First of all by tidying up the many regulations and orders made under the Factories Act 1961.

Does it affect any other Act?
Yes! Eventually it will also supersede the Offices, Shops and Railway Premises Act 1963.

Will the Health and Safety at Work Act eventually cover all the areas covered by the other two Acts?
Yes! It will also cover much more; for the first time health and safety legislation has been extended to protect those employed in education, research, medicine, the leisure industry and some parts of the transport industry. Altogether it is estimated that 8 million workers who were previously excluded will now be protected by the Act.

How long will it take to replace the existing Acts?
Repeal, amendment, revision and updating of existing legislation will continue over a period of years.

Does the Act make specific provisions for particular industries?
The Act as it stands outlines the general duties of employers, employees, etc; detailed provisions will be contained in regulations, orders and codes of practice which will be introduced in time.

What are the general aims of the Act?
The main provisions of the Act are directed towards:
    (a) maintaining or improving standards of health, safety and welfare of persons at work
    (b) protecting persons other than persons at work, against risks to health or safety arising out of, or in connection with, the activities of persons at work
    (c) controlling the storage and use of explosives or highly flammable or otherwise dangerous substances to prevent their illegal acquisition, possession and use
    (d) controlling the emission of noxious or offensive substances
    (e) setting up a Health and Safety Commission and Executive to be responsible to the Secretary of State for Employment and other ministers for administrating the legislation.

What are the general duties of employers?
Every employer has a duty to ensure, as far as is reasonably practicable, the health, safety and welfare of his employees. Additionally, every employer or self-employed

person has a duty to ensure that persons, other than employees who may be affected by his activities, are not exposed to risks to their health and safety.

In particular every employer has a duty to ensure, *as far as is reasonably practicable*:
- (a) the provision and maintenance of plant and systems of work that are safe and without risk to health
- (b) arrangements for safety and freedom from risks to health in connection with the use, handling, storage and transport of articles and substances
- (c) the provision of such instruction, training and supervision as is necessary to guarantee the health and safety at work of employees
- (d) the maintenance of any place of work in a condition that is safe and without risks to health and to provide safe means of access and egress
- (e) the provision of a working environment that is safe and free from risks to health, with adequate facilities and arrangements for welfare at work.

What are the employees' duties in connection with safety and health at work?

Every employee while at work has a duty:
- (a) to take reasonable care for his own health and safety and that of others who may be affected by his acts and omissions at work
- (b) to co-operate with his employer (or any other person) to enable any duty or requirement under the Act to be complied with.

What are the functions and duties of the Health and Safety Commission, the Health and Safety Executive and the Inspectorate?

The Health and Safety Commission must ensure that adequate advice and information on health and safety matters are available and that research and training are undertaken as necessary and that new regulations are prepared when needed. It must keep the Secretary of State for Employment informed of its work and carry out his directions.

The Commission can also arrange for investigations and inquiries into accidents, incidents and anything else which it considers requires investigation and can obtain any information needed to carry out its functions. It can also approve and issue codes of practice containing practical guidance made by itself or prepared by other bodies.

The Health and Safety Executive is responsible to the Commission for carrying out its functions according to the Commission's directions. It has a specific duty of making adequate arrangements for the enforcement of the relevant statutory provisions.

The Inspectorate — it is the duty of the Executive, local authorities or any other authority to make adequate arrangements for the enforcement of the relevant statutory provisions, ie the requirements of this Act, etc. The staff of the previous factories, mines, quarries, explosives, nuclear installations and alkali works inspectorates have been transferred to the Executive to carry out this enforcement.

What action can a Health and Safety Inspector take in respect of breaches of the Health and Safety at Work orders?

If, in the opinion of the Inspector, the work activity being carried on involves the immediate risk of serious personal injury to employees, he may serve the employer with a "Prohibition Notice" requiring the employer to halt the activity until the fault is remedied.

Where the Inspector is of the opinion that the breach does not involve the immediate risk of serious personal injury he may issue an "Improvement Notice" which permits production to continue but requires the employer to remedy the fault within a specified period.

What provisions have been made in respect of work safety committees?
Employers are required to consult representatives of the employees with a view to making and maintaining arrangements which will enable them and their employees to co-operate effectively in promoting and developing the health and safety at work of the employees and in making sure the measures are effective.

Recognised independent trade unions may appoint safety representatives from among employees. Their general function is to consult with the employer on health and safety matters. In addition their specific functions include investigation of hazards and dangerous occurrences and workplace inspections.

(For further information on health and safety aspects a book entitled *Croner's Health and Safety at Work* is available from the publishers of this book.)

The Factories Act 1961

This Act consolidated the previous Factories Acts of 1937, 1948 and 1959. In addition to the detailed legislation contained in the Act hundreds of regulations have been introduced over the years covering health, safety and welfare matters.

Briefly, the term "factory" within the meaning of the Act refers to any premises, including open air premises, in which, or within the precincts of which, by way of trade or for purposes of gain, persons are employed in manual labour in any process for or incidental to any of the following purposes and to or over which the employer of the person employed therein has the right of access or control, namely:
   (a) the making of any article or of part of any article
   (b) the altering, repairing, ornamenting, finishing, cleaning, or washing, or the breaking up or demolition of any article
   (c) the adapting for sale of any article
   (d) the slaughtering of cattle, sheep, goats, horses, asses or mules
   (e) the confinement of the aforementioned animals while awaiting slaughter in premises which are not part of a farm or part of a market.

The definition then continues to include many more premises in which persons are employed in manual labour.

The Offices, Shops and Railway Premises Act 1963

The Act introduced health, safety and welfare provisions to many premises not previously covered by the Factories Act.
NB Details of the Factories Act 1961 and the Offices, Shops and Railway Premises Act 1963 have not been given because, as previously mentioned, these Acts will be gradually superseded by the Health and Safety at Work Act 1974. Readers who wish to keep up-to-date with changes in health and safety legislation and

the introduction of codes of practice are advised to consult *Croner's Reference Book for Employers* or *Croner's Reference Book for the Self Employed and Smaller Business.*

Special Note on Social Legislation Questions

Despite the fact that the syllabus clearly states with reference to social legislation, that "At the end of the course the candidate should be able to: State the main objectives of the following:" and lists 20 pieces of legislation, questions of detail rather than of the main objectives continue to be asked in the examination.

Certain specific requirements of the Factories Act have appeared and these are given below, in case they should be used again:

Space per person — 400 cubic feet minimum
First-aid — One first-aid box per 150 persons. One certified first-aider if more than 50 persons are employed.

It is also disturbing to note that examination candidates are asked to judge from a set of facts whether or not the situation described constitutes discrimination. These situations are presumably based on decided cases and without turning this book into a treatise on race relations law it is impossible to cover all the decided cases and the reasons for decisions.

As a general guide, when tackling this type of question, you should ask yourself: Was this regulation/rule/condition of employment, etc, one which applied to all the workers and which only adversely affected an individual or group of individuals because his or their race or religion differed from that of the majority or, was it aimed specifically at placing him/them at a disadvantage.

If the former, then it would probably not be regarded as discrimination, if the latter, it most certainly would be.

You should also take note of any cases reported in the press or shown on television, especially if the judge's reasons for his decision are reported.

Company Safety Policy

Employers with five or more employees are required to have a health and safety policy statement which is a written statement detailing the arrangements for health and safety in the work place.

Employers are required to set out their own policy having regard to the nature of their working areas. In transport operations, for example, due notice should be given to the use of equipment, eg driving fork lift trucks, stepping into and out of vehicle cabs; working on loading banks where vehicles may have to reverse into confined spaces; the type of goods handled, such as dangerous goods; employees lifting cartons, bales, etc; the supply of protective clothing especially fluorescent type jackets for night workers, etc.

The health and safety policy should be drawn up in co-operation with the management team and other employees (including the trade union safety representatives) who are in a position to know where problem areas exist. The statement should be signed by the managing director or the most senior person in the company and dated so that it is periodically reviewed in the light of changed circumstances or new conditions. It should be displayed prominently on company noticeboards and copies given to any contractors or other people who may be working on the premises either regularly or for long periods.

PART II

Certificate of Professional Competence (International)

CHAPTER 13
(Module D)
Law

Legislative Sources

What is the difference between an EC directive and an EC regulation?
An EC *directive* is a general instruction issued by the Council and the Commission to a Member State with the intention of achieving a particular objective. It is binding on the Member State which is, however, free to select its own method of reaching that objective, eg EC Council Directive 74/561 relating to admission to the occupation of road haulage operator, requires that an operator shall be professionally competent. It was left to the British Government, through the Secretary of State for Transport, to draw up and implement regulations which would enable professional competence to be determined.

An EC *regulation* is a precise instruction that is directly applicable to all Member States and is binding in its entirety, eg Regulations 3820/85 and 3821/85 of the Council lay down the EC requirements in respect of driving time, rest periods and breaks, drivers' records, etc.

What are the main EC bodies and how do they regulate and control?
The most important bodies which affect road transport are:

The Council of Ministers — for general discussions this consists of the Foreign Affairs Ministers of each of the 12 Member States, but for Transport Policy meetings it consists of the 12 Ministers of Transport. The Council has the sole right to make decisions. Usually these decisions must be unanimous but in some instances a qualified majority is permissible.

The Commission of the EC — the individual Commissioners who together make up the Commission are appointed by each Member State. As Commissioners they act independently of their own States, in the interests of the Community as a whole. Under the Treaty of Rome they have the exclusive right and duty to submit proposals to the Council of Ministers. (The Council considers each proposal and communicates its decision to the Commission for action, eg to issue a directive or make regulations.)

The Committee of Permanent Representatives (COREPER) — as its title indicates this committee is composed of permanent representatives (ambassadors) from the Member States, unlike the Council, where the Ministers are non-permanent. It makes representations to the Commission (from which proposals may eventually emanate) and engages in continuous discussion with that body on current problems. It prepares briefs for the Ministers, ie doing the groundwork on which the Council makes its decisions. It is therefore a permanent working body, assisting both the Council and the Commission.

The Court of Justice — suitable judges are nominated from the legal systems of Member States to serve on the Court. It has sole authority to interpret the Treaty and to appraise the legality of all decisions, actions or administrative regulations and has the power to issue directives to Governments or people but it has no powers to impose fines or apply sanctions.

The Economic and Social Committee — is concerned with the financial and social well-being of the Community. Social policies envisage the harmonisation of standards of living, working conditions, etc. The Committee is concerned not only with harmonisation within an industry but also with the effects of that industry on other sections of the Community, eg the beneficial effect that an efficient transport system can have on standards of living.

The Assembly (European Parliament) — consists of 518 elected Members of the European Parliament (MEPs). It is responsible for approving the budget of the Commission and has the power to dismiss the Commission by a two-thirds majority on a vote of censure. It has little legislative power and is really confined to giving opinions on draft legislation, making recommendations and communicating information.

What are the main provisions of the Common Transport Policy (CTP) that affect road haulage?

The main provisions can be summarised as follows:
1. To remove obstacles to the free circulation of transport services.
2. To harmonise the laws and regulations affecting road haulage.
3. To devise controls to limit uneconomic competition.
4. To devise guidelines which will enable transport to play its part in achieving the socio-economic aspirations of the Community, ie to balance the need for economic operation with the social and environmental considerations of the Community.

Why is transport so important to the aims of the Community?

The CTP was not formulated in isolation but in the knowledge that transport is an essential factor which affects all aspects of community life and therefore has an important part to play in achieving the objectives of other Community policies.

How does it affect these policies?

Generally the benefits derived from efficient transport services far outweigh any adverse effects:

Regional policy — the problems of under-developed or depressed areas can often be assisted by the development of good transport links and efficient transport services, by encouraging new industries to locate in those areas and moving people and products to and from the areas cheaply and efficiently.

Social policy — employees in the same sort of transport employment should have similar basic working conditions and transport services to people in different countries should reach uniform minimum standards.

Fiscal policy — the taxation of vehicles and fuel should be harmonised so that operators in one country are not at a disadvantage compared with those in other countries of the Community.

Environmental policy — while transport is essential to the economic well-being of the Community, its effects on the environment must be recognised and contained within acceptable limits.

Energy policy — transport is a major user of energy. The economic use of fuel is essential during a time of decreasing world reserves of fuel and high costs to Community Member States.

External policy — the Community must not operate in isolation. Development of world trade and understanding is essential for future prosperity and peace. Transport has an important part to play in achieving these aims.

What are the main international Conventions and Agreements which affect road haulage?

Because most of these Conventions and Agreements have French titles and are fairly lengthy, they are usually referred to by abbreviations, but the full English title indicates the purpose of the Convention, etc.

1. Customs Convention on the International Transport of Goods 1975, TIR (Transports Internationale Routiers)
Possession of a TIR carnet exempts a carrier from normal Customs examination at frontiers.

2. Convention on the Contract for the International Carriage of Goods by Road 1956, CMR (Convention Relative au Contrat de Transport Internationale de Marchandises par Route)
This Convention which governs the conditions of contracts for the international carriage of goods by road was incorporated into British law by the Carriage of Goods by Road Act 1965.

3. International Agreement on the Carriage of Dangerous Goods by Road 1968, ADR (Accord Dangereux Routiers)
Countries which are party to this agreement permit the transport of dangerous goods by road through their territories, without hindrance, provided they are packed and labelled in accordance with Annex A to ADR and are carried in vehicles complying with the provisions of Annex B.

4. International Agreement on the Transport of Perishable Foodstuffs ATP
The International Carriage of Perishable Foodstuffs Act 1976 enables the requirements of this agreement to be enforced in this country in respect of international carriage. (It does not apply to journeys which are wholly domestic, nor to international journeys entailing sea crossings exceeding 150km.)

5. International Convention on the Taxation of Road Vehicles engaged on International Journeys 1957
Goods vehicles registered in the United Kingdom will not be charged any vehicle taxes while in any other country which is party to the Convention.

6. European Agreement concerning the work of crews of vehicles engaged in International Road Transport (AETR)
Drivers operating to countries outside the European Community but who are a party to this agreement must observe certain "hours of work" rules — see page 168.

Hours and Conditions of Work

What are the basic requirements concerning drivers' hours under EC Regulation 3820/85?
These fall into three main groups:
- (a) daily driving hours and compulsory breaks
- (b) weekly driving hours
- (c) rest periods.

What are the regulations concerning daily driving hours?
Total driving must not exceed **4½ hours** (after which a break must be taken) and the daily total must not exceed **nine hours** except that on two days per week it may be extended to **10 hours**.

What breaks must be taken?
Breaks must be taken as follows:
- (a) a break of at least **45 minutes** must be taken after **4½ hours** total driving, or
- (b) **two** or **three** shorter periods of not less than **15 minutes** duration, totalling **45 minutes** during the total driving period or partly within or immediately following it.

What are the maximum permitted weekly driving hours?
This is no longer laid down in the regulations but taking a total of six daily driving periods the maximum total driving in one week can be **56 hours** but since the regulations *do* stipulate a total driving time in a fortnight **(90 hours)** the second week would not allow more than **34 hours** maximum.

What are the regulations regarding rest periods?
The daily rest period must be:
- (a) not less than **11 hours** in a 24 hour period, but
- (b) this may be reduced to **nine hours** on three days per week provided the reduced period(s) is made up before the end of the following week.

When the daily rest period as (a) above is not reduced the driver can break up the rest period into two or three parts (minimum one hour) during the 24 hours, provided one period is of at least eight hours' duration. In such cases the total rest must be increased to 12 hours.

Are there any variations when the vehicle carries two drivers?
Where a vehicle is double manned each driver must have a rest period of not less than eight consecutive hours during each period of 30 hours.

Can the daily rest periods be taken on the vehicle?
It depends on whether or not a bunk is fitted — where there is no bunk, the daily rest period must be taken away from the vehicle but where a bunk is fitted, it may be taken there, *provided the vehicle is stationary*.

Are there provisions for journeys involving the use of ferries or trains?
Where journeys involve the use of ferries or trains, crew members may interrupt their *daily rest periods* not more than once, provided they comply with the following conditions:
- (a) that part of the daily rest period spent on land may be taken before or after that part of the daily rest period taken on board the ferry or train
- (b) the period between the two parts must be as short as possible and must not exceed one hour before embarkation or after disembarkation
- (c) crew members must have access to a bunk or couchette during both parts of the rest period
- (d) where the daily rest period is interrupted in this way, it must be increased by two hours
- (e) when time spent on board a ferry or train is not counted as part of a daily rest period it will instead be regarded as a break in driving.

What are the specified weekly rest periods?
A weekly rest period of **45 hours** must be taken by every crew member but this may be reduced to **36 hours** where the vehicle is normally based, or to **24 hours** if taken elsewhere. Each reduced rest period must be made good by the driver taking an equivalent rest period *en bloc* before the end of the *third week* following the week in question.

Are there any provisions for emergencies?
In the event of an emergency, or in circumstances outside a driver's control, the driving and rest periods may be waived to allow the driver to reach a suitable stopping point or, in certain circumstances, his destination. Details of the occurrence must be noted in the daily record sheet, or on the tachograph chart.

What are the EC age limits for HGV drivers?
Drivers of 18 and under 21 years of age may not drive vehicles, including vehicles with trailers or semi-trailers attached, weighing over 7.5 metric tonnes gross unless they hold a certificate of professional competence which means, where Great Britain is concerned, the ordinary driving licence and HGV licence. These licences are recognised by the other Member States.
  The minimum age for a driver's mate is 18 years.

Are any drivers exempt from the regulations?
The regulations do not apply to drivers of goods vehicles, including goods vehicles with any trailer or semi-trailer attached which does not exceed 3.5 metric tonnes gross.

What records must be kept of drivers' hours?
All vehicles, except those which have a gross permitted weight not exceeding 3.5 tonnes or which are exempt from the regulations, are required to be fitted with a calibrated EC tachograph which must be operated in accordance with EC regulation 3821/85.

What is the AETR agreement?
This is an international agreement concerning drivers' hours, etc and covers journeys to certain non-EC countries.

Which countries are parties to the agreement?
The United Kingdom and other EC Member States are parties to the agreement plus the following non-EC countries:
 Austria, Czechoslovakia, East Germany, Norway, Sweden, USSR and Yugoslavia.

What are the basic rules applying under AETR regulations?
When travelling to any of the above mentioned countries from the United Kingdom the following rules should be observed even though the journey may include travel through EC Member States:

Maximum continuous driving — four hours, but may be extended to 4½ hours to enable the driver to reach a convenient stopping place or his destination.

Maximum daily driving — eight hours, but may be extended to nine hours on two days per week. (This concession does not apply to excepted vehicles, ie articulated vehicles or drawbar trailer combinations which exceed 20 tonnes maximum permitted weight.)

Maximum weekly driving — 48 hours in any period of seven consecutive days.

Maximum fortnightly driving — 92 hours in any period of 14 consecutive days.

Breaks from driving — excepted vehicles (see above), one hour must be taken after four hours of continuous driving, or two breaks of 30 minutes each spread over the daily driving period in such a manner that at no time is four hours continuous driving exceeded. For all other vehicles, after four hours continuous driving a break of at least 30 minutes must be taken, or two breaks of 20 minutes, or three breaks of 15 minutes during this period, or partly immediately following it.

Daily rest periods — 11 consecutive hours in a 24 hour period, but this may be reduced on two days per week to nine consecutive hours if taken at home base or eight consecutive hours if taken away from home base. Double manned (without bunk) not less than 10 consecutive hours in a 27 hour period. Double manned (with bunk) not less than eight consecutive hours in a 30 hour period. Any reduction in rest periods must be made good.

Weekly rest periods — 24 hours immediately preceded or followed by a daily rest period.

Emergencies — In the event of an emergency or circumstances outside a driver's control the driving and rest periods may be waived to enable the driver to reach a suitable stopping place or, in certain circumstances, his destination.

Record keeping on international journeys

What method of record keeping is required for international journeys?

EC Member States require drivers of vehicles exceeding 3.5 tonnes gross weight to record their hours of work on the tachograph chart. AETR member countries allow drivers the option of a tachograph or individual record book. (Since the regulations on the keeping of records are common to both national and international operations, information on this subject can be found in Chapter 2 of this book.)

CHAPTER 14
(Module D)
Access to the International Market

Permits, quotas and tariffs
Most countries will allow foreign vehicles to circulate provided that they comply with the maximum weight and dimensions applicable to that particular country. For vehicles which exceed those weights and dimensions, special authorisation is required and for vehicles carrying dangerous goods, special certification is required.

Although some countries allow freedom of access to foreign operators, others still require them to obtain permits before the vehicle can enter the country.

Are permits required for both "hire or reward" and "own account" operations?
Some countries require permits for both "hire or reward" and "own account" operations whilst others concentrate on "hire or reward" only. Where permits are not required for "own account" operations the vehicle must carry a document giving the full details and nature of the business, load carried, route, final destination, etc.

Which European countries require permits for "own account" operations?
Czechoslovakia, Turkey, USSR, Yugoslavia.

Which countries require "own account" documents?
These are required for journeys to and from, or for transit through, Austria, France, West Germany, Hungary, Italy, Portugal and Spain.

What information must be shown in the "own account" document?
This varies from country to country but includes the following at least:
   (a) name of operator and nature of business
   (b) details of goods being carried
   (c) loading and unloading points
   (d) type and registration number of vehicle being used
   (e) the route.

Are there any countries which stipulate certain conditions for "Own Account" transport operations?
France requires goods to be carried in a vehicle owned by the operator or in his possession under a hire purchase agreement or a vehicle on hire.

In Italy the requirements are that: the goods carried must be the property of the undertaking, or sold, bought, hired, purchased, extracted, processed or repaired by them; they are being carried to or from the undertaking, etc; the vehicle is being driven by an employee of, and the vehicle itself is owned by, the undertaking, and the carriage of the goods is no more than ancillary to their overall activities.

What types of permits are available?
1. Bilateral, ie between two countries
2. EC (European Community)
3. ECMT (European Conference of Ministers of Transport)

Bilateral permits apply when two countries having concluded a bilateral road haulage agreement, wish to regulate the number of journeys made by goods vehicles of either country. Such permits also cover vehicles which are merely in transit and not delivering or collecting goods in that country.

Which countries have signed bilateral agreements with the United Kingdom?

The United Kingdom has concluded bilateral agreements with the following countries:

*Austria	Belgium	Bulgaria	*Czechoslovakia
Denmark	East Germany	Eire	Finland
*France	Greece	*Hungary	*Italy
Luxembourg	Netherlands	Norway	Poland
*Portugal	Romania	*Spain	Sweden
Switzerland	*Turkey	*USSR	*West Germany
*Yugoslavia			

However, only countries marked* require permits for "hire or reward" operations.

How are permits obtained?

Application for permits must be made to:
 The International Road Freight Office (IRFO)
 Westgate House
 Westgate Road
 Newcastle-upon-Tyne NE1 1TW
 (Tel: (091) 2610031)

Do permits cover more than one journey?

Both "journey" and "period" permits are issued depending upon the need. A "journey" permit is valid for one return journey unless otherwise stated. Transit journeys through a country (outward and return) count as one complete journey. "Period" permits can be used for an unlimited number of journeys during their validity.

Which countries issue journey permits which cover more than one journey?

Permits for **France** allow one, two, three or four return journeys.

Permits for **West Germany** allow for multiple journeys, eg two, three or four return journeys, valid for a period of six months.

Are permits transferable?

Permits cannot be used by or transferred to any other haulier or operator and they can only be used for vehicles currently authorised on an operator's licence.

What happens to permits after use, or if unused?

Permits must be returned, properly completed, to the International Road Freight Office within 15 days of the end of the journey or, if unused, within 15 days of their expiry.

What is the situation with regard to permits for West Germany, Hungary, Italy, Portugal, Spain, Turkey (transit) and Yugoslavia (transit)?

These countries operate a general quota system and the total number of permits available is usually insufficient to meet the demand although increases in the number of permits in the last two years has eased the situation. However, the problem is aggravated in the case of Italy by the need to obtain transit permits for either West Germany or France in order to reach that country.

How are these quota permits allocated?

Allocation is done by means of a block system under which operators are normally guaranteed at least the same number of permits one year as they received the previous year, as long as they use at least 75% of their allocation over a three year period.

Is it possible to transit France and West Germany without a permit?

Both France and West Germany operate road/rail "Kangourou" or "Piggy back" services for which a road/rail certificate can be obtained exempting the operator from the need for a permit.

In France the "Kangourou" service is operated and applies only to unaccompanied trailers or semi-trailers and must be used for both outward and return journeys.

In West Germany the company Kombiverkehr operates a "piggy back" service which allows complete vehicles and unaccompanied trailers or semi-trailers to operate without permits; such journeys within the country are permit free providing that a reasonable proportion of the journey both outward and return is via the "piggy back" service.

In all instances the road/rail certificate must accompany the vehicle and be stamped by the rail authorities as proof that the vehicle has been carried on the train.

Road/rail certificates are available from the IRFO.

What is the situation regarding journeys to East Germany?

A special quota of West German permits (short distance transit quota permits) is available for use when travelling to East Germany (German Democratic Republic) and to qualify for these British operators must route their vehicles only via the West German ports of Bremen, Bremerhaven or Hamburg and across the border into East Germany at the Lauenburg-Horst or Schlutup (Lübeck)-Selmsdorf crossing points.

Does a permit allow an operator to load and deliver within the same country?

No! This is called cabotage and is not allowed. Some countries, however, will allow British operators to pick up and deliver return loads to third countries, provided that the laws of that third country permit.

NB Proposals to permit limited cabotage within the EC by nationals of EC Member States are due to take effect from July 1990. "Cabotage permits" will allow hauliers to collect and deliver goods in a Member State provided they comply with the requirements on terms and conditions (including tariffs) etc, of the country in which they are operating. Permits will be valid for either one or two months.

Do countries allow empty vehicles to enter in order to pick up loads?

In most cases there are no problems, but France will only allow empty vehicles to enter for this purpose if contracts have been agreed in advance.

What are multi-lateral permits?

These permits are issued by (a) the European Economic Commission and (b) countries which are parties to the European Conference of Ministers of Transport (ECMT). They allow tramping, in the case of (a) between Member States of the EC and (b) between countries who are members of the ECMT.

The EC also issues Removal Permits. These allow United Kingdom operators (employing specialist staff) engaged in household removals to operate between Member States.

Can EC permits be used for journeys between the United Kingdom and other Member States?

Yes! However, they may not be used for transit through EC countries to pick up loads in countries outside the EC, or for unaccompanied trailer or semi-trailer operations.

Are they "journey" permits?

Each permit is valid for one calendar year and can be used with only one vehicle at a time.

Is there any restriction on the number of journeys made during that period?

There is no limit to the number of journeys made during the validity of the permit.

Which countries are members of the European Conference of Ministers of Transport (ECMT)?

Austria, Belgium, Denmark, Eire, Finland, France, West Germany, Greece, Italy, Luxembourg, Netherlands, Norway, Portugal, Spain, Sweden, Switzerland, Turkey, United Kingdom and Yugoslavia.

Do the same conditions apply to ECMT permits as apply to EC permits?

They are, broadly speaking, the same but some ECMT permits may be valid for less than a year and some member countries restrict their use.

What United Kingdom legislation applies to permits?

The International Road Haulage Permits Act 1975 allows regulations to be made with respect to the forgery, carriage and production of licences, permits, authorisations, etc relating to the international carriage of goods by road.

Who, in Great Britian, is empowered to require the production of permits?

Traffic examiners are given powers to require a driver to produce the prescribed document; to detain the vehicle whilst inspecting and copying the document; and to enter any premises where it is believed a vehicle subject to the regulations is kept or where the document may be found.

What is the penalty for contravening these regulations?
Any contravention of the regulations without a good reason can result in the operator being fined. A driver who refuses to comply with the requirements of an examiner, or wilfully obstructs him in the course of his duty, can also be prosecuted and fined.

Can an examiner prevent a vehicle from leaving the country?
If he thinks a vehicle is being used for international journeys and that the driver or owner of the vehicle has refused or failed to comply with the regulations, he has the power to prohibit the vehicle from being taken out of the United Kingdom.

What is the penalty for using forged permits?
It is an offence for anyone to use or possess forged or altered permits with intent to deceive and conviction carries a penalty of up to two years in prison. In addition the offence can result in the revocation of the operator's licence.

What specific regulations have been made in the United Kingdom with regard to permits for Austria, France, West Germany or Italy?
The Goods Vehicle (International Road Haulage Permits) Regulations 1975 (SI 1975 No. 2234) make it an offence to use a goods vehicle on journeys from the United Kingdom to, or in transit through, these countries unless a valid permit has been issued.

Permits must be carried on the vehicle and Department of Transport examiners have powers to prohibit the departure of vehicles from the United Kingdom if the regulations are not being complied with.

What are Forked (Bracket) Tariffs?
Bracket tariffs are tariffs laying down the maximum and minimum rates for the carriage of goods between two Member States.

The bracket spread is 23% of the maximum rate and between the upper and lower limits rates may be freely negotiated.

What is the purpose of these tariffs?
The purpose of these tariffs is that they should avoid the abuse of dominant positions and damaging competition, ie to provide users with transport at reasonable rates, yet ensuring a fair return for carriers.

Who determines rates?
The Road Haulage Association has been officially designated as the body to represent professional hauliers in this country in bi-lateral negotiations with similar organisations in other EC Member States.

On what basis are the rates determined?
"The base rate (the mid-point between the upper and lower limits) shall be fixed having regard both to the average cost of the transport operation concerned, including the general expenses of the business for a properly managed undertaking enjoying normal conditions of use of its carrying capacity and to market conditions and shall be such as to provide a fair return to carriers".

Are other organisations consulted?

Before publication of the rates, organisations representing users and services ancillary to transport are consulted. The Freight Transport Association and the Institute of Freight Forwarders have been designated for this purpose.

Are the tariffs obligatory on hauliers and users?

Although the EC proposed that the tariffs should be compulsory, many countries failed to introduce them and a revised system of **reference tariffs** and **compulsory tariffs** was proposed. **Compulsory tariffs**, if introduced, would replace the forked (bracket) tariffs, while **reference tariffs** would be recommended rates only and not obligatory.

If the tariffs should eventually become obligatory will there be any provisions for exceptions?

The EC rules allow for special contracts in writing between a carrier and another party at transport rates outside the upper or lower limits of the relevant tariff brackets provided that:

 (a) circumstances exist which were not taken into account at the time when the tariffs where fixed, in particular, where a special contract is made in response to the requirements of competition or where it is entered into for a certain period
 (b) the tonnage to be carried under such contract within any three month period must be not less than 500 metric tonnes
 (c) contracts must, in all cases, be such as to maintain or increase the carrier's trading returns.

Details of all such special contracts must be communicated to the competent authorities for publication and communication to any other States concerned.

NB Whilst these tariffs operate in a number of EC Member States and between Member States they have not been enforced in this country and this section is included so that the student may have knowledge of the existence of such tariffs.

International Transport Documentation

The range of documents which a driver must carry when engaged on international operations can be considerable and varies according to the countries visited. The documents required can be roughly grouped into:
 (a) those applicable to the driver
 (b) those applicable to the vehicle
 (c) those applicable to the load.

What personal documents does the driver need?

(1) Driving licences — a British driving licence is valid in many, though not all, Western European countries and in some Middle East countries. Therefore, unless it is certain that the British driving licence is valid in the countries to be visited, an International Driving Permit must be carried and this is essential for Bulgaria, East Germany, Hungary, Poland and Spain although Spain will accept the EC model British driving licence.

NB The RAC and the AA are responsible for issuing International Driving Permits.

(2) Passports and visas — passports are required for all countries. Entry visas are not required for EC countries but are required for some East European countries and

some Middle East countries, viz:

Bulgaria	Czechoslovakia	East Germany	Hungary	Iraq
Iran	Jordan	Kuwait	Lebanon	Poland
Romania	Saudi Arabia	Syria	Turkey	USSR

Applications for visas should be made to the Embassies in the United Kingdom of the country or countries to be visited.

(3) Drivers' records — most countries insist that records of drivers' hours of work must be carried and this is usually in the form of the tachograph charts.

(4) Bail bond — a form of additional insurance essential for drivers visiting Spain. In the event of an accident Spanish police usually hold all the parties until responsibility has been established. Bail bond cover of £1500 will probably secure the release of the driver and vehicle, pending investigation.

(5) Letter of authorisation, — most countries require the driver to carry a letter of authorisation if he is not the owner of the vehicle.

(6) Money — although the need will not necessarily arise in connection with documentation, this is nevertheless a convenient place to point out the need for drivers to carry with them an adequate supply of money. Many countries impose "on the spot" fines for offences in connection with the vehicle and its load, which can be quite heavy. Failure to pay the fines and, in particular, those resulting from accidents, can result in the driver being detained until the money is forthcoming.

What documents are needed in connection with the vehicle?

Depending upon the particular country to which the goods are being carried, or through which the vehicle is passing, any of the following may be required:

(a) Permit and Journey Record
(b) Carnet de Passage en Douane
(c) International Insurance Certificate (Green Card) or Third Party Insurance Certificate
(d) Operator's Licence
(e) Rail/Road Certificate
(f) Vehicle Registration Document (form V5)
(g) Letter of Authorisation to drive the vehicle if driver is not the owner.

The vehicle must also display a nationality plate, eg GB plate, at the rear.

These documents and the procedures relating to their use are described in detail elsewhere in the text.

What documents are needed in connection with the goods?

The obligatory documents are usually those connected with Customs formalities, eg:

(a) Single Administrative Document (SAD)
(b) TIR Carnet (not recognised between EC countries) or, when not applicable, the appropriate Customs form
(c) ATA Carnet (or Community Carnet) for temporary importations

Also required are:

(d) CMR Consignment notes for all "hire or reward" operations
(e) ADR Certificate (for dangerous goods) if applicable
(f) ATP Certificate (for perishable goods) if applicable.

In addition to these documents, dealt with elsewhere in the text, the documents described below may be carried, usually for commercial purposes:

Bill of Lading

This is the most important document used in shipping and probably the most useful commercial document as it fulfils three functions.

1. It is a receipt for goods and may be either:
   (a) a "shipped bill", ie a receipt for goods actually loaded on board, or
   (b) a "received" or "received for shipment" bill, ie the shipping company acknowledges receipt of the goods but does not certify that they have been loaded on board.

   A received bill is sometimes regarded as being of somewhat lower status than a shipped bill; because there is no guarantee that the goods have actually been shipped it is not usually acceptable in connection with letters of credit.
2. It is *prima facie* evidence of the contract of affreightment, ie although it is not itself the contract which is made when space is booked or the goods are accepted for shipment, it usually contains the terms and conditions of that contract.
3. It is a document of title, transferable by endorsement, ie it is good, though not indisputable, proof of ownership of the goods and that ownership can be transferred to another party by a simple endorsement of the bill of lading, eg:

   Please deliver to: J Brown & Co Ltd

   Signed: S Jones

   For: Arthur Smith & Co Ltd.

This simple act is sufficient to transfer the ownership of goods worth thousands of pounds, without the need for any other formality.

Bills of lading are issued by the shipping company, although they are usually prepared by the shipper. When the goods have been shipped (or received for shipment) the details of the bill of lading are checked against the tally made at the time of shipment or receipt and, if correct, a number of "original" copies, usually three, are signed by the master or his agent. Once one of these signed copies has been endorsed to the effect that no further charges are due, it becomes a "released" bill of lading and the document of title against which the shipping company will deliver the goods on arrival at the destination port.

House or Groupage Bill

This is not a true bill of lading because it is not issued by a shipping company but by a freight forwarder (shipping and forwarding agent), eg when a freight forwarder organises a groupage service, only one bill of lading is issued by the shipping company in respect of the container, etc which may contain consignments from several shippers. The freight forwarder receives the bill of lading and, in turn, issues "house" bills to the individual shippers. These do not have the legal status of bills of lading and might more properly be called Certificates of Shipment. However, despite its misnomer, the term "house bill" has become so well established that there is little chance of its use being discontinued.

Invoice

This is a document listing goods sent to a purchaser with their price and charges. In international trade much more information is likely to be included on the invoice, viz:

the terms of sale, packing specifications; the vessel on which the goods are shipped; import and export licences where applicable.

Consular invoice — Some countries require special invoices to be used. These are frequently made out on a prescribed form, often in the language of the country for which the goods are destined and must be "legalised" (approved) by the consulate of the country concerned.

Certificate of Insurance
According to the terms under which goods are sold for export, exporters may be responsible for ensuring that goods are adequately covered by insurance. A certificate of insurance is sent with the bills of lading to the buyer or his agent as proof that insurance cover has been arranged.

ECGD certificate
One of the risks that an exporter faces is non-payment for his goods. This is where the Export Credit Guarantee Department, a Government department, becomes involved. To encourage exporters the ECGD assists them in two ways.
1. It insures them against the risk of non-payment either because the buyer has defaulted or for some other reason, eg the collapse of a country's economy or seizure of power by an opposition group.
2. By guaranteeing repayment to banks it encourages them to offer credit to exporters at favourable rates.

There are many types of ECGD policy, but they can be divided into two main groups:
(a) comprehensive short term policies — these cover short term trade of a repetitive nature relating to standard types of goods
(b) specific policies — these relate to non-repetitive trade such as civil engineering projects where risks are spread over a number of years and where the exporter needs to secure long term credit.

The ECGD certificate is proof to interested parties, eg banks and finance houses, that the Department will act as guarantor for any loans offered.

Customs entry forms
Almost every country in the world exercises some form of control through its Customs Authority over goods entering or leaving its territory. In order to obtain clearance through Customs, information concerning the goods must be submitted to them (entered) on the appropriate customs entry forms, usually known simply as "entries".

Entries must be submitted even when there is no duty payable because, in addition to their use in the revenue collecting process, entries yield statistical information vital to governments.

What is meant by the SITPRO system of aligned documents?
An unfortunate but unavoidable feature of international trade is the large amount of paperwork involved. On examination it becomes obvious that a great deal of the information contained in individual documents is the same as that contained in the others. This means that a lot of time is spent in typing or writing the same information on numerous documents, each of which has a separate purpose. Frequently the information required on one document is copied from that contained in another, giving rise to the possibility of error or omission.

SITPRO (Simplification of International Trade Procedures Board), an organisation funded by the Department of Trade, has created a system of aligned documentation to overcome these problems.

In aligned documentation, a standardised system of forms is used, so that the same information, eg sender's name and address, description of goods, weight, value, etc appears in the same "box" on each of the individual documents. This means that a complete set of documents can be produced from one typing or, where a large number of documents is involved, can be run off from one master copy. Where master copies are used, there is no limit to the number of documents or copies that can be produced and each is as clear as the original.

Where certain information is not required on a particular document or where it is considered advisable that it should not be shown, eg the value of the goods, a system of masking enables this information to be excluded.

Fiscal Charges

What is the purpose of the International Convention on the Taxation of Road Vehicles 1956?
Under the provisions of the Convention, vehicles of States party to the Convention are exempt from excise duties when travelling to, or in transit through, each other's territory.

Which countries are party to the convention?
Austria, Belgium, Bulgaria, Czechoslovakia, Denmark, Finland, France, West Germany, Hungary, Republic of Ireland, Luxembourg, Netherlands, Norway, Poland, Portugal, Romania, Sweden, Switzerland, Turkey, Yugoslavia.

Are British vehicles exempt from vehicle tax in any other countries?
British vehicles are exempt from vehicle tax in a number of other countries either because the country does not levy vehicle taxes on foreign vehicles, or as a result of bi-lateral agreements between those countries and the United Kingdom.

Is it necessary to display vehicle excise tax discs abroad?
Tax discs are proof that the vehicle tax has been paid in the home country. Failure to display them can result in the imposition of vehicle tax and fines in foreign countries.

In which countries are additional time, mileage and/or tonnage taxes levied?
Additional taxes are levied as follows:

Austria — tonne/kilometre tax charged on maximum permissible pay load on loaded or partly loaded vehicles but not on empty ones
Finland — only where vehicles remain for more than one year
Hungary — British vehicles are exempt from taxes unless they exceed the following weights:
(a) single axle load of more than 10 tonnes
(b) double axle load of more than 16 tonnes (ie vehicles with axles 2m or less apart)
Norway — a kilometre tax is payable

Romania — a weight tax is payable on vehicles operating in excess of 38 tonnes
Sweden — a tonne/kilometre tax is payable on all diesel-engined goods vehicles
Switzerland — road tax on vehicles based upon a percentage of the annual rate
Turkey — road charges based on weight and distance travelled; excess charges are levied on vehicles exceeding Turkish maximum weights or dimensions. These charges are applicable when in transit through the country
Yugoslavia — a tax based on gross weight is levied on vehicles in transit through the country.

Which countries impose surcharges on fuel in vehicle tanks carried across their borders?
Tax is charged on fuel carried in excess of the following duty-free allowances:
- Austria — 200 litres
- Finland — 400 litres
- France — 300 litres
- W. Germany — 200 litres
- Norway — 200 litres.

Are there any other fuel restrictions?
In Bulgaria, Czechoslovakia, Hungary and the USSR fuel can only be obtained by either coupons or vouchers purchased at the respective borders.

CHAPTER 15
(Module D)
Business and Financial Management of the Undertaking Consignment Notes and Carrier's Liability

What is the purpose of the CMR Convention?
This Convention governs the *contracts* between carriers engaged in the international carriage of goods by road and their customers. It does not seek to interfere with the rates for the job but to regulate the conditions under which the contract is carried out in order to ensure uniformity of law between all countries which are parties to the Convention.

Does this mean that conditions in private contracts are void?
Insofar as they conflict with the provisions of the Convention, they are void and the Convention applies. Where they do not conflict they are perfectly valid.

How does the Convention regulate and ensure uniformity?
It defines *inter alia*:
- (a) the rights and duties of the carrier, consignor and consignee
- (b) time limits for claims and actions
- (c) the carrier's defences against claims
- (d) the limits of liability.

It requires the issue of consignment notes and specifies the information that must be shown therein.

How is an international journey by road defined in the Convention?
It states that "this Convention shall apply to every contract for the carriage of goods by road for reward when the place of taking over the goods and the place designated for delivery, as specified in the contract, are situated in two different countries of which at least one is a contracting country — irrespective of the place of residence and nationality of the parties", ie it applies to any international carriage by road which starts or finishes in the United Kingdom irrespective of which country the load is going to or coming from.

NB Journeys between the United Kingdom and the Republic of Ireland are specifically excluded.

What vehicles does it cover?
For the purpose of the Convention "vehicle" means motor vehicles, articulated vehicles, trailers and semi-trailers as defined in Article 4 of the Convention on Road Traffic dated September 19, 1949.

Does this mean that a British haulier running loaded trailers to and from a port in this country is engaged in international road carriage, even though his tractor never leaves this country?
Most definitely! Provided that the loaded trailers are destined for (or have come from) another country and have remained loaded throughout the journey, he is engaged in one leg of an international carriage.

Does the Convention have the force of law in this country?
It was incorporated into British law by the Carriage of Goods by Road Act 1965.

Is it an offence against United Kingdom law not to comply with the provisions of the Convention?
Failing to comply, eg by not completing the required consignment notes, does not constitute an offence in this country, but in any claim for damages the claim and any subsequent court action would be governed by the provisions of the Convention even if one or both of the parties were unaware of its existence.

In some Continental countries the use of CMR consignment notes is obligatory and operators could find themselves in difficulties if they are not available.

What is the position if part of the journey is by sea, rail, inland waterway or air?
The Convention applies to the whole of the journey except:
- (a) in cases of loss or damage, where that loss or damage could only have resulted from the use of that other mode of transport, eg damage by salt water during carriage by sea, when carried on deck
- (b) when it becomes impossible to carry out the contract in the manner designated and another mode of transport has to be used, in which case special rules apply under Articles 12 and 14 of the Convention.

Are any types of goods exempt from the provisions of the Convention?
It does not apply to:
- (a) carriage performed under the terms of any international postal convention
- (b) funeral consignments
- (c) furniture removals (this presumably means household effects, not trade furniture).

What are the requirements relating to consignment notes?
Article 5 states that the consignment note must be made out in triplicate and signed by the carrier and sender as follows:

First copy — for the sender
Second copy — for the consignee
Third copy — for the carrier.

Are there official forms which must be used?
The Convention does not specify any particular forms and presumably any form which complies with the requirements would be acceptable. However, the International Road Transport Union (IRU) has prepared a CMR consignment note which is widely used and readily recognised in member countries. For convenience, ease of completion and to avoid possible queries by officials, it is recommended that this form (or one which follows it very closely) should be used.

Where can copies of the form be obtained?
In this country they can be obtained from either the Freight Transport Association or the Road Haulage Association.

They are made up in sets of four with coloured lines on a white background for ease in identification:

First copy (for sender) . . . . Red
Second copy (for consignee) . . . . Blue
Third copy (for carrier) . . . . Green
Fourth copy (for file). . . . . Black

What information must be shown on the consignment notes?
The information which *must* be given is:
 (a) the date of the consignment note and the place at which it is made out
 (b) the name and address of the sender
 (c) the name and address of the carrier
 (d) the place and date of taking over the goods and the place designated for delivery
 (e) the name and address of the consignee
 (f) the description in common use of the nature of the goods and the method of packing and, in the case of dangerous goods, their generally recognised description
 (g) the number of packages and their special marks and numbers
 (h) the gross weight of the goods or their quantity otherwise expressed
 (i) charges relating to the carriage (carriage charges, supplementary charges incurred from the making of the contract to the time of delivery)
 (j) the requisite instructions for Customs and other formalities
 (k) a statement that the carriage is subject, notwithstanding any clause to the contrary, to the provisions of the Convention.

NB If the statement in (k) is omitted, the carrier will be liable for any additional expense to the consignor caused by this omission — but where IRU standard forms are used, this is incorporated in the printing.

In addition to the information specified in (a)–(k) above, the following information must be included if relevant:
 (a) a statement that transhipment is not allowed
 (b) the charges which the sender undertakes to pay
 (c) the amount of "cash on delivery" charges
 (d) a declaration of the value of the goods and the amount representing special interest in delivery
 (e) the sender's instructions to the carrier regarding insurance of the goods
 (f) the agreed time limit within which the carriage is to be carried out
 (g) a list of the documents handed to the carrier.

Any other information which may be useful to the carrier, consignor or consignee may be entered on the consignment note.

What is meant by "special interest in delivery"?
Sometimes goods which in themselves have little value, may give rise to considerable losses if they are lost, damaged or delayed, eg a spare part for a broken-down machine — if this does not arrive safely it may result in losses of perhaps hundreds of pounds per day until it is safely installed. A consignor or consignee may have a special interest in its safe arrival. A sum may be agreed between the consignor and the carrier, above the carrier's maximum liability, as the amount which will be claimed if the goods do not arrive safely. If the carrier agrees to accept this higher liability, he will be entitled to charge a higher rate for accepting the risk, ie a form of insurance premium. If he is not prepared to accept the risk, the consignor must seek insurance cover elsewhere.

What is the carrier's liability for loss or damage?
The carrier's liability for loss or damage is limited to 8.33 units of account per kg of gross weight short and "in addition, the carriage charges, Customs duties and other

charges incurred in respect of the carriage of goods, shall be refunded in full in case of total loss and in proportion to the loss sustained in case of partial loss ...".

NB The Carriage by Air and Road Act 1979, s.4, amended paragraph 3 of Article 23 of the CMR by replacing the gold franc with Special Drawing Rights and this change came about in the United Kingdom on December 28, 1980. However, it should be borne in mind that not all countries who are signatories to the CMR have replaced the gold franc with SDRs.

What are "Special Drawing Rights" and how is conversion into a national currency made?

Special Drawing Rights are as defined by the International Monetary Fund and converted into the national currency of the State of the Court seised of the case on the basis of the value of the currency on the date of the judgement or the date agreed upon by the parties.

How are SDRs converted into Sterling?

It is necessary to refer to the financial press daily to ascertain the rate of SDRs to Sterling for that particular day and the basis of conversion is as follows:

eg on January 5, 1990 (Financial Times) 1 SDR = £1.23816

therefore, 8.33 x £1.23816 = £10.3138 per kg

or £10,313.80 per tonne (1000kg)

Is there any special significance in the phrase "in addition, the carriage charges, Customs duties and other charges incurred, etc"?

In the case of *James Buchanan & Co Ltd v Babco Forwarding 1976*, a lorry load of whisky bound for Teheran was stolen in England, the carrier admitting liability. The value of the whisky was £7000 before duty, but the exporter was required to pay the duty of £30,000 under the provisions of the Customs & Excise Act 1952, because the goods had not been exported. The carrier agreed liability for the £7000 but disputed liability for the £30,000 duty. The decision of the Court of Appeal, subsequently confirmed by the House of Lords, was that the carrier was liable for the £30,000 under Article 23(4) of the Convention.

The significance of this decision as far as the carrier is concerned is that when carrying dutiable goods, he must ensure that his CMR insurance is adequate to cover any duty that might be incurred if his load is stolen due to his (or his servant's) negligence.

Can the carrier exempt himself from this liability by a clause in his conditions?

No! Any condition inserted with a view to exempting or lessening liability beyond what is allowed under the Convention is void and would be disregarded by a court.

Can a carrier agree to accept a higher liability than that set by the Convention?

The Convention provides for a higher value or a "special interest in delivery" to be *agreed* between the sender and the carrier and inserted in the consignment note. The carrier is entitled to make an extra charge if he accepts this greater liability. He should, of course, notify his insurer and obtain cover for the additional amount.

In the event of a dispute as to the value of goods how is this determined?

First of all, the value of the goods may be different at the start and finish of the carriage, so the Convention states that the value "shall be calculated by reference to the value of the goods at the place and time at which they were accepted for carriage".

The Convention goes on to say that "the value of the goods shall be fixed according to the commodity exchange price or if there is no such price, according to the current market price, or if there is no commodity exchange price or current market price, by reference to the normal value of goods of the same kind and quality".

In what circumstances can a carrier avoid liability, ie what are his defences against a claim for damages?

A carrier is liable for the total or partial loss of goods or damage to them from the time he takes over the goods until the time of delivery and for delay to the goods unless the damage or delay was caused by:

(a) the wrongful act or neglect of the claimant
(b) the instructions of the claimant given otherwise than as the result of a wrongful act or neglect of the carrier
(c) inherent vice of the goods
(d) through circumstances which the carrier could not avoid and the consequences of which he was unable to prevent.

In addition, the carrier is relieved of liability if the loss or damage arose from one of the following special risks:

(a) use of open unsheeted vehicles when their use has been expressly agreed and specified in the consignment note
(b) the lack of, or defective condition of, packing in the case of goods which, by their nature, are liable to wastage or to be damaged when not packed or not properly packed
(c) handling, loading, stowage or unloading of the goods by the sender, the consignee or persons acting on behalf of the sender or the consignee
(d) the nature of certain kinds of goods which particularly expose them to total or partial loss or to damage, especially through breakage, rust, decay, desiccation, leakage, normal wastage, or the action of moth or vermin
(e) insufficiency or inadequacy of marks or numbers on the packages
(f) the carriage of livestock.

How is delay defined?

Delay in delivery is said to occur when the carrier fails to deliver the goods within the agreed time limit or, when no time limit has been agreed, within a reasonable time.

What is the extent of the carrier's liability for delay?

His liability is limited to a sum not exceeding the carriage charges unless, of course, a sum to represent "special interest in delivery" has been agreed and additional charges paid.

What happens if the goods fail to arrive?

If the goods have not been delivered within 30 days of the agreed time limit or, if no time was agreed, within 60 days from the time the carrier took over the goods, the person entitled to claim can treat them as lost and claim accordingly.

Where more than one carrier is involved in the carriage who is liable if there is a claim for damage?
When the carriage involves successive carriers, the carrier who was carrying the goods at the time the loss or damage occurred is liable. If it is not possible to determine which carrier was responsible for the loss or damage then all carriers share the liability, *pro rata* to their shares of the carriage charges.

How is the liability shared?
Each carrier is liable in proportion to the share of the payment for carriage which is due to him, unless they have agreed a different apportionment.

What happens if one of the carriers is unable to pay, ie he is insolvent?
The share due from him, or such part as is unpaid, must be divided among the remaining carriers in the same proportions as above.

Who is entitled to claim for damages?
This will be "the person entitled to dispose of the goods". Under the Convention and in line with the law prevailing in most European countries, the sender has the right to exercise control over the goods until the consignee is handed the second copy of the consignment note, unless other arrangements have been agreed between them and noted in the consignment note.

This means that either the sender or the consignee (or some other person who is the actual owner of the goods) may claim, depending upon the circumstances of each case.

Does the right to exercise control mean that the sender is entitled to change the instructions to the carrier after he has handed the goods to him, eg en route?
The sender (or other person entitled to dispose of the goods) can ask the carrier to: stop the goods in transit; change the place at which delivery is to take place; deliver the goods to a consignee other than the one indicated in the consignment note, etc at any time prior to delivery to the consignee but he must not divide up the consignment.

Against which carrier should a claim be made?
Claims may only be brought against the first carrier, the last carrier or the carrier who was performing the portion of the carriage during which the loss or damage occurred (if known). This last carrier is frequently referred to simply as the "performing carrier".

What is the time limit for claims?
The consignee is required to check the goods with the carrier and in the case of:
- (a) *apparent damage*, ie obvious from external appearance, etc, he must "make reservations", that is sign for them as damaged, short delivered, etc *at the time of checking* or notify the carrier the same day. If he fails to do this it will be *prima facie* evidence that the goods were received in good condition. In the case of:

(b) *damage not apparent* reservations in writing must be made to the carrier within seven days of checking (Sundays and public holidays excepted).

In the event of disputes what is the time limit for bringing an action?

Where a dispute cannot be settled and one or both of the parties decide to have the matter resolved in court, the action must commence within one year, or in cases of wilful misconduct, within three years.

Where can an action be brought?

In legal proceedings arising out of carriage under the Convention, the plaintiff may bring an action in any court or tribunal of a contracting country *designated by agreement* between the parties and, in addition, in the courts or tribunals of a country within whose territories:
- (a) the defendant is ordinarily resident, or has his principal place of business, or the branch or agency through which the contract of carriage was made
- (b) the place where the goods were taken over, or where the place designated for delivery is situated.

What duties does a consignor have?

The consignor has a duty to ensure that all necessary information is included in the consignment note and will be responsible for all expenses, loss and damage sustained by the carrier by reason of the inaccuracy or inadequacy of the information.

He will also be liable to the carrier for damage to persons, equipment or other goods and for any expenses due to defective packing, unless the defect was apparent or made known to the carrier at the time he took over the goods and the carrier made no reservations about it.

The sender is also responsible for attaching to the consignment note or handing to the carrier all documents necessary for Customs and other formalities.

Are there any special provisions for dangerous goods?

The sender has to inform the carrier of the exact nature of the danger when he hands dangerous goods to him and, if necessary, the precautions to be taken. If this information is not noted in the consignment note the sender must prove (if it becomes necessary) that the carrier knew of the exact danger by some other means.

If the carrier discovers that he is carrying dangerous goods which had not been declared, they may be unloaded, destroyed or rendered harmless by the carrier without compensation and the sender will be liable to the carrier for all expenses, loss or damage.

Are there any other general points the carrier should note?

Anything out of the ordinary, eg declaration of value, special arrangements between the consignor and consignee, reservation as to the condition of the goods, etc must be noted in the consignment note so that all the parties are aware of them.

In particular, on taking over goods from a consignor or from a preceding carrier, the carrier must give a receipt for goods and, where necessary, reservations as to the condition of the goods must be noted on the consignment note. Unless this is done the carrier may find himself liable for damage to goods that occurred prior to the goods coming into his possession, eg if the following carrier signs for goods "damaged" the preceding carrier may be held liable if he took them over already damaged but failed to record this on the consignment note.

Insurance Abroad

The aim of the EC Directive 72/166 is to ensure that the laws of Member States relating to insurance against civil liability in respect of the use of motor vehicles shall approximate with one another and that Member States will enforce the obligation to insure against such liability. This aim is directed towards the broader objective of liberalising the movement of persons and motor vehicles travelling between Member States.

Why is it necessary to have frontier controls of compulsory insurance cover against civil liability in respect of the use of motor vehicles?

This is to safeguard the interests of persons who may be victims of accidents caused by vehicles from other countries by ensuring that those vehicles have the required insurance cover.

Does British compulsory third party insurance meet the requirements of other EC countries?

Yes. Third party insurance covers liability for death, injury, emergency hospital treatment and third party property damage.

How does Directive 72/166 liberalise the movement of vehicles and people?

By abolishing the checks on Green Cards (international certificate of insurance) for vehicles normally based in one Member State entering the territory of another Member State. This arrangement has been extended to cover the aforementioned States with which the EC has concluded reciprocal arrangements.

How has this concession been made possible?

By means of an agreement between the national insurer's bureaux whereby each national bureau guarantees compensation in accordance with the provisions of national law in respect of any loss or injury giving entitlement to compensation caused in its territory by one of those vehicles, whether or not insured.

Who administers the agreement?

The Motor Insurers' Bureau in the United Kingdom acts as Secretariat for the scheme.

Does this mean that a Green Card is no longer necessary for travel abroad?

Although no longer necessary for frontier checks in the EC and other countries party to the Agreement, it is still advisable to carry the Green Card because it may be necessary as proof of insurance cover in case of accident.

How does the Green Card system work?
An international certificate of insurance (Green Card) is issued by insurers on behalf of a national bureau in accordance with Recommendation 5 adopted by the Sub-Committee of the Inland Transport Committee of the United Nations Economic Commission for Europe.

On application and on payment of an additional premium, insurers will extend policies for use on the Continent, including sea journeys of up to 65 hours' duration, and will issue a Green Card as proof of cover.

Does the Green Card cover both the vehicle and the trailer?
Yes! However, where a trailer is used, this should be specified separately on the Green Card.

Is a vehicle which is exempt from insurance in this country similarly exempt abroad?
It is an offence for a person to use, in a Member State or any of those countries mentioned above, a vehicle which, though exempted from insurance in this country, does not have a policy covering the risks required to be covered by the laws of the Member State or other country concerned. Vehicles exempt from insurance in this country include those whose owners have deposited cash or securities to the value of £15,000 with the Supreme Court.

Is any additional insurance required?
Third party insurance does not, of course, provide protection against damage to the carrier's own vehicle, nor is the owner covered if it is stolen and additional cover should be obtained either by extending the third party insurance to cover fire and theft or better still by means of a Comprehensive policy. Goods in transit insurance will also be necessary to cover loss or damage to the load carried.

Is goods in transit (GIT) insurance obligatory abroad?
It is in some countries but unless the carrier is prepared to risk having to meet very large claims himself then he should ensure that he has valid GIT cover. It is essential that the operator should arrange for this GIT cover to be extended to cover his liability when operating abroad.

What level of cover is needed?
Most operators in this country limit their liability in accordance with the RHA Conditions of Carriage, giving them a maximum liability of £800 per tonne on the gross weight of the goods carried. This is clearly inadequate for international operations. Remember that even if carrying to or from countries that are not parties to the CMR Convention, under the Carriage of Goods by Road Act 1965, the provisions of the Convention will still apply and that means a high maximum liability on a per tonne basis, *plus* "carriage charges, customs duties and other charges incurred in respect of the carriage of goods". In the *James Buchanan & Co Ltd* case it can be seen how much the additional charges can amount to so it is essential to ensure that the GIT policy covers such risks. Some GIT policies specifically exclude high risk loads such as spirits and tobacco so the haulier must be certain that his policy covers such loads, or that the insurer will extend the cover, before accepting loads of this sort.

What is a European Accident Statement?

This is a form signed by both drivers involved in an accident which constitutes an agreed statement of facts concerning the accident.

What happens to the forms after they have been signed?

Each driver sends his copy of the form to his insurance company with the accident report.

Customs Practice and Formalities

What are the sources of information on Customs Conventions and taxation and the documents required?

The principal Customs Conventions affecting the road haulier are:

(a) the Customs Conventions on the International Transport of Goods 1959 and 1975 (TIR)

(b) the International Customs Convention on the Temporary Importation of Road Vehicles 1956.

The tax convention on road vehicles is the International Convention on the Taxation of Road Vehicles engaged on International Journeys 1957.

Operators who require detailed information of these Conventions can obtain copies from HMSO. (Summaries of the Conventions which affect road hauliers and any important amendments to them are given in *Croner's Road Transport Operation*.)

Information concerning United Kingdom Customs and Excise requirements can be obtained from a booklet published by direction of the Commissioners of HM Customs and Excise, which gives a general survey of the Customs Law of the United Kingdom, obtainable from HMSO. Detailed information on specific subjects is contained in Public Notices which can be obtained from the Secretary, HM Customs and Excise, New Kings Beam House, 22 Upper Ground, London SE1 9PJ or from any office of HM Customs and Excise.

Information concerning the Customs requirements of other countries, changes in tariffs, etc can be obtained from the Department of Trade and Industry.

Why are Customs entries required for exports, since no duty is payable?

Although goods for export are not subject to Customs duties, nevertheless it is necessary, for various reasons, for some form of official control to be exercised over them and for details of the goods to be recorded. Information is collected by HM Customs for statistical purposes and they must also ensure that any necessary licences have been obtained and that prohibited goods do not leave the country, etc.

Consequently under the provision of the Customs and Excise Management Act 1979, European Community legislation, and the Finance Act 1981, exporters are responsible for ensuring that, unless excepted, a statistical declaration or entry is made to Customs and Excise for all goods being exported.

Which goods are exempted from entry requirements?
Entries are not required for the following: postal exports unless under outward processing authorisation or from a bonded warehouse; ships stores for consumption on voyage; personal, professional or household effects on temporary exportation in baggage; touring vehicles temporarily exported; unexamined through baggage exported as cargo; road and rail vehicles and freight containers used for the carriage of goods; certain goods on through air waybills; diplomatic mail; free of charge commercial samples exported in baggage, samples, etc, under ATA Carnet; temporarily imported aircraft spares re-exported by registered operators; goods in transit or transhipment goods.

What is the procedure for export declaration and clearance?
There are five main procedures:
1. Pre-entry
2. Simplified Clearance Procedure (SCP)
3. Local Export Control (LEC)
4. Period Entry (Exports) Scheme (PE(E)).
5. Low Value Procedure.

What is pre-entry and when is it necessary?
Pre-entry is the completion and presentation of an export declaration to Customs and Excise prior to clearance of the goods for shipment and is the basis of official export documentation. For certain goods pre-entry is mandatory and the appropriate official form must be fully completed.

Which goods are required to be pre-entered?
Pre-entry is required for goods exported from a bonded warehouse, goods in transit, other dutiable goods, goods for which export licences are required, eg arms, drugs, antiques, etc.

Can pre-entry be used for goods other than those on the mandatory list?
Other goods can be entered on a **voluntary** pre-entry basis, in which case the pre-entry code will be inserted on the SAD (see page 194). If they are not known at the time, the following details may be omitted from the entry: date of sailing/flight; ship's name/flight no; dock/wharf/station; port/airport of export; flag code; port code. In such cases Customs and Excise will complete the document as part of the official procedure.

At the time the goods are sent forward, the pre-entry, together with the appropriate commercial document, such as the National Standard Shipping Note (NSSN) for seafreight, the Air Waybill for airfreight, or CMR consignment note for road freight, will be sent with the goods to the loader — usually the shipping line or airline — who will present the goods and pre-entry to Customs for acceptance and authorisation to export (cleared to load).

NB With pre-entry, registration with Customs is **not** required, records do **not** have to be maintained and there are no post-shipment requirements.

When is the Simplified Clearance Procedure (SCP) used?
The SCP is an alternative to pre-entry, except where mandatory pre-entry applies and involves the completion and presentation of an approved commercial transport

document, eg a National Standard Shipping Note etc, or a partially completed SAD, or a form C271 as a pre-shipment advice.

After shipment, an export declaration giving full details must be submitted to HM Customs within 14 days by the exporter or agent whose CRN appears on the pre-shipment advice using SADs (Single Administrative Documents — see page 194), paper schedules or magnetic tapes to Customs headquarters at Southend or by direct input to DEPS (Departmental Entry Processing System).

What is CRN?

This stands for Customs Registered Number. Before an exporter or agent can use the SCP system, he must first apply to HM Customs for registration and allocation of a CRN.

The pre-shipment advice and the subsequent export declaration must both show the reference number of the particular consignment, known as the Export Consignment Identifier (ECI) and consists of the CRN (a five digit number) followed by the commercial reference (which must not exceed nine characters) and must identify the consignment absolutely.

At the time the goods are sent forward to the loader they must be accompanied by the pre-shipment advice which must have the ECI in the appropriate box, and the loader will present the goods to Customs for acceptance and authorisation to export.

How does Local Export Control (LEC) operate?

This is a procedure which provides for clearance of goods at an exporter's premises. To operate this procedure exporters must obtain HM Customs approval. Before this approval is given, certain conditions, including a prescribed volume of traffic, must be met.

Traders using the scheme authenticate their own SADs for Community Transit purposes. Customs control is exercised from the local customs office and is based mainly on a periodic verification of the company's records supplemented by occasional visits during packing for export. Application to use the facility must be made to the local customs officer.

What is the Period Entry (Exports) Scheme PE(E)?

This is a scheme for authorised exporters who use computers for stock control and accounting purposes and regularly export large quantities of goods. The scheme allows users to submit periodic schedules to Customs on computer-produced media giving details of goods exported.

What is the procedure for low value goods?

Provided the goods are not required to be pre-entered there are simplified procedures for:
— low value goods which are exported in a single consignment and have a total value of less than £475 and a total net weight of not more than 1000kg.
— goods of no statistical interest (Non-Stat) which are listed in Customs Notice 275 Appendix C.

These goods can be declared for export purposes by using a commercial document or a SAD completed as a pre-shipment advice but with the ECI (Export Consignment Identifier) replaced either by the statement "LV" followed by the value in pounds sterling or Non-Stat as appropriate.

There are a number of other procedures for specialised uses which it is not relevant to mention here.

(Readers seeking more detailed information on export entry procedure or export procedure generally, are advised to consult *Croner's Reference Book for Exporters.*)

The Single Administrative Document (SAD)

Goods moving between the UK and another EC country are normally the subject of three customs declarations, one each for export, transit and import purposes. Until January 1988 Community Transit (CT) documents were standard throughout the EC but import and export forms varied in each Member State, even though the information declared on them was similar.

The need to simplify documentation, facilitate trade and for the computerised communication of customs data within and between commerce and Government in the EC, resulted in the development of a Single Administrative Document (SAD) which took advantage of those similarities of information requirement throughout the EC and is used as an export, transit and import declaration for any consignment moving within the Community.

To cater for situations in which the use of a SAD to perform all three of its intended functions for a particular transaction is not, for whatever reason, practical, it is possible to use separate copies of the form for the individual functions (export, transit or import) of the document or any combination of them. These separate copies are called split-use sets.

How many copies are there of the form and what are their functions?

The SAD set consists of eight copies. The function of each copy is as follows:

Copy 1 (Copy for the country of dispatch/export) remains at the office of departure for the purposes of control and may also be used for other export control purposes.

Copy 2 (Statistical copy — country of dispatch/export) is the copy of the export declaration for statistical purposes.

Copy 3 (Copy for the consignor/exporter) is the exporter's or agent's copy or may be retained by the Community Transit principal.

Copy 4 (Copy for the office of destination) is for Customs in the Member State to act as evidence that the goods are (or are not) in free circulation (ie to indicate whether Customs duty is payable).

Copy 5 (Copy for return-CT) is returned from the office of destination to Customs in the Member State of destination to provide evidence that the goods reached their destination intact.

Copy 6 (Copy for the country of destination) is used in the Member State of destination as the customs import declaration on arrival.

Copy 7 (Statistical copy — country of destination) is the copy of the import declaration for statistical purposes in the Member State of destination.

Copy 8 (Copy for consignee) is for retention by the importer or his agent and in the UK, will serve as the VAT copy for goods cleared at locations which are not served by the Customs computerised entry processing system (DEPS).

Copies 1-3 therefore, remain in the Member State of despatch, whilst copies 4-8 travel forward with the goods.

The copies for statistical use are edged in green at the right-hand margin to facilitate recognition. Certain boxes are also shaded in green to indicate that they are used for CT.

Each set is printed on self-copying paper. However, because some items can change while the goods are en-route the set is treated so that those items do not copy through.

On arrival any missing information must be added before the document is signed by the importer or his authorised agent and presented to Customs.

It is important to understand that signing the form at this stage commits the signatory to all the information declared on it, including that which was entered at export.

Must the importer (or his agent) use the SAD prepared by the exporter as the import declaration?

No. Because most of the SADs completed in other European countries are not in English, it is difficult to verify the accuracy of the information and most importers submit their own split-use set for the import declaration.

What is the legal effect of lodging a SAD with Customs?

Article 8(a) of EC Regulation 678/85 provides that:

"The lodging with a customs office of a declaration signed by the declarant or his representative shall indicate that the person concerned is declaring the goods in question for the procedure applied for and, without prejudice to the possible application of penal provisions, shall be equivalent to the engagement of responsibility under the provisions in force in Member States, in respect of:
— the accuracy of the information given in the declaration,
— the authenticity of the documents attached, and
— the observance of all the obligations inherent in the entry of the goods in question under the procedure concerned."

This means that, although there is no pre-printed declaration on the form as to the accuracy of the information it contains, the fact that the SAD has been submitted is of itself a legal declaration to that effect.

Customs Entry and Clearance of Imports

Unless a haulier intends to offer a regular entry preparation and clearance service to his customers and employ specialised staff for this purpose, he should avoid taking on this responsibility because of the pitfalls awaiting anyone without the necessary knowledge and expertise. Instead, where a customer requires these services, the haulier should employ a freight forwarder or recommend one to his customer. Nevertheless if the haulier has an understanding of the basic documents and procedures, he may be able to avoid frustrating delays and possibly lost journeys by detecting obvious errors and omissions. But remember that under the CMR Convention it is the sender's responsibility to ensure that the carrier has all the necessary documentation.

What documents are required for the clearance of imports through Customs?

The following is a selection of documents that may be required:

(a) Customs entry form — there were, until a few years ago, a large number of forms each having a specific use depending upon the class of goods and the circumstances of the importation but these separate forms have been replaced by the Single Administrative Document, which also incorporates the requirements of the Community Transit System.

(b) the original invoice and a copy for Customs, plus an extra copy if VAT is payable
(c) packing lists if the invoice does not show the contents of the packages
(d) an import licence, if necessary
(e) a Certificate of Origin for certain classes of goods entitled to preferential treatment
(f) a form C105 A or B for goods liable for *ad valorem* duty and valued at over £1000 and for certain goods liable for VAT and deliverable to non-registered customers
(g) EC "T" forms, where applicable.

How is "clearance" obtained?

The SAD and supporting documents must be presented to the Customs Officer at the point of entry (or ICD). At computerised locations data may be fed into the Customs computerised Departmental Entry Processing System (DEPS). The input of data by traders is known as Direct Trader Input (DTI). The officer checks the correctness of the documents and the rate of duty paid, etc and at his discretion may require the packages containing the imported goods to be opened so that he can check the contents against the information given.

What is the Community Transit System?

The Community transit system is an EC customs procedure which controls and facilitates the movement of goods from one part of the Community to another.

What is its purpose?

It serves three purposes:
(a) it indicates the Community status of the goods
(b) it establishes control over the movement of goods which are subject to special controls regarding end use, destination or exportation
(c) it acts as a through transit scheme to enable goods to cross frontiers without being inspected and delayed at Customs posts.

How does the status of goods differ?

There are three categories of goods in circulation in the EC: goods which have been "wholly produced" within the EC (mainly agricultural and mineral); and goods that have been manufactured from materials wholly produced in the EC which are classed as being in *free circulation*. Also included in the latter category are goods which have been imported into the EC and which have paid all Customs duties, charges and levies (eg CAP) and are therefore entitled to move anywhere within the Community without payment of additional duties at frontiers.

Goods that are *not in free circulation* are those that come from countries outside the Community and are therefore liable to full Customs duties and charges when crossing frontiers into the EC countries. The third category applies to goods which are in free circulation in Spain (ES) and Portugal (PT) and which are therefore eligible for the appropriate transitional rate of duty when imported into other Member States.

How are these differences in status indicated?
The following codes are used to indicate status:
T1 — Applies to goods which are not in free circulation.
T2 — Applies to goods which are in free circulation.
T2ES and T2PT — Apply to goods which are in free circulation in Spain and Portugal respectively.

What is an EUR1?
An EUR1 is a form which indicates that goods are of EC or EFTA origin and qualify for preferential rates of duty.

How does the CT procedure work?
The full Community Transit procedure applies when goods have to pass through one of more Member States en route to another Member State. The SAD acts as the transit document, in particular copies 4 and 5 (see page 194). Copy 4 is for Customs in the state of destination. Copy 5 is returned from the office of destination to Customs in the Member State of despatch to provide evidence that the goods reached their destination intact. The insertion of one of the codes above in Box 1 of the form, indicates the status of the goods.

How is control exercised over the goods during transit?
Under the CT procedure each Member State has designated customs offices at which movements under the full CT procedure begin and end. These offices are called "offices of departure" and "offices of destination" respectively. Offices through which goods may enter a country in the course of a movement within the Community are called "offices of transit". Copies of the SAD will need to be produced to Customs at the various offices together with transit advice notes (TANs).

Is there any difference if goods only pass across one frontier, ie directly from one Community State to another?
In this case, or if goods pass from one Community State, to a non-Community State, and then to a second Community State (and the TIR procedure is being used) then the full CT procedure does not apply.

Prior to the introduction of SAD, Movement Certificates were used in these circumstances. Now the procedure is called the T2L procedure, the codes used being:
T2L for goods in free circulation
T2LES for goods eligible for Spanish transitional rates of duty
T2LPT for goods eligible for Portuguese transitional rates of duty.

How are the T forms numbered?
When the United Kingdom first entered the EC there were three forms but on acquiring full status these were reduced to two, the T1 and T2. A further development has been to produce one form which will serve as either T1 or T2 in the appropriate "box".

T1 — indicates that the goods are not in free circulation and will be liable to full Customs duties and charges when crossing frontiers.

T2 — indicates that the goods are in free circulation in the Member States of the EC and are therefore not liable to duty when crossing frontiers.

Is there a time limit for full community transit movement?
Yes! It is laid down by the office of departure and is normally 14 days.

What are Community guarantee vouchers?
These relieve companies from having to produce individual guarantees or deposits to cover possible customs claims when moving goods through Member States under the full CT procedure. They are valid in all Member States and Austria and Switzerland (who are also parties to the Community Transit system) and are available from authorised guarantors.

Who are authorised guarantors in the United Kingdom?
The Freight Transport Association, the Road Haulage Association, and the Prudential Assurance Co Ltd.

What is the purpose of a Community Carnet?
When goods are exported for temporary use in another Member State and are then to be returned to the United Kingdom the SAD can be replaced by a Community Carnet. There are restrictions on the goods Carnets can cover and the people who can use them. Carnets are obtainable from offices of HM Customs and Excise.

Are there any other carnets that an operator may require?
Most European countries permit the temporary importation of foreign goods vehicles free of duty and deposit and without guaranteed Customs documentation. In some countries, however, a Carnet de Passage en Douane is required.

Which countries require a Carnet de Passage en Douane?
A Carnet is required for each commercial vehicle or trailer entering: Iran, Iraq, Jordan, Kuwait, Lebanon, Saudi Arabia, Syria, Turkey and other Middle East countries.

France requires Carnets for unaccompanied trailers and unregistered trailers, eg semi-trailers and drawbar trailers but this does not apply to "plated" trailers.

Greece requires Carnets for vehicles staying more than 10 days.

Italy requires Carnets for vehicles remaining for more than three months.

Portugal requires Carnets for vehicles remaining for more than one month.

What facility is obtained by the possession of a Carnet de Passage en Douane?
It authorises the movement of the vehicles to and from the country or countries specified in the application.

Who issues these Carnets?
The Carnet de Passage en Douane is issued in the United Kingdom by the Automobile Association or the Royal Automobile Club.

How long does the Carnet last?
Under the general acceptance of the FIA the Carnet lasts for one year but as requirements vary in certain countries, the uninterrupted period for each country in one year is six months after which users should apply (to the Customs of the countries where vehicles intend to operate) for permission to use the Carnet for the remaining six months.

What type of Carnet allows temporary importation of goods?
Many countries permit the temporary importation of certain specified goods under cover of an ATA Carnet (Carnet de Passage en Douane pour l'Admission Temporaire).

What type of goods are permitted under the ATA Carnet?
1. Samples
2. Professional equipment
3. Goods for exhibitions and fairs

Must the goods be accompanied?
No! The Carnet can be used both with accompanied and unaccompanied goods.

Which countries accept the ATA Carnet?
It is accepted in the following countries:
Austria, Belgium, Bulgaria, Cyprus, Czechoslovakia, Denmark, Finland, France, W. Germany, Gibraltar, Greece, Hungary, Iran, Irish Republic, Israel, Italy, Luxembourg, Netherlands, Norway, Poland, Portugal, Spain, Sweden, Switzerland, Turkey, United Kingdom, Yugoslavia.

Who issues ATA Carnets?
They are available from major Chambers of Commerce.

What is the validity of Carnets?
They are valid for 12 months from the date of issue.

TIR Convention

What is the purpose of the TIR Convention?
The Convention (Transports Internationale Routiers) is designed to facilitate the international movement of goods by road transport and to simplify Customs requirements where a journey involves crossing more than one frontier.

How is this achieved?
Prior to the operation of the Convention, vehicles and their loads were subject to examination at each frontier crossing on an international journey and security for duty had to be lodged even though the vehicle might only be in transit through a country. Under a TIR Carnet the complete journey can be undertaken free from Customs delays and inconveniences, subject to compliance with the conditions of the Convention.

What are the conditions which must be met?
1. The vehicle, trailer or container must satisfy the conditions of the Convention.
2. The vehicle, etc and its load, will have been examined and sealed at the Customs Office of departure.
3. The vehicle and load will be accompanied by a valid TIR Carnet.

What is the significance of the TIR Carnet?
The Carnet serves as a Bond for the goods carried on the vehicle and is guaranteed by the Trade Association by which it is issued. Any duty for which an operator

becomes liable will be paid by the guarantor (the Association) and recovered from the carrier concerned.

Who issues TIR Carnets in the United Kingdom?
They are issued and guaranteed by the Road Haulage Association and the Freight Transport Association.

Does the Carnet cover both outward and return journeys?
The Carnet is valid only for the outward load. If a return load has been arranged, then a separate Carnet must be obtained and should be taken on the outward journey.

How is the Carnet used?
At each stage of the journey, ie the Office of Departure, Transit Offices and Office of Destination, Customs will extract a voucher from the Carnet and stamp and sign the counterfoil, creating a complete record of the journey.

What is the validity of TIR Carnets?
The 14 volet Carnet is valid for two months and the 20 volet for three months. They must be returned in time to the issuing authority whether or not renewal of Carnet is required.

Which countries recognise the TIR Convention?

Afghanistan	Greece	Norway
Albania	Hungary	Poland
Austria	Iran	Portugal
Belgium	Ireland, Republic of	Romania
Bulgaria	Israel	Spain
Canada	Italy	Sweden
Cyprus	Japan	Switzerland
Czechoslovakia	Jordan	Tunisia
Denmark	Kuwait	Turkey
Finland	Luxembourg	United Kingdom
France	Malta	USA
East Germany	Morocco	USSR
West Germany	Netherlands	Yugoslavia

Are TIR Carnets valid for journeys from the United Kingdom to another EC country?
No! TIR Carnets are not valid for journeys to or within EC countries and the Community Transit System (T forms) must be used. But TIR Carnets are valid for crossing EC countries to or from non-EC countries.

How is TIR approval for vehicles and containers obtained?
Application for the vehicle to be inspected is made to the Clerk of the Licensing Authority for the area in which the vehicle is available for inspection, on form GV62, obtainable from the Department of Transport or any Area Traffic Offices.

Who is responsible for examining vehicles?
Department of Transport examiners carry out a detailed examination to ensure that

the vehicles meet the construction and equipment requirements of the Convention before issuing a Certificate of Approval.

Where is this examination conducted?

For existing vehicles the examination is carried out at the operator's premises. In the case of new vehicles, manufacturers are prepared to arrange for vehicles to be examined before delivery to the customer, if the customer requests this.

Containers are granted Certificates of Approval in a similar manner. These containers will also need to meet the requirements of the International Container Convention.

Where vehicles and containers are manufactured to identical design specifications as part of a production series, type approval will be given on application by the manufacturer after inspection of an initial production unit. Individual certificates of approval for further units will be issued without further inspection, except for spot checks.

What is the validity of a Certificate of Approval?

The Certificate of Approval must be renewed every two years and must always be carried on the vehicle when it is operating under a TIR Carnet.

How is TIR approval indicated on the vehicle or container?

When a vehicle or container has been approved, it must display to the front and rear a plate showing the letters TIR in white on a blue background.

What are the technical conditions that must be met in order to obtain approval?

These are too detailed to be given in full here, but Article 1 of the Regulations states the general requirements:
1. Approval for the international transport of goods by road vehicle under Customs seal may be granted only for vehicles constructed and equipped in such a manner that:
   (a) Customs seals can be simply and effectively affixed thereto
   (b) no goods can be removed from or introduced into the sealed part of the vehicle without obvious damage to it or without breaking the seals
   (c) they contain no concealed spaces where goods may be hidden.
2. The vehicles shall be so constructed that all spaces in the form of compartments, receptacles or other recesses which are capable of holding goods, are readily accessible for Customs inspection.
3. Should any empty spaces be formed by the different layers of the sides, floor and roof of the vehicles, the inside surfaces shall be firmly fixed, solid and unbroken and incapable of being dismantled without leaving obvious traces.

Can TIR certificates be transferred when an "approved" vehicle is sold?

They are not transferable and the new owner must have the vehicle re-certified.

What is the AGR Convention

This is a convention which governs the system of numbering for road networks in Europe.

Financial Aspects of Operation

What are exchange rates?
Exchange rates are quite simply the rates at which we can exchange British currency (Sterling) for foreign currency, eg Francs, Marks, Kroner, etc. These rates are not constant, but fluctuate from day to day. When more of a particular currency is obtained per pound than in the recent past, the pound is said to be "strong" against that particular currency and if the reverse is the case then the pound is said to be "weak".

What effects do these fluctuations have on British operators engaged in international road haulage?
Generally speaking when the pound is strong the operator's costs go down and when it is weak they go up.

What examples of this effect are there?
Those which are most immediately noticeable are in respect of fuel and drivers' subsistence allowances. Although prices may not have altered in Continental countries if the pound is weak we will get less of a particular currency for each pound and therefore will have to pay more (in terms of pounds), eg for the same quantity of fuel. Similarly it will cost the driver more for food and accommodation. The same will apply to any goods or services that have to be paid for in foreign currencies.

Apart from costs, do fluctuating exchange rates present any other difficulties?
Fluctuations in exchange rates make it difficult to quote for jobs any distance in the future. A fall in the exchange rate could mean that increased costs may wipe out a large part of the operator's profit.

A weak pound then, is detrimental to the road haulage operator?
Sudden falls constitute the danger. When the exchange rate remains relatively stable, the operator will allow for the costs in his quotations. In one way a weak pound may benefit him. When other currencies are strong against the pound, British goods will be cheaper in foreign countries and foreigners will be anxious to buy British. This will mean a constant flow of goods to European countries and present the British operator with a regular demand for his services.

Apart from the extra costs due to adverse exchange rates, what other additional costs must be met by an operator involved in international haulage?
The list is quite extensive. The following are some of the common ones.
1. Cost of providing and preparing documentation required.
2. Cost of permits (when necessary).
3. Cost of sea crossing.
4. Higher goods in transit insurance premiums to cover CMR requirements.
5. Cost of obtaining foreign currency, ie bank commission.
6. Loss of interest on driver's float. Because the driver may be away for several weeks, he must be provided with a substantial sum to cover subsistence to purchase fuel and to meet eventualities. Where a number of drivers are

involved it can mean tying up thousands of pounds of capital that could otherwise be earning interest.
7. Circulation taxes, fuel taxes, ton/mileage taxes, motorway tolls, etc are charged in many European countries.
8. Spot fines can be incurred even by the most careful drivers. (Often drivers are of the opinion that they are unjustly imposed but have to pay them to avoid more costly delays.)
9. Lower vehicle and driver utilisation because in many countries HGVs are banned from the roads at weekends and public holidays.
10. "Palm-greasing" or, to give it its proper name, bribery. However much it is frowned upon in official quarters, it becomes almost unavoidable in many Middle East countries, unless the operator is prepared to face long delays.
11. Communications — because of the distance involved and the need for drivers to keep in touch, telephone and telex charges will be high.

This list is by no means complete but it does give a good indication of the much higher costs involved in international operations compared with operations of a purely domestic nature.

Systems and Services

The syllabus requires the candidate to be able to state the advantages and disadvantages of a number of systems and services. Whether a system offers advantages or suffers disadvantages depends to a large extent on the circumstances peculiar to the individual user. Many of the claimed advantages accrue to the exporter or importer and make little difference to the road haulier.

The following observations will not be universally accepted because so much depends upon individual circumstances and preferences and they result from a series of discussions with a number of users and operators. Readers must determine for themselves the extent to which the statements made are valid. They are put forward as a basis for further thought and discussion.

A. The use of freight forwarders

Advantages
1. Freight forwarders are experts in the preparation of customs entries and other documentation. Their services should be employed whenever the prospective user does not possess the necessary expertise.
2. Because of the wide range of services offered (see Chapter 10) they can relieve the customer of all worries concerning documentation, insurance, packing, transport, etc as required.

Disadvantages
1. Costs may be higher than if all arrangements are made by the importer or exporter himself.
2. The operation is no longer under the customer's control. He does not know to what extent costs or delays are unavoidable or, alternatively, due to failings on the part of the freight forwarder.

B. Unitisation

This expression is often used purely to cover the use of pallets, but more properly it should be used as a general term to cover all forms of unit loads, eg containers, pallets, Lancashire flats, etc.

Containers

Advantages
1. Less handling, therefore:
    (a) lower labour costs
    (b) less damage (lower insurance premiums).
2. Faster transit times.
3. Easily transferred from one mode of transport to another. Standardisation of container dimension has permitted standardisation of handling equipment.
4. Multiple height stacking possible, reducing storage space required.
5. Reduces pilferage.

Disadvantages
1. High cost of containers and container hire.
2. High cost of specialised handling equipment.
3. Weight of container reduces payload.
4. Although petty pilferage is reduced, hi-jacking is made easier.
5. Although there are fewer insurance claims, those that do arise are likely to be very heavy.
6. If containers are unevenly loaded, or weights incorrectly declared, the road haulage operator may unwittingly operate illegally.

Pallets

Advantages
1. Less handling than with individual packages, though more than required with containers.
2. Less damage, due to less frequent handling and protection afforded by pallet and strapping, but protection is not as great as that afforded by containers.
3. Easier stacking and better utilisation of height in warehouses, etc.
4. Pilferage more difficult and easily detected.

Disadvantages
1. May cause space loss on vehicles and in ships.
2. Short life of pallets — continuous replacement and repair expensive.
3. Problems with return of pallets (particularly in respect of overseas shipments) and pallet losses.

C. Groupage

Groupage means the consolidation or grouping together of a number of small consignments destined for separate consignees into one unit load for the major part of their journey. The groupage operator (often a road haulier) offers a regular service or services to specified destinations at fairly frequent intervals. He consolidates the individual consignments into a unit load and transports it to the common destination, where the load is broken down for local distribution of the individual consignments.

Advantages
1. More frequent service than available with conventional vessels.
2. Faster transit time on specialised vessels than on conventional services.
3. Small consignments attract high minimum rates on conventional cargo ships. The groupage operator is able to obtain the benefit of a lower rate for a bulk shipment and pass part of the saving on to the shipper.
4. Less likelihood of delay through Customs, etc than with conventional shipments.
5. When on driver accompanied vehicles, less likelihood of loss or temporary loss in transit sheds.

Disadvantages
1. If the groupage service is not sufficiently frequent or well-supported, consignments may be delayed until an economic load is available.
2. Delays can occur if other consignments in the load have not been properly documented.

D. LCL (Less than container load)

This is a form of groupage service offered by container shipping companies or Combined Transport Operators (CTOs). Consignments which are too small to merit the exclusive use of a container are consolidated with other small consignments to form a container load.

Advantages
1. Derive almost all the advantages of shipment in individual containers, eg fast transit, protection, etc.
2. Although LCL rates are higher than full container rates they are much cheaper than using a container only partly loaded.

Disadvantages
1. Additional cost of transport to and from ICDs.
2. Transit time may be extended until a full container load is obtained.
3. Delays in clearance may be experienced if other consignments in the container do not comply with Customs requirements.

E. Roll-on, roll-off (Ro-Ro) services

Advantages
1. Much faster transit time than applies with conventional shipping.
2. Less likelihood of delays in Customs clearance.
3. Less likelihood of damage due to fewer handling operations.
4. If vehicle is accompanied, the driver is able to sort out any difficulties that may arise.
5. Door-to-door service.

Disadvantages
1. Difficult to obtain return loads, so charge for transport of goods must cover vehicle costs both ways.
2. Essential to ensure that vehicle is acceptable for the vessel booked, eg does not exceed height limitations.
3. Permits may be needed to enable the road vehicle to operate.

F. Train Ferry

Advantages
1. Useful when exporter and importer have rail sidings.
2. Overcomes need for permits.

Disadvantages
1. If no private sidings, then transport to and from rail terminals and transhipment is necessary.
2. Being unaccompanied, consignor loses control over goods, delays may not be quickly identified, and problems of documentation, etc are more difficult to resolve.

G. Road/Rail

Advantages
1. Avoids need for permits.
2. Avoids weekend restrictions.
3. Less fatigue for driver.

Disadvantages
1. More expensive than all road transit.
2. Transit time may be longer than all road transit.
3. Possibility of trailer damage and loss of spares.

Ferry Routes

Information concerning ferry routes may be obtained from British Rail and shipping companies involved.

A list of companies operating Ro-Ro services is published in *Croner's Road Transport Operation*.

CHAPTER 16
(Module D)

Vehicle Construction, Weights and Dimensions

What are the sources of information on regulations governing construction weights and dimensions?
Vehicles which comply with the British construction and use regulations are subject to occasional change and before engaging in international operations operators should check if there is a possibility that any vehicle may infringe the regulations. The most authoritative sources are, of course, the transport authorities of the countries concerned. Members of the RHA and FTA can obtain information from the advisory services provided by those organisations. (Subscribers to *Croner's Road Transport Operation* will find that this information is continually updated for their convenience.)

Harmonisation

How does EC Regulation 156/70 on the harmonisation of technical standards affect British operators?
One of the objectives of the Common Transport Policy is to harmonise the framework of laws and regulations within which the different modes and undertakings operate. Life for the international operator would be even more difficult than it is today if every European country operated rules and regulations that bore no relationship to those applied by its neighbours. We have already seen that great progress has been made throughout Europe (and in some cases much further afield) through international Conventions and Agreements to bring about uniformity in the law relating to the carriage of goods.

Having achieved a broad agreement in connection with the carriage of goods, it is logical to seek common standards for the vehicles which convey these goods. The alternative would be that a vehicle constructed and operated in accordance with the regulations in force in its country of origin could be adjudged illegal in any other country because its lights were an inch too high or too low, or its brakes were 1 or 2% less efficient than required in a particular country.

EC regulations on the harmonisation of technical standards are designed to effect this uniformity in construction and use regulations to ensure that vehicles which comply with the minimum standards laid down will be acceptable in all Member States.

The EC has been particularly concerned to direct its attentions to those aspects of construction and use of vehicles that affect the safety of operations. For this reason, early in the programme of technical harmonisation, EC Regulation 156/70 and subsequent directives and amendments have been introduced to ensure standards of safety in the braking requirements for road vehicles.

Traffic Restrictions and Special Requirements

The following is a summary of traffic restrictions which apply in European countries.

Austria
On Saturdays after 15.00 hours and all day Sundays, vehicles with trailers and vehicles above a loaded weight of 7.5 tonnes permitted gross weight are not allowed to operate. This also applies on public holidays.
Vehicles exceeding 3500kg must carry at least two wheel chocks.
A warning triangle must be carried.
Snow chains must be carried during winter months.
A first-aid kit must be carried.

Belgium
No general restrictions on road transport during Sundays and public holidays.
A warning triangle must be carried.

Bulgaria
Abnormal loads restricted to weekdays only 08.00 to 18.00 hours Monday to Friday.
A warning triangle must be carried.

Czechoslovakia
Transit of road vehicles is permitted at weekends and public holidays but these should be kept to a minimum from 14.00 hours on Friday to 21.00 hours on Sunday. Further restrictions are in force between April and September.
A warning triangle must be carried.
Snow chains must be carried during winter months. Road signs indicate when they must be used.

Denmark
No restrictions
A warning triangle must be carried

Finland
No restrictions.
A warning triangle must be carried.
Snow chains must be carried during winter months.

France
Goods vehicles over 7.5 tonnes laden weight are not allowed to circulate on Sundays and Bank Holidays from 06.00 to 22.00 hours. Vehicles carrying dangerous goods are banned from the roads from midday Saturday to midnight Sunday. The restriction also applies on holiday eves. Refrigerated vehicles may circulate during weekends and public holidays provided they are at least 3/4 full of perishable goods. Lower speed limits are in force for vehicles carrying dangerous goods.
A warning triangle and first-aid kit must be carried.
A complete set of replacement light bulbs must be carried.
Snow chains should be carried in winter months, especially if journeys are in regions bordering Italy and Switzerland.

East Germany
No restrictions.
A warning triangle and first-aid kit must be carried.
A complete set of replacement bulbs must be carried.

West Germany
Transit of goods vehicles over 7.5 tonnes laden weight is generally prohibited at weekends and public holidays.
Such vehicles are also prohibited from using motorways and certain Federal Highways from 07.00 hours on Saturday to 22.00 hours on Sunday from late June to early September.
A warning triangle and a flashing yellow light must be used in emergencies.
A first-aid kit must be carried.

Greece
Transit of goods vehicles is prohibited from 18.00 hours on Saturday to 24.00 hours on Sunday, except for perishable goods.
A warning triangle and a first-aid kit must be carried.

Hungary
Transit of road vehicles is allowed on Sundays and public holidays except on motorways which may not be used from 12.00 hours on Saturday to 24.00 hours on Sunday. The restriction also applies from 12.00 hours on the eve of a public holiday until 24.00 hours on the last day of a holiday.
A warning triangle must be carried.
Drinking and driving — the slightest trace of alcohol results in a heavy fine. Spot checks are carried out.

Republic of Ireland
Transit of goods vehicles is allowed on Sundays and public holidays.
Attendance at Customs posts is only available from 09.00 hours to 17.00 hours except on prior request and on payment of a fee.
Clearance is available at Dun Loaghaire on Sundays for Ro-Ro traffic.

Italy
Goods vehicles exceeding 5 tonnes maximum weight are prohibited from circulating on Sundays and public holidays from 07.00 hours to 22.00 hours.
A warning triangle must be carried.

Luxembourg
No restrictions.
A warning triangle must be carried.

Netherlands
No restrictions.
A warning triangle must be carried.
Vehicles must not operate with illuminated headboards.

Norway
In view of the nature of the terrain there are restrictions on the size of vehicles and the types of roads that may be used.
A warning triangle must be carried.
Snow chains must be carried and may only be fitted to tyres in perfect condition.
It is forbidden for a driver to smoke whilst driving.

Poland
No restrictions.
A warning triangle must be carried.

Portugal
There is a general ban on goods vehicles using certain main roads and motorways at weekends and on public holidays.
A warning triangle must be carried.

Romania
Restrictions on goods vehicle movements apply on Sundays and public holidays from May to September.

Spain
The transit of goods vehicles is prohibited on Sundays and public holidays, except those carrying perishable foodstuffs.
Dangerous goods are banned from all roads from midday Saturday to midnight Sunday and all day on public holidays.
Two warning triangles must be carried.
Spare bulbs for headlights, sidelights and rearlights should be carried.
A bail bond to cover against accidents should be taken out with the operator's insurance company.

Sweden
No general restrictions except in Stockholm where movement of vehicles exceeding certain weights and/or dimensions are banned from the "controlled zone" during certain hours of the day.
A warning triangle must be carried.
A complete set of replacement bulbs should be carried.

Switzerland
Transit of goods vehicles is banned on Sundays and public holidays and at night throughout the year from 22.00 to 05.00 hours.
A warning triangle must be carried.
Horns must not be sounded in built-up areas unless safety demands it.
Snow chains must be carried from October to the end of April.

Turkey
No restrictions on Sundays or public holidays.
Time limits apply for vehicles in transit through the country.
Two warning triangles must be carried.

Yugoslavia
There are restrictions on commercial vehicle movement in different regions of the country — mainly summer weekends and over public holidays.
A warning triangle must be carried (two are required if a trailer is being towed).
A complete set of replacement bulbs should be carried.

NB In the event of involvement in an accident or a breakdown on the road in most countries in Europe, the driver must warn oncoming traffic by placing a red triangular warning sign to the rear of his vehicle.

Dangerous Goods

What regulations apply to the carriage of dangerous goods by road abroad?
The European Agreement for the International Carriage of Dangerous Goods (Accord Dangereux Routiers) usually known by the abbreviation ADR has as its objective the safe packing and carriage by road of dangerous items.

How does the agreement operate?
The parties to the agreement undertake to permit the transport of dangerous goods by road through their territories, without hindrance, provided they are carried in compliance with the provisions of the Annexes to the agreement.

What do the Annexes cover?
Annex A lays down rules for the packing and labelling of dangerous substances.

Annex B provides for the examination and certification of tank vehicles (embracing rigid vehicles, articulated vehicles and semi-trailers) used for the carriage of such goods, together with certain explosives-carrying vehicles.

How is evidence supplied that the regulations have been met?
The contracting parties to the agreement will accept a valid ADR certificate as evidence of compliance with the requirements of the agreement and with regulations in force in their country of origin.

Which countries are parties to the agreement?
The contracting parties are: Austria, Belgium, Denmark, Finland, France, Federal German Republic (W. Germany), German Democratic Republic (E. Germany), Hungary, Italy, Luxembourg, the Netherlands, Norway, Poland, Portugal, Spain, Sweden, Switzerland, the United Kingdom and Yugoslavia.

Who is responsible for certifying vehicles and tanks?
Examination of the vehicle and of any tank fitted to it will be carried out by separate authorities. Examination of any tank fitted to a vehicle will be made by inspecting organisations approved by the Health and Safety Executive.

Examination of the vehicle itself will be carried out by Department of Transport examiners at HGV testing stations.

Is it possible to have both ADR and plating and testing carried out simultaneously?
This is possible provided that both application forms are submitted together. There is an additional fee for ADR certification over and above the vehicle testing fee.

How frequently must vehicles and tanks be re-certified?
ADR vehicle certificates are valid for 12 months. For tanks the period varies, according to the classification of the tank, from six months to six years.

What will the tank inspection cover?
The factors to be considered will vary according to the particular commodities likely to be carried by a tank in its specified class. It will be tested for corrosion, cracking at attachment points, seams and valve connections. Hydraulic testing, low pressure air testing and non-destructive examination may be expected.

What does the vehicle examination involve?
The requirements for the vehicle itself are extensive and include such items as wiring circuits and electrical equipment (which must be firmly attached and protected from overloading), positioning of the vehicle exhaust and fuel tank. Screw-in bulbs must not be used and lamps recessed inside the body of the vehicle must be protected by strong cages or grids. Plastics, if used in the construction of the cab must be of an approved type.

Are there any other requirements?
It is not possible to cover the full requirements of the ADR Agreement as this extends to some 424 pages (copies are available from HMSO) but the following is an outline of the general requirements.

Vehicle operation and equipment
Two fire extinguishers must be carried on the vehicle, one suitable for dealing with engine fires and the other for fires in the load. A *third* extinguisher may also be necessary on articulated vehicles or those drawing a trailer — when a loaded trailer is left to stand uncoupled on a public highway it must have an extinguisher suitable for dealing with a fire in the load.

ADR vehicles must carry a tool kit for emergency repairs and at least one scotch or chock of a size suited to the weight of the vehicle and diameter of the wheels.

On the Continent (but not in Great Britain) two amber lights of the continuous flashing type must be carried and these must operate independently of the vehicle. When a vehicle halts at night or in bad visibility and its normal lights are not working, one amber light must be placed in the road 10m ahead of the vehicle and the other 10m behind the vehicle.

Markings
The International Carriage of Dangerous Goods (Rear Marking of Motor Vehicles) Regulations 1975 allow vehicles carrying dangerous goods on international journeys to display a rectangular plate at the rear of the vehicle whilst travelling in the United Kingdom.

The plate must be of orange reflex reflecting material and measure 40cm long by at least 30cm high with a black border not more than 15mm wide. The plate may be divided by a black horizontal line to show the identification number of the danger risk (the "Kember" Lazard identification) in the top half (two or three figures) and the identification number (if any) of the substance (four figures) in the bottom half. All figures must be 10cm high and 15mm thick.

Vehicles carrying substances on the Continent are required to show two rectangular orange plates 40cm each side, one at the front and one at the rear of the vehicle.

Driver instruction
Crews must be instructed on safety aspects of ADR vehicle movements, eg vehicles must not be parked in built-up areas, except in an emergency.

Crews must also be instructed in the action to be taken and treatment to be given in the event of persons coming into contact with the substance being carried; the measures to be taken in case of fire and, in particular, the extinguishing methods and agents that may be used; and the measures to be taken in case of breakage or deterioration of the packages or substances being carried, particularly when they have been spilled on the road.

A driver of a tank vehicle or a vehicle carrying tank containers exceeding 3000 litres capacity must hold a certificate showing that he has completed a training course in the requirements connected with the carriage of dangerous goods.

Where a vehicle carrying a dangerous substance is halted and may be a source of special danger if the crew is unable to deal with it quickly they should notify the nearest competent authorities.

The driver must be provided with written instructions concerning the nature of the load and the safety measures which must be observed. The Tremcard (Transport Emergency Card) scheme, operated by the European Council of Chemical Manufacturers' Federations safisfies the ADR requirements.

Tremcards are A4 size and show the name and physical properties of the substance, the protective devices to be carried (eg goggles) and the action to be taken in an emergency. The card also gives the telephone number and address of the organisation(s) from whom additional information can be obtained.

Packaging and labelling
Dangerous goods accepted for international carriage must be packed and labelled in accordance with the ADR requirements. These cover the types of packs which can and cannot be used for particular substances, the strength of packing materials and the manner in which they must be cushioned. Packages must be marked and labelled in the prescribed manner.

What are the sources of information on ADR?
In addition to the ADR Agreement obtainable from HMSO, explanatory notes for goods vehicle operators (ADR-2) together with supplementary information and application forms for the test (ADR-3) can be obtained from the Department of Transport, Dangerous Goods Branch, 2 Marsham Street, London SW1P 3EB.

Perishable Goods

The International Carriage of Perishable Foodstuffs Act 1976
This Act incorporates into British Law the Agreement on the International Carriage of Perishable Foodstuffs and on the Special Equipment to be Used for Such Carriage, usually known by the abbreviation ATP (Accord Transports Perissables).

What is the scope of the legislation?
It covers journeys made by road or rail and sea crossings of less than 150km. It does not cover domestic operations or perishable goods sent by air.

What are the main provisions of the act?
The act covers such matters as: regulation of standards; examination and testing; type approval of equipment; examiners' powers; offences and legal proceedings.

How does the Act regulate standards?
The Act itself does not specify standards, but *Section 1*:
- (a) provides for regulations to be made on standards for transport equipment, ie goods vehicles, railway wagons and containers
- (b) prescribes foodstuffs or classes of foodstuffs as perishable foodstuffs and the temperature limits for the conveyance of such foodstuffs
- (c) prescribes the various classes and different standards of transport equipment to be used and may exempt transport or perishable foodstuffs from all or any of the regulations as required.

Sections 2 and 3 cover the examination and testing of transport equipment by qualified persons appointed by the Secretary of State; the issuing of Certificates of Compliance and designates marks to such equipment attaining the prescribed standards. They also cover the provision and maintenance of testing stations and test apparatus and designate suitable premises for testing, etc.

What kinds of goods are covered by the regulations?
The agreement covers quick-frozen, deep-frozen, frozen and non-frozen foodstuffs but does not apply to fresh vegetables and soft fruit.

For how long does the Certificate of Compliance last?
The Certificate of Compliance is valid for six years.

What powers are given to examiners?
Examiners have the power to enter and inspect any transport equipment used, or believed to be used, for the international carriage of foodstuffs and any premises where such equipment is kept or believed to be kept. They have the power to detain any vehicle for as long as is necessary to complete the inspection and to require the driver to produce a certificate covering the vehicle and container.

Failure to comply with any of these conditions, or obstructing the examiner, are offences which can result in prosecution and fines.

What other offences are there in connection with the carriage of perishable foodstuffs?
Sections 7–10 concern offences relating to using, causing, or permitting the use of, transport equipment where a certificate of compliance is not in force or where the designating mark is not exhibited; fixing to or leaving designated marks on transport equipment not covered by a certificate of compliance; forging and altering certificates, and making false statements in order to obtain certificates.

Such offences can result in prosecution and fines.

What powers do examiners have in relation to foreign vehicles?
An examiner may prohibit the driving of a foreign goods vehicle if the required certificate of compliance cannot be produced, or if the vehicle, or use of the vehicle, does not comply with the regulations.

The driver may be directed to remove the vehicle under prohibition to a designated place, until the examiner is satisfied that appropriate action to rectify the situation has been taken.

Failure to comply with the directions given by an examiner is an offence and can incur a fine on summary conviction.

A constable in uniform may arrest without warrant any person suspected of failing to comply with such directions.

CRONER'S ROAD TRANSPORT OPERATION
A loose-leaf reference book with monthly updates.

Well known throughout the road haulage industry this authoritative book is indispensable to all companies who operate commercial vehicles in the UK and on the Continent of Europe. CRONER'S ROAD TRANSPORT OPERATION is designed to give simple, speedy and accurate reference to the rules and regulations as they apply to road transport and includes information on Operator's Licensing – CPC requirements – C & U regulations – plating and testing of vehicles – excise licensing – driving licences (incl. H.G.V.) – speed limits – new drivers' hours regulations and record keeping (tachographs) – carriage of dangerous goods – special type vehicles etc., etc. Also included is a section covering European countries which provides details of documents required, speed limits, etc., etc.

The legislation affecting hauliers is constantly changing – this book keeps you up-to-date with monthly amendments in the form of revised pages.

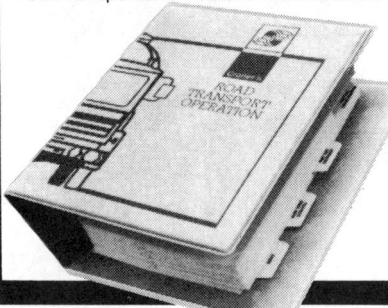

To order this book, see a copy on ten days free approval or request further details, please write to:
Croner Publications Ltd.,
Croner House, London Road, Kingston-upon-Thames, Surrey KT2 6SR
Tel: 081-547 3333 Fax 081-547 2638

CRONER'S COACH AND BUS OPERATIONS
A loose-leaf reference book updated every three months.

The law demands that operators of coaches and buses must have a detailed knowledge of the rules and regulations governing them and that these rules are applied on a day to day basis. The rules are complex and contained in many and varied statutes, regulations and orders. This loose-leaf service draws together and keeps up to date all the information you need to comply with the law *and* run a cost effective operation.

The Transport Act 1985 is now in force and 'deregulation' of bus services, etc. commenced in late October '86. The impact of this new legislation is included in the appropriate sections.

Part 1:– Definition and Classification – Taxis and Hire Cars – Driver Licensing – Operators Licensing and Qualifications – PSV Drivers' Hours and Records – PSV Fitness, Equipment and Use – Speed Limits – Offences and Penalties – Use of Vehicles – Financial Information (UK).

Part 2:– Covers Europe with information on Authorisations – EC Waybills – VAT – Speed Limits – Drivers' Hours – Medical treatment – Documentation, etc., etc.

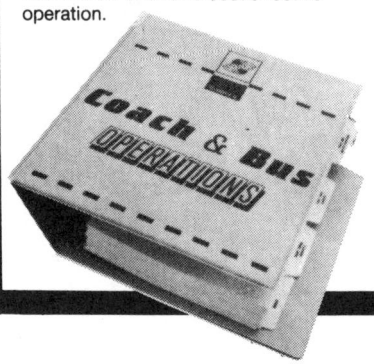

To order this book, see a copy on ten days free approval or request further details, please write to:
Croner Publications Ltd.,
Croner House, London Road, Kingston-upon-Thames, Surrey KT2 6SR
Tel: 081-547 3333 Fax 081-547 2638

PART III

Self-Examination Tests

These questions are in the same form as those you will be asked to answer in the examination. There is only one correct answer to each question and in the examination you will be asked to mark your answer on a separate sheet by inserting the correct letter in the answer box, in pencil, eg:

1. In a leap year, the number of days in February is:

(A) 28
(B) 29
(C) 30
(D) 31

| 1 | B | | 2 | | | 3 | | | 4 | |

It is suggested that in answering the questions that follow you adopt the same procedure, recording your answers on a separate sheet, instead of marking your book. In this way you will be able to work the tests several times, as revision, without being influenced by your previous answers.

Chapter 1

1. Legislation providing for the licensing of Transport Managers was first introduced in:

    (A) The Road Traffic Act 1960
    (B) The Carriage of Goods by Road Act 1965
    (C) The Transport Act 1968
    (D) The Road Traffic Act 1972

2. An own account operator has depots in three traffic areas, each operating under its own restricted operator's licence. How many CPC holders will be required?

    (A) None
    (B) One
    (C) Two
    (D) Three

3. A hire or reward operator has three depots in the same traffic area. Unless the Licensing Authority agrees otherwise, how many CPC holders will he require?

    (A) None
    (B) One
    (C) Two
    (D) Three

4. Which of the following statements is correct?

    (A) A CPC qualification can only be acquired by passing a DTp examination.
    (B) A CPC qualification can only be acquired by passing a DTp examination or through grandfather rights.
    (C) Certain professional qualifications exempt the holder from taking a CPC examination.

5. If the qualified operator or manager dies or is incapacitated, unless a special dispensation is granted by the Licensing Authority, he must be replaced within:

    (A) 1 month
    (B) 3 months
    (C) 6 months
    (D) 1 year

6. The examination for determining "professional competence" is set by:

   (A) The Department of Transport
   (B) The Department of Education and Science
   (C) The Chartered Institute of Transport
   (D) The Royal Society of Arts

7. A hire or reward operator solely engaged in international operations (who does *not* qualify for grandfather rights):

   (A) Does not need to pass an examination
   (B) Must pass an EC examination
   (C) Need only pass an international examination
   (D) Must pass both national and international examinations

8. To cater for different sizes of fleets:

   (A) There are 4 levels of examination
   (B) There are 3 levels of examination
   (C) There are 2 levels of examination
   (D) No distinction is made and there is only one level of examination

9. How often are the CPC examinations held?

   (A) Once a year
   (B) Twice a year
   (C) Three times a year
   (D) Four times a year

10. Subject to suspension or revocation, a Certificate of Professional Competence will be valid for:

    (A) Life
    (B) 10 years
    (C) 5 years
    (D) 3 years

Chapter 2

1. No driver may drive without a break for rest or refreshments for more than a total of:

   (A) 5½ hours
   (B) 5 hours
   (C) 4½ hours
   (D) 4 hours

2. A break of at least 45 minutes must be taken after the maximum period of driving. Which one of the following is an acceptable alternative if taken during and immediately following the maximum period of driving?

(A) Three breaks of 15 minutes each
(B) One break of 30 minutes and two of 10 minutes each
(C) One break of 20 minutes, one of 15 minutes, and one of 10 minutes

3. Except where concessions apply, the maximum daily driving allowed under Community rules is:

(A) 8 hours extended to 9 hours twice a week
(B) 8½ hours extended to 9½ hours twice a week
(C) 9 hours extended to 10 hours twice a week
(D) 9½ hours extended to 10½ hours twice a week

4. Under the Community hours rules, total driving times must not exceed:

(A) 80 hours in any 2 consecutive weeks
(B) 86 hours in any 2 consecutive weeks
(C) 90 hours in any 2 consecutive weeks
(D) 94 hours in any 2 consecutive weeks

5. The definition of a week is:

(A) The period between 00.00 hours Monday to 24.00 hours Sunday
(B) The period between 00.00 hours Saturday to 24.00 hours Friday
(C) The period between 00.00 hours Sunday to 24.00 hours Saturday
(D) Any period of 7 consecutive days

6. If a vehicle is double-manned, the daily rest period for both drivers must not be less than:

(A) 8 hours during each period of 30 hours
(B) 9 hours during each period of 27 hours
(C) 8 hours during each period of 27 hours
(D) 9 hours during each period of 30 hours

7. The speed recorded by a tachograph must be accurate to:

(A) within 10% at all speeds
(B) within 10% at speeds above 10 mph
(C) within ± 6 kilometres per hour at speeds above 10 kph
(D) within ± 6 kilometres per hour of the actual speed at all speeds

8. Drivers on Community journeys should retain their completed tachograph charts for:

(A) The current week and for the last day of driving in the previous week
(B) 2 days
(C) 7 days
(D) The current week and for the last 3 days of the previous week

9. Employers must keep completed tachograph charts for at least:

(A) 3 months
(B) 6 months
(C) 1 year
(D) 18 months

10. If a tachograph chart is damaged whilst being used it:

(A) Must be destroyed as soon as possible
(B) Can be either retained or destroyed as the driver wishes
(C) Must be returned to the employer, together with the replacement chart

Chapter 3

1. On roads other than dual carriageways and motorways, the maximum permitted speed for goods vehicles not exceeding 7.5 tonnes GVW is:

(A) 30 mph
(B) 40 mph
(C) 50 mph
(D) 60 mph

2. On motorways, except where lower limits are in force, the maximum permitted speed for articulated vehicles is:

(A) 40 mph
(B) 50 mph
(C) 60 mph
(D) 70 mph

3. On motorways, a goods vehicle with a GPW exceeding 7.5 tonnes and any vehicle drawing a trailer is allowed to use the third lane:

(A) Under no circumstances
(B) Only to pass slow moving traffic
(C) Only if it is safe to do so
(D) Only to pass an abnormally wide load

4. In which of the following cases is a vehicle *prohibited* from stopping on the hard shoulder of a motorway

   (A) In the case of illness of the driver
   (B) To render assistance to another person who has broken down
   (C) For the driver to take an official rest break
   (D) In case of accident

5. For which of the following offences may a traffic warden issue a fixed penalty ticket?

   (A) Driving a vehicle uninsured
   (B) Exceeding the speed limit
   (C) Using a vehicle with illegal tyres
   (D) Making a "U" turn in an unauthorised place

6. When a fixed penalty ticket has been issued, the recipient has the option of paying the fine within:

   (A) 7 days
   (B) 14 days
   (C) 28 days
   (D) 1 month

7. A double yellow line parallel to the kerb indicates

   (A) No waiting during the working day (as indicated on nearby signs)
   (B) No waiting at other times (as indicated on nearby signs)
   (C) No waiting during the working day and at other times (as indicated on nearby signs)
   (D) No waiting at any time

8. Loading bans at peak hours (actual times shown on lamp-post signs) are indicated by:

   (A) Single yellow marks at kerbsides
   (B) Double yellow marks at kerbsides
   (C) Treble yellow marks at kerbsides
   (D) Single yellow lines in gutter

9. In which of the following circumstances is a traffic warden empowered to demand the production of driving licences?

   (A) When he has reason to believe the driver has been drinking.
   (B) When he has reason to believe a vehicle is unsafe, eg having an illegal tyre.
   (C) When employed at a car pound, he has reason to believe that an offence has

been committed by the vehicle obstructing, waiting, being loaded or unloaded on a road.

(D) When he has reason to believe the driver is under age.

10. In which of the following circumstances has an offence *not* been committed?

(A) Leaving a vehicle unattended without stopping the engine and securely applying the handbrake.
(B) Parking a goods vehicle exceeding 1525kg unladen weight without lights on a road subject to a 30 mph speed limit.
(C) Parking a demolition vehicle on a clearway to carry out a clearing operation.
(D) Parking a goods vehicle not exceeding 1525kg unladen weight, in the approach zone of a zebra crossing.

Chapter 4

1. For which of the following offences does the penalty include obligatory disqualification from driving unless the court considers there are special reasons?

(A) Being in charge of a motor vehicle while unfit through drink or drugs
(B) Exceeding the speed limit
(C) A second conviction of reckless driving within three years of the first
(D) Using a vehicle uninsured against third party risks

2. A driver disqualified for less than 10 years, but not less than four years may apply to have the disqualification removed:

(A) After 1 year
(B) After 2 years
(C) After 4 years
(D) When half the disqualification period has expired

3. An endorsement for a drinking and driving offence must remain on a driving licence for:

(A) 3 years
(B) 4 years
(C) 7 years
(D) 11 years

4. The "prescribed limit" of alcohol in the breath in connection with drinking and driving offences is:

(A) 35 microgrammes of alcohol per 100 millilitres of breath
(B) 35 milligrammes of alcohol per 100 millilitres of breath
(C) 80 microgrammes of alcohol per 100 millilitres of breath
(D) 80 milligrammes of alcohol per 100 millilitres of breath

5. If a driver is convicted of a first offence of driving a vehicle while under the influence of drink or drugs and no special circumstances exist, the court is obliged to disqualify him for a minimum period of:

(A) 6 months
(B) 12 months
(C) 2 years
(D) 3 years

6. A driver altered a certificate of insurance with the intention of deceiving the insurance company but they were not deceived. In consequence the driver could be charged with:

(A) Attempted forgery
(B) Forgery
(C) Making false statements
(D) No offence

7. In connection with which of the following offences is the employer likely to be charged as well as the driver?

(A) Speeding
(B) Driving without a licence
(C) Leaving a vehicle in a dangerous position
(D) Failure to comply with a traffic direction by a police constable

8. A driver who is disqualified under the totting-up procedure, having been disqualified once before in the previous three years, will, unless there are special circumstances, be disqualified for a minimum period of:

(A) 6 months
(B) 1 year
(C) 2 years
(D) 3 years

9. If a vehicle is ordered to proceed to a weighbridge and is then found not to be overloaded, the Highway Authority, on whose behalf the weighing requirement was made, shall pay any loss suffered if the journey involved was more than:

(A) 1 mile
(B) 2 miles
(C) 3 miles
(D) 5 miles

10. If a driver is convicted on the same occasion of three offences carrying two, three and four points respectively, the number of points endorsed on his licence will be:

(A) 2
(B) 3
(C) 4
(D) 9

Chapter 5

1. A driver must stop, give his name and address, the name and address of the owner of the vehicle, and the identification marks of the vehicle, to any person having reasonable grounds for requiring them, if involved in an accident in which:

(A) He alone suffers injury
(B) His vehicle is damaged but there is no damage to the other vehicle
(C) A dog carried in his vehicle is injured
(D) A horse carried in a trailer pulled by the other vehicle is injured

2. A driver is involved in an accident involving damage to another vehicle, and a minor injury to a passenger in that other vehicle. Who is entitled to demand production of the driver's licence?

(A) A police constable called to the scene
(B) A traffic warden who witnessed the accident
(C) The driver of the other vehicle
(D) The injured passenger

3. If, following an accident, the policy-holder neglects to inform the insurance company within the period stipulated in the policy, the insurance company may invalidate the claim in respect of injury suffered by:

(A) The policy holder (or his driver)
(B) The policy holder (or his driver) and third parties
(C) Third parties only

4. A vehicle owner is not required to take out third party insurance if he has deposited:

(A) £10,000 with the Motor Insurers' Bureau
(B) £10,000 with the Supreme Court
(C) £15,000 with the Motor Insurers' Bureau
(D) £15,000 with the Supreme Court

5. A driver is not required to report an accident involving injury to which of the following animals?

(A) Dog
(B) Cat
(C) Horse
(D) Cow

6. On a sign indicating that a road tanker is carrying inflammable liquids, which of the following colour combinations would be used?

(A) Red and white
(B) Orange and black
(C) Red and black
(D) Black and white

7. When collecting a tank trailer carrying a corrosive liquid a haulier must receive details of:

(A) The customer's insurance company
(B) The risks created by the liquid
(C) Locations of safe parking spaces
(D) The operator's licence of the trailer owner

8. The Code of Practice on the safe loading of vehicles states that to prevent movement of the payload in a sideways direction, a load restraint device should be capable of withstanding a force equal to:

(A) 25% of the total weight of the load
(B) 50% of the total weight of the load
(C) 75% of the total weight of the load
(D) The total weight of the load

9. If a load shifts or falls from a heavy goods vehicle, who is liable to be prosecuted for having an "insecure load?"

(A) Only the person who loaded the vehicle
(B) Both the driver and the haulage operator
(C) The driver only
(D) The haulage operator only

10. On long journeys horses must be fed and watered at least every:

(A) 6 hours
(B) 8 hours
(C) 10 hours
(D) 12 hours

Chapter 6

1. For the purpose of operator licensing, a goods vehicle is defined as a vehicle used for the carriage of goods in connection with a trade or business which exceeds 3.5 tonnes GPW or, if unplated:

    (A) 1525kg unladen weight
    (B) 1550kg unladen weight
    (C) 1575kg unladen weight
    (D) 1750kg unladen weight

2. A motor tractor is a vehicle not constructed to carry a load having an unladen weight:

    (A) Exceeding 3525kg but not exceeding 5000kg
    (B) Exceeding 5000kg but not exceeding 6350kg
    (C) Exceeding 6350kg but not exceeding 7370kg
    (D) Exceeding 7370kg but not exceeding 11,690kg

3. Gross kerbside weight (GKW) is:

    (A) The total weight of an unladen vehicle with body, less driver, ready for operation on the road
    (B) The total weight transmitted to the road by a laden vehicle
    (C) The total maximum all-up weight of a rigid vehicle together with its loaded drawbar trailer
    (D) The weight of a motor vehicle only, plus fuel, water, tools and any towing bracket

4. What is the maximum permitted weight of a two-axled drawbar trailer?

    (A) 16,260kg
    (B) 17,000kg
    (C) 18,000kg
    (D) 24,390kg

5. The maximum length of a road train comprising of a vehicle and one trailer is:

    (A) 15m
    (B) 18m
    (C) 24m
    (D) 25.9m

6. Where a motor vehicle is drawing a trailer by means of a tow-rope or chain, the distance between their nearest points must not exceed

(A) 3m
(B) 4m
(C) 4.5m
(D) 5m

7. The maximum permitted overhang of a goods vehicle must not exceed what percentage of its wheelbase?

(A) 30%
(B) 40%
(C) 50%
(D) 60%

8. The maximum permitted height of a goods vehicle is:

(A) 14 feet
(B) 14 feet 6 inches
(C) 15 feet
(D) Not specified

9. If a vehicle is found to be overloaded, the form issued by a DTp examiner or other authorised officer will be:

(A) GV60
(B) GV160
(C) GV9C (PG9C)
(D) GV219

10. At what width does written notice have to be given to the Secretary of State for Transport, when wide loads are being carried on the road?

(A) Exceeding 2.9m
(B) Exceeding 3.05m
(C) Exceeding 4.3m
(D) Exceeding 5m

Chapter 7

1. When exceptional circumstances prevent the plating and testing of a vehicle by the due date, an exemption certificate may be issued with a maximum validity of:

(A) 3 months
(B) 6 months
(C) 9 months
(D) 12 months

2. Where a rearward projecting load exceeds 3.05m, but does not exceed 5m:

 (A) An end marker board must be fitted
 (B) End and side marker boards must be fitted
 (C) End and side marker boards must be fitted and an attendant carried
 (D) End and side marker boards must be fitted, an attendant carried and two days' notice given to the police

3. Which of the following vehicles must be fitted with a rear marking having the words LONG VEHICLE in black lettering on a yellow reflective background with a red fluorescent border?

 (A) A rigid goods vehicle 12m long
 (B) A trailer combination exceeding 11m but not exceeding 13m
 (C) An articulated combination 12m long
 (D) An articulated combination exceeding 13m long

4. Headlamps must be fitted at a minimum height from the ground of:

 (A) 300mm
 (B) 400mm
 (C) 500mm
 (D) 600mm

5. Most vehicles first used on or after April 1, 1980 must be fitted with at least:

 (A) 2 rear foglamps fitted independently
 (B) 1 rear foglamp
 (C) 1 spotlamp
 (D) 2 foglamps

6. Which of the following vehicles is permitted to carry one or more blue flashing lights?

 (A) Breakdown vehicles
 (B) Snow clearance vehicles
 (C) Blood transfusion service vehicles
 (D) Road clearance vehicles

7. A goods vehicle examiner can issue a delayed prohibition notice permitting a maximum delay of:

 (A) 5 days
 (B) 7 days
 (C) 10 days
 (D) 14 days

8. When a vehicle which has been subject to a prohibition notice is presented for clearance and is found to be fit for service, the examiner will issue a:

(A) GV9B (or PG9B)
(B) GV9C (or PG9C)
(C) GV10 (or PG10)
(D) GV219

9. Records of inspections and maintenance must be kept for a minimum period of:

(A) 12 months
(B) 15 months
(C) 18 months
(D) 2 years

10. It is a statutory requirement for goods vehicles to be inspected for defects:

(A) Every 2 weeks
(B) Every 4 weeks
(C) Every 6 weeks
(D) At regular intervals of either time or mileage

Chapter 8

1. An operator's licence must be held for the operation of all goods vehicles which exceed:

(A) 1.5 tonnes unladen weight
(B) 2 tonnes unladen weight
(C) 3.5 tonnes gross plated weight
(D) 7.5 tonnes kerbside weight

2. In order to engage in international hire or reward operations a haulier would require:

(A) A standard international operator's licence only
(B) A standard national/international operator's licence
(C) A multi-national operator's licence
(D) A universal operator's licence

3. In establishing good repute, the Licensing Authority will take into consideration any relevant convictions by the applicant, his partner or the company within the preceding:

(A) 3 years
(B) 4 years
(C) 5 years
(D) 11 years

4. In the "statement of intention" that forms part of the application for an operator's licence, the applicant gives certain undertakings. Which of the following is *not* included?

(A) He will ensure that his drivers observe the drivers' hours regulations
(B) He will ensure that proper records are kept
(C) He will ensure that he does not overcharge for his services
(D) He will ensure that his vehicles are kept fit and serviceable

5. A company holds a "restricted" operator's licence. This permits it to:

(A) Deliver and collect all goods for hire or reward or own account in the United Kingdom only
(B) Deliver and collect all goods, its own and for hire or reward in the United Kingdom and internationally
(C) Deliver and collect its own goods in the United Kingdom only
(D) Deliver and collect its own goods in the United Kingdom, and internationally

6. A company carrying goods for hire or reward has four bases in the Metropolitan Traffic Area. How many "O" licences does it require?

(A) One
(B) Two
(C) Three
(D) Four

7. One of the following is *not* entitled to object to the grant of an operator's licence.

(A) The National Union of Railwaymen
(B) A local authority
(C) The Freight Transport Association
(D) A magistrate

8. Responsibility for advertising an "O" licence application rests on:

   (A) The applicant
   (B) The licensing authority
   (C) The local authority
   (D) The planning authority

9. An operator uses his home as his office, but parks his vehicles in a yard which he shares with another operator, and has them maintained at a local garage. He stores most of his records at the office of the accountant who prepares his income tax returns. His operating centre is:

   (A) His home
   (B) The yard where he parks his vehicles
   (C) The garage where his vehicles are maintained
   (D) His accountant's office

10. An application for an operator's licence must be made on form:

    (A) GV79
    (B) GV80
    (C) GV85
    (D) GV90

Chapter 9

1. A sole trader is responsible for the debts of a business:

   (A) Only to the extent of the value of its assets
   (B) The value of the assets of the business, and an additional £50,000
   (C) To a maximum of £100,000
   (D) To the full extent of his personal wealth

2. The minimum number of shareholders required by a public limited company is:

   (A) 2
   (B) 7
   (C) 20
   (D) 50

3. The rules governing the internal working of a company are embodied in:

   (A) The Memorandum of Association
   (B) The Certificate of Incorporation
   (C) The Articles of Association
   (D) The company prospectus

4. A debenture as shown on a balance sheet is:

   (A) A current liability
   (B) Part of the risk capital of the company
   (C) Part of the loan capital of the business
   (D) A short term loan

5. Which of the following is a statement of the assets and liabilities of a business at a given date?

   (A) The trading account
   (B) The operating account
   (C) The profit and loss account
   (D) The balance sheet

6. Working capital ratio is the ratio of:

   (A) Fixed assets to total capital employed
   (B) Creditors to debtors plus cash at bank
   (C) Authorised capital and issued capital
   (D) Current assets to current liabilities

7. Which of the following is *not* an example of fixed costs?

   (A) Licences
   (B) Insurance
   (C) Repairs and maintenance
   (D) Depreciation

8. An operator buys a lorry for £14,000 and estimates that its resale value after 6 years will be £2000. How much must the operator set aside for the depreciation of the vehicle, using the straight line method?

   (A) £1500
   (B) £2000
   (C) £2200
   (D) £2500

9. The ratio of liquid assets to current liabilities is obtained by calculating the:

(A) Working capital ratio
(B) Current ratio
(C) Liquidity ratio
(D) Cash ratio

10. Return on capital employed is the best method of calculating a haulage company's:

(A) Level of profitability
(B) Working capital
(C) Capital reserves
(D) Liquidity

Chapter 10

1. The document made out by the seller advising the buyer of the amount due in respect of a particular transaction is called:

(A) An advice note
(B) A quotation
(C) An invoice
(D) A statement

2. Which of the following types of insurance would cover an operator for claims for death or injury to a pedestrian arising out of the defective loading of a vehicle?

(A) Goods in transit
(B) Consequential loss
(C) Public liability
(D) Third party insurance

3. If a driver's mate is injured while being carried on his employer's vehicle, compensation for his injury would be covered by:

(A) Fidelity guarantee insurance
(B) Third party insurance
(C) Employer's liability insurance
(D) Consequential loss insurance

4. The Motor Vehicles (Third Party Risks Deposits) Regulations 1967 provide for a deposit to be made to the Supreme Court as an alternative to a motor insurance policy. The sum required is:

   (A) £50,000
   (B) £30,000
   (C) £15,000
   (D) £10,000

5. To cover himself for loss of trade following a fire at his premises an operator would need to take out which of the following:

   (A) Fire insurance
   (B) Third party insurance
   (C) Employer's liability insurance
   (D) Consequential loss insurance

6. To insure himself against losses arising from the dishonesty of his employees, an operator should take out a:

   (A) Fire and theft policy
   (B) Comprehensive policy
   (C) Employer's liability policy
   (D) Fidelity policy

7. A restrictive "night risk clause" contained in a "goods in transit" policy means that

   (A) Goods of high value cannot be transported at night unless an additional premium is paid
   (B) Goods can only be transported during daylight hours
   (C) Goods will automatically be covered against the additional risks of transporting them at night
   (D) A goods vehicle must not be left unattended at night unless fitted with an approved anti-theft device

8. A person wishing to make regular deposits of small sums into a bank in order to save for a holiday and at the same time to earn interest would open:

   (A) A deposit account
   (B) An investment account
   (C) A current account
   (D) A savings account

9. If a person wishes a cheque to be paid only into a specified account, the type of cheque which should be used is:

   (A) An open cheque
   (B) A bearer cheque
   (C) A cheque crossed "& Co"
   (D) A cheque crossed "A/C payee"

10. The system under which instead of paying by cheque, creditors are paid any money owed them direct into their bank accounts, is known as:

    (A) Direct debit
    (B) Standing order
    (C) Credit transfer
    (D) Direct credit

Chapter 11

1. Common Law was established in the reign of William the Conqueror. It applied:

   (A) Only to common land
   (B) To the common people but not to nobility
   (C) To certain parts of the country only
   (D) To all. It was so called because it was common (the same) to all the land

2. The rule of judicial precedent provides that:

   (A) The status of a judge is determined by his length of service
   (B) The decision of a judge takes precedence over Common Law
   (C) The decision of a judge is binding on all other judges of an equal or inferior status
   (D) Equity always prevails over Common Law

3. An instruction originating from the European Community calling upon Member States to take action to achieve a broadly stated aim is called:

   (A) A regulation
   (B) A recommendation
   (C) A directive
   (D) A requirement

4. Which of the following statements concerning contracts is true?

   (A) Unless it is signed a contract is not binding
   (B) All contracts must be in writing (writing includes typewriting, printing, etc)
   (C) Contracts with aliens are illegal (even in peacetime)
   (D) Contracts may be oral, written or implied by the conduct of the parties

5. An employer is liable for the acts of his servants committed while acting within the scope of their employment. In which of the following is the employee not acting "within the scope of his employment".

   (A) A driver deviates 50 miles from his authorised route to visit a sick relative and while off the route is responsible for an accident
   (B) A fitter testing a vehicle on the road engages in a race with another driver, though this practice has been forbidden by his employers, and damages the vehicle which was being maintained under contract
   (C) A clerk from the traffic office moves a lorry which was causing an obstruction and damages a visitor's car
   (D) A driver omits to sheet-up a load, though he has standing instructions to do so and the load is damaged by rain

6. In connection with the law of contract, consideration means:

   (A) The parties must think carefully before they make their contract
   (B) The parties must behave fairly towards each other
   (C) Each party must derive a benefit from the contract
   (D) The way each party interprets the contract

7. In which of the following circumstances is there an enforceable contract?

   (A) X says "I will sell you this watch for £15" and Y says "All right, providing you throw in a new watch strap"
   (B) X writes to Y saying "You can have my car which you were interested in for £500. If I don't hear from you within a week I'll assume that we have a deal". Y does not reply within a week
   (C) X telephones Y and offers him a load if he will do the job for £50. Y says "I'll do it for £60". X says "OK"
   (D) X writes to Y offering to sell him a car for £700. Y replies "I accept. I'll give you £200 down and the rest in instalments"

8. The duty of care which the occupier of premises owes to a visitor who is lawfully on those premises means:

   (A) The visitor must take the premises as he finds them
   (B) The occupier need only warn the visitor of concealed dangers on the premises
   (C) The occupier is always liable if the visitor is injured while on the premises
   (D) The occupier must take such care as is in all circumstances of the case reasonable

9. A car owner living nearby repeatedly parks his car on a wide road but in such a manner that it restricts the access to a haulage operator's premises. The most likely action that could be brought against him would be for:

(A) Public nuisance
(B) Private nuisance
(C) Trespass
(D) Public liability

10. A group of children have regularly entered your yard to play after working hours. You have given up trying to keep the fence repaired because no sooner is it mended than they break it open again. A small child falls into an unlit, unguarded inspection pit and is injured. Which of the following is most likely?

(A) You will not be liable because it is not reasonable to continually repair the fence
(B) You will not be liable because the children were trespassers
(C) You will not be liable because it is the parents' responsibility to control their children
(D) You will be held liable because you knew of their habit and therefore should have repaired the fence and effectively guarded the pit

Chapter 12

Which of the following statements does *not* describe an objective of the Sex Discrimination Act 1975:

(A) To ensure that both sexes have equal opportunities to be selected for a job (unless inappropriate)
(B) To ensure that both sexes have equal opportunities for promotion
(C) To ensure that both sexes shall receive equal pay for doing the same job
(D) To ensure that in redundancy cases one sex shall not be discriminated against in favour of the other

2. The Act which established the principle of Industrial Training Boards was:

(A) The Education Act 1948
(B) The Employment and Training Act 1953
(C) The Industrial Training Act 1964
(D) The Employment and Training Act 1973

3. Under current employment legislation an employer must give an employee a written statement of his main conditions of employment

   (A) Prior to commencing employment
   (B) As soon as he commences employment
   (C) Within 4 weeks of commencing employment
   (D) Within 13 weeks of commencing employment

4. The Advisory, Conciliation and Arbitration Service (ACAS) is

   (A) A department of the CBI
   (B) A department of the TUC
   (C) A section of the Department of Employment
   (D) A statutory institution

5. Industrial Tribunals have authority to hear cases concerning legislation relating to

   (A) Redundancy
   (B) Drivers' hours
   (C) Social security
   (D) Industrial injuries

6. When a Health and Safety inspector issues an "improvement" notice this means that the system of work referred to

   (A) Must not continue and failure to carry out the improvement will result in a fine being imposed by the inspector concerned
   (B) Must not continue until the improvement is made
   (C) May continue providing the improvement is made within a specified period of time.
   (D) May continue provided a trade union safety representative agrees to the specified improvement

7. A male employee aged 25 who has lost his job through redundancy is entitled to redundancy pay if he has normally worked for 16 hours per week or more, for a minimum period of:

   (A) 6 months
   (B) 1 year
   (C) 2 years
   (D) 5 years

8. The maximum period for which an employer is required to pay an employee Statutory Sickness Pay is:

(A) 26 weeks
(B) 28 weeks
(C) 13 weeks
(D) 4 weeks

9. What period of notice is an employee with 2 years service required to give his employer?

(A) 1 week
(B) 2 weeks
(C) 3 weeks
(D) 4 weeks

10. Under the Disabled Persons Employment Acts, employers of 20 or more persons are required to employ a quota of disabled people. The normal standard quota is:

(A) 1% of the workforce.
(B) 2% of the workforce.
(C) 3% of the workforce.
(D) 5% of the workforce.

Trial Examination (National — Module A)

You should not attempt this examination until you have thoroughly studied the preceding chapters.

Record your answers on a separate sheet of paper in case you should wish to attempt the examination a second time.

1. What is the maximum speed limit on a de-restricted single carriageway road?

    (A) 40 mph
    (B) 50 mph
    (C) 60 mph
    (D) 70 mph

2. For which of the following offences may a traffic warden issue a fixed penalty ticket?

    (A) Exceeding the speed limit
    (B) Having a tyre with an illegal tread
    (C) Leaving a vehicle parked at night without lights or reflectors
    (D) Driving without due care and attention

3. It is an offence, subject to obligatory disqualification to drive or attempt to drive a vehicle when above the statutory limit for breath alcohol. That limit is:

    (A) 35 milligrammes of alcohol per 100 millilitres of breath
    (B) 35 microgrammes of alcohol per 100 millilitres of breath
    (C) 80 milligrammes of alcohol per 100 millilitres of breath
    (D) 80 microgrammes of alcohol per 100 millilitres of breath

4. The name of the document that sets out the objects of a company is:

    (A) The Memorandum of Association
    (B) The Articles of Association
    (C) The Certificate of Incorporation
    (D) The Certificate of Trading

5. Which of the following would be the best source of short-term capital for a transport operator wishing to cover a temporary cash-flow problem?

    (A) An issue of shares
    (B) An issue of debentures
    (C) A bank loan
    (D) A bank overdraft

6. Debentures are:

    (A) A form of short-term loan
    (B) Part of the fixed assets of a company
    (C) Part of the share capital of a company
    (D) Part of the loan capital of a company

7. The best method of ascertaining the profitability of a company is to examine:

    (A) Its gross profit
    (B) Its liquidity ratio
    (C) The ratio of net profit to capital invested
    (D) The ratio of current assets to current liabilities

8. Which of the following is a fixed cost?

    (A) Tyres
    (B) Vehicle excise licence
    (C) Maintenance
    (D) Lubricating oil

9. Effective stock control means that:

    (A) Every spare part that might be needed is always in stock
    (B) Capital is not tied up in unnecessarily high stock levels
    (C) The company is always ready to take advantage of bulk purchase offers
    (D) Spares are never ordered until they are needed

10. When carriage charges are to be paid by the consignee, the conditions of sale would refer to this as:

    (A) Carriage on account
    (B) Carriage deferred
    (C) Carriage forward
    (D) Carriage included

11. A transport operator's employee is injured and his vehicle is damaged. The judgement debt is unsatisfied (ie the uninsured driver is unable to pay the damages awarded against him). In these circumstances, under Compulsory Third Party Insurance legislation:

    (A) The operator can claim under his own Motor Vehicle insurance for damage to his vehicle, and under Employers' Liability insurance for the injuries to his driver
    (B) The operator can claim under his own Motor Vehicle insurance for damage to his vehicle, but no compensation can be obtained in respect of his employee's injuries
    (C) The driver can recover damages from the Motor Insurers' Bureau, but the operator cannot recover from them
    (D) Both the operator and the driver can recover the amount of the unsatisfied judgement debt from the Motor Insurers' Bureau

12. An excess clause in a Motor Vehicle Insurance Policy means that:

   (A) The operator ceases to be covered if he makes an excessive number of claims (ie beyond a stipulated number) in a year
   (B) The operator is not covered for the excess over a stipulated sum
   (C) An initial amount of a claim (eg first £50) will be met by the operator
   (D) The operator will be covered for amounts in excess of the maximum payable under an ordinary policy by the payment of an additional premium

13. For day to day business an operator would use which of the following types of bank account?

   (A) Savings account
   (B) Deposit account
   (C) Current account
   (D) Loan account

14. When a Minister of Transport introduces a new Construction and Use regulation, this is an example of:

   (A) Ministerial legislation
   (B) Delegated legislation
   (C) EC law
   (D) Statute law

15. An agent accepts a booking on behalf of a transport operator. The operator is fully committed and fails to carry out the contract.

   (A) The operator would be liable for any losses sustained by the customer by reason of the operator's failure to complete the contract
   (B) The operator has no liability and the customer must seek redress from the agent
   (C) The operator is only liable if he confirmed acceptance of the booking in writing
   (D) The operator can avoid his liability if he can show that the agent exceeded his authority in accepting the order

16. In which of the following could a transport operator avoid liability for the act of his servant (employee)?

   (A) As there were no drivers available, a traffic clerk, *without his employer's knowledge*, moved a vehicle which was causing obstruction, and damaged a visitors vehicle and its contents
   (B) Two fitters who had been carrying out maintenance on a customer's vehicles decided to have a race with them, despite previous warnings against this practice, and were involved in a collision causing extensive damage
   (C) A driver who had received several verbal warnings concerning speeding, and had been given a written warning that a further occurrence would result in dismissal, ignored the warning, and crashed the vehicle doing extensive damage to property adjoining the road

(D) A driver deviated from his normal route in order to visit his girl friend and while off his normal route was involved in an accident, due to his negligence. His employer can avoid liability because deviation renders a contract void *ab initio*

17. The maximum number of employees that may be employed before it is necessary to employ a qualified first-aider is:

(A) 20
(B) 50
(C) 100
(D) 150

18. In which of the following circumstances is an employer required to give an employee time off from work with pay?

(A) A trade union representative on official union business
(B) An employee called for jury service
(C) An employee who is a local magistrate, for court duty
(D) An employee who is a school governor, to attend a governor's meeting

19. An employee who qualifies for redundancy pay would receive for each year of service between the ages of 41 and 64:

(A) ½ weeks' pay
(B) 1 weeks' pay
(C) 1½ weeks' pay
(D) 2 weeks' pay

20. An employer of more than 20 persons is required to employ a quota of disabled persons. This quota may be varied according to the suitability or unsuitability of the employment, trade or industry, but the standard quota is:

(A) 2% of the workforce
(B) 3% of the workforce
(C) 4% of the workforce
(D) 5% of the workforce

Trial Examination (National — Module B)

1. The driver of a 38 tonne articulated lorry, operating under Community rules may replace the 45 minutes break following 4½ hours total driving, by:

   (A) 2 breaks of 15 minutes
   (B) 3 breaks of 10 minutes
   (C) 3 breaks of 15 minutes
   (D) 2 breaks of 20 minutes

2. Under Community rules the daily driving period must not exceed:

   (A) 8 hours (extended to 9 hours not more than twice each week)
   (B) 8½ hours (extended to 9½ hours not more than twice each week)
   (C) 9 hours (extended to 10 hours not more than twice each week)
   (D) 9½ (extended to 10½ hours not more than twice each week)

3. The fortnightly driving period must not exceed:

   (A) 112 hours in any 2 consecutive weeks
   (B) 108 hours in any 2 consecutive weeks
   (C) 106 hours in any 2 consecutive weeks
   (D) 90 hours in any 2 consecutive weeks

4. Where journeys involve the use of ferries or trains, crew members may interrupt their daily rest periods provided that the rest period is:

   (A) Interrupted only once and 1 hour is added to the total daily rest period
   (B) Interrupted only once and 2 hours are added to the total daily rest period
   (C) Interrupted not more than twice and 1 hour is added to the total daily rest period
   (D) Interrupted not more than twice and 2 hours are added to the total daily rest period

5. Where a vehicle is double-manned the minimum daily rest period for each driver is:

   (A) 8 hours in 30 hours
   (B) 10 hours in 30 hours
   (C) 8 hours in 27 hours
   (D) 10 hours in 27 hours

6. Tachographs must be re-calibrated at approved centres in the United Kingdom every:

   (A) 1 year
   (B) 2 years
   (C) 3 years
   (D) 6 years

7. A driver must retain his completed tachograph charts for:

   (A) The last two days
   (B) The last seven days
   (C) The current week and also for the last day of the previous week on which he drove
   (D) 28 days

8. Operators must retain completed tachograph charts for:

   (A) 15 months
   (B) 12 months
   (C) 6 months
   (D) 3 months

9. A tachograph must be accurate to:

   (A) Plus or minus 6 mph of the actual speed at speeds in excess of 10 mph
   (B) Plus or minus 10 mph of the actual speed at speeds in excess of 6 mph
   (C) Plus or minus 6 kph of the actual speed at speeds in excess of 10 kph
   (D) Plus or minus 6 kph of the actual speed at all speeds

10. The minimum age at which a driver can hold an HGV Class 1 licence is:

    (A) 17 years
    (B) 18 years
    (C) 21 years
    (D) 25 years

11. The minimum age for drivers' mates is:

    (A) 16 years
    (B) 17 years
    (C) 18 years
    (D) 21 years

12. If a driving licence cannot be produced on request by a Department of Transport examiner, it must be produced at the office of the examiner or at an office of a specified Licensing Authority within:

    (A) 10 days
    (B) 7 days
    (C) 5 days
    (D) 3 days

13. On roads other than dual carriageways or motorways, goods vehicles not exceeding 7.5 tonnes gross weight are restricted to a speed of:

   (A) 60 mph
   (B) 50 mph
   (C) 40 mph
   (D) 30 mph

14. The maximum speed at which an articulated vehicle exceeding 7.5 tonnes is permitted to operate on motorways is:

   (A) 40 mph
   (B) 50 mph
   (C) 60 mph
   (D) 70 mph

15. For which of the following offences would a fixed penalty fine *not* be appropriate?

   (A) Using a vehicle with defective tyres
   (B) Failing to display a current excise licence
   (C) Motor racing on the highway
   (D) Parking a vehicle in a "no waiting" area

16. A loading ban throughout the working day (normally 08.30 to 18.30 hours) is indicated by:

   (A) Single yellow lines in the gutter
   (B) Single yellow marks at the kerbside
   (C) Double yellow marks at the kerbside
   (D) Treble yellow marks at the kerbside

17. How many points can a driver licensed under the Young HGV Driver Training Scheme accumulate before he is liable to have his special licence withdrawn?

   (A) 2 penalty points
   (B) 3 penalty points
   (C) 4 penalty points
   (D) 5 penalty points

18. An HGV licence holder can only have that licence suspended by

   (A) A Chief Constable
   (B) A magistrate
   (C) A Licensing Authority
   (D) A traffic examiner.

19. The definition of an articulated vehicle states that when the semi-trailer is attached with its load uniformly distributed the percentage of the load to be borne by the drawing vehicle is:

(A) 10%
(B) 20%
(C) 25%
(D) 30%

20. A wide tyre is one which has an area of contact with the road having a width of not less than:

(A) 200mm
(B) 250mm
(C) 300mm
(D) 350mm

21. Horns may not be sounded when a vehicle is stationary on a road nor when it is in motion on a restricted road at night between:

(A) 22.30 hours and 7.30 hours
(B) 23.30 hours and 7.00 hours
(C) 22.30 hours and 7.00 hours
(D) 23.30 hours and 7.30 hours

22. Spray suppression equipment must be fitted to the wheels of each axle of vehicles first used from April 1, 1986 which exceed:

(A) 3.5 tonnes maximum gross weight
(B) 5 tonnes maximum gross weight
(C) 7.5 tonnes maximum gross weight
(D) 12 tonnes maximum gross weight

23. The term "axle spread" used in weight calculations concerning rigid vehicles means the distance between the:

(A) Inner axles
(B) Outer axles
(C) Two rear axles
(D) Two front axles

24. The maximum permitted length of a rigid goods vehicle is:

(A) 12m
(B) 13m
(C) 15m
(D) 18m

25. A vehicle not constructed to carry a load, having an unladen weight not exceeding 7370kg is called:

(A) A heavy motor car
(B) A motor tractor
(C) A light locomotive
(D) A heavy locomotive

26. When P=Payload, D=the distance from the centre of load to the rear axle and W=wheelbase, the formula for calculating the load on the front axle is:

(A) $\dfrac{P \times D}{W}$

(B) $\dfrac{P+D}{W}$

(C) $\dfrac{P \times W}{D}$

(D) $\dfrac{W-D}{P}$

27. Where a motor vehicle is drawing a trailer by means of a tow-rope or chain the distance between the nearest points

(A) Must not exceed 3m
(B) Must not exceed 4m
(C) Must not exceed 4.5m
(D) Is not specified

28. The overall width of a vehicle and its load must not exceed

(A) 2.3m
(B) 2.5m
(C) 2.7m
(D) 2.9m

29. The maximum overhang of a goods vehicle must not exceed

(A) 60% of the wheelbase
(B) 40% of the wheelbase
(C) 30% of the wheelbase
(D) 20% of the wheelbase

30. In the case of a four-wheeled rigid goods vehicle overhang is measured from the centre line through the rear axle to:

(A) The rearmost part of the chassis
(B) The rearmost lamp
(C) The rearmost part of the vehicle
(D) The rearmost part of the vehicle and its load

31. When a vehicle is shown to be overloaded the form issued by a DTp examiner is:

(A) GV9
(B) GV10
(C) GV120
(D) GV160

32. A Category 2 special types vehicle (with a total weight not exceeding 80,000 kg) when operating on a dual-carriageway is restricted to a speed limit of:

(A) 20 mph
(B) 30 mph
(C) 35 mph
(D) 40 mph

33. Highway and bridge authorities must be notified when the gross weight of a vehicle or any combination of vehicles and trailers exceeds:

(A) 72,600kg
(B) 72,000kg
(C) 80,000kg
(D) 76,600kg

34. The *second* means of braking of rigid vehicles (with more than two axles) and all articulated vehicles registered on or after January 1, 1968 must have an efficiency of:

(A) 15%
(B) 20%
(C) 25%
(D) 40%

35. The maximum period for which an examiner can issue a delayed prohibition is:

(A) 5 days
(B) 7 days
(C) 10 days
(D) 14 days

36. From the lowest part of the illuminating surface, the minimum height at which a headlamp may be fixed is:

(A) 600mm
(B) 500mm
(C) 400mm
(D) 300mm

37. The total weight of a vehicle with body ready for operation on the road and inclusive of fuel, water, tools and any towing bracket, but exclusive of its load is called:

(A) Kerbside weight
(B) Unladen weight
(C) Tare weight
(D) Gross plated weight

38. For which of the following vehicles would an operator's licence be required?

(A) A four-wheeled rigid goods vehicle of 3250kg GPW
(B) A local authority refuse collection vehicle of 7500kg GPW
(C) A four-wheeled rigid goods vehicle of 5000kg GPW
(D) A dual-purpose vehicle of 1500kg unladen weight

39. A four-wheeled goods vehicle with a GPW of 1500kg will pay vehicle excise duty based on:

(A) Gross plated weight
(B) Kerbside weight
(C) Unladen weight
(D) Same rate as a car

40. A vehicle operating under a Recovery Vehicle Licence will cease to be covered by that licence if:

(A) It is used to carry goods which were being carried in the broken down vehicle prior to its breakdown, during removal of the vehicle for repair
(B) Removing a broken down vehicle from premises to which it had been taken for repair, to other premises for repair or scrapping
(C) For towing or carrying one trailer which had been towed or carried by the vehicle prior to its breakdown, during removal of the vehicle for repair
(D) After recovering a broken down vehicle, the recovery vehicle is used to deliver the goods previously carried in the broken down vehicle

Chapter 13

1. An instruction issued by the EC with the intention of achieving a broadly stated objective, leaving the Member State free to select its own method of reaching that objective, is called:

    (A) A recommendation
    (B) A regulation
    (C) A directive
    (D) A decision

2. The international convention that covers the carriage of dangerous goods by road is the:

    (A) ADR
    (B) ATC
    (C) ATA
    (D) ATP

3. If a Member State fails to comply with an EC directive, the Court of Justice may impose a fine for each month the State fails to comply, not exceeding:

    (A) £100,000
    (B) 100,000 francs
    (C) 100,000 SDRs
    (D) Has no power to impose a fine

4. An HGV driver, driving under EC Regulation 3820/85, is restricted to 9 hours daily driving. However this daily driving period may be extended to:

    (A) 10 hours not more than once a week
    (B) 10 hours not more than twice a week
    (C) 11 hours not more than once a week
    (D) 11 hours not more than twice a week

5. When a vehicle carries two drivers, the daily rest period must be not less than:

    (A) 8 hours in a 30 hour period
    (B) 9 hours in a 30 hour period
    (C) 9 hours in a 27 hour period
    (D) 10 hours in a 27 hour period

6. On a day when the daily rest period is not reduced, it may be divided into 2 or 3 parts, providing certain conditions are met. Which of the following meets those conditions?

    (A) One period of 5 hours and one period of 6 hours
    (B) Two periods of 6 hours each
    (C) One period of 8½ hours and one period of 3½ hours
    (D) One period of 8 hours, one period of 3½ hours and one period of ½ hour

7. This week a driver has driven a vehicle for a total of 48 hours. The maximum number of hours he can drive next week is:

    (A) 42 hours
    (B) 44 hours
    (C) 46 hours
    (D) 48 hours

8. When the daily rest period is interrupted to accommodate a train journey or ferry crossing, the daily rest period must be increased by:

    (A) 30 minutes
    (B) 1 hour
    (C) 1 hour, 30 minutes
    (D) 2 hours

9. Provided the time lost is compensated for during the following three weeks, the weekly rest period of 45 hours may be reduced, when taken away from the home base, to:

    (A) 40 hours
    (B) 36 hours
    (C) 30 hours
    (D) 24 hours

10. Which of the following statements does *not* apply when driving under AETR rules?

    (A) Maximum weekly driving, 48 hours in any period of seven consecutive days
    (B) Maximum continuous driving 4 hours, extendable to 4½ hours to enable a driver to reach a convenient stopping place or his destination
    (C) Daily rest period of 11 hours, may be reduced to 9 hours three times a week
    (D) Weekly rest period 24 hours immediately preceded or followed by a daily rest period

Chapter 14

1. Which of the following is a document of title?

    (A) CMA consignment note
    (B) Bill of lading
    (C) ECGD Certificate
    (D) Standard shipping note

2. The organisation funded by the Department of Trade to create a system of aligned documentation is:

    (A) AETR
    (B) COREPER
    (C) ECMT
    (D) SITPRO

3. Which of the following countries is not a party to the International Convention on the Taxation of Road Vehicles 1956.

    (A) Czechoslovakia
    (B) East Germany
    (C) Romania
    (D) Poland

4. A tonne/kilometre tax is levied on British goods vehicles entering:

    (A) Austria
    (B) Belgium
    (C) Netherlands
    (D) Luxembourg

5. Which of the following statements concerning EC multilateral permits is correct?

    (A) Is required for both hire or reward and own account operations
    (B) Is required for own account operations only
    (C) May be used for unaccompanied trailer or semi-trailer traffic
    (D) May not be used for unaccompanied trailer or semi-trailer traffic

6. In which of the following countries is a permit required for "own account" operations:

    (A) Poland
    (B) Holland
    (C) Czechoslovakia
    (D) Sweden

7. Unused permits must be returned after expiry to the International Road Freight Office within:

(A) 7 days
(B) 10 days
(C) 14 days
(D) 15 days

8. It is an offence under the Goods Vehicles (International Road Haulage Permits) Regulations to transport goods for hire or reward, without a valid permit from the United Kingdom to which of the following countries?

(A) Switzerland
(B) Italy
(C) Belgium
(D) Holland

9. ECMT permits are valid in:

(A) EC and EFTA countries only
(B) Most West European States and one in Eastern Europe
(C) West European States only
(D) EC countries only

10. A period permit allows a vehicle

(A) One return journey
(B) One return journey within a specified period
(C) A fixed number of journeys in a given period
(D) As many journeys as it can undertake in one year

Chapter 15

1. Before publication of "forked" tariffs between the United Kingdom and other EC Member States, organisations representing users and services ancillary to transport are consulted. In the United Kingdom the representative bodies are the Freight Transport Association and:

(A) The Road Haulage Association
(B) The National Chamber of Commerce
(C) The Institute of Export
(D) The Institute of Freight Forwarders

2. In addition to road journeys, the Green Card gives cover for sea journeys which do not exceed:

(A) 50 hours
(B) 65 hours
(C) 75 hours
(D) 150km

3. The maximum liability for carriers under the CMR Convention is:

(A) £800 per tonne
(B) 8.33 SDRs per tonne
(C) 8.33 SDRs per kilo
(D) £1000 per ton

4. Under the CMR Convention a carrier is not liable for loss, damage or delay to goods:

(A) If the value exceeds £6000 per tonne and the value of the goods has not been declared
(B) Unless the carrier or his servants have been guilty of wilful misconduct
(C) If caused by circumstances which the carrier could not foresee and the consequences of which he was unable to prevent
(D) If an official CMR consignment note is not used

5. Under the CMR Convention a carrier's liability for delay is limited to a sum linked with the amount of the carriage charges, unless a "special interest in delivery" has been declared. This amount is equal to:

(A) The amount of the carriage charges
(B) Twice the amount of the carriage charges
(C) Three times the amount of the carriage charges
(D) Four times the amount of the carriage charges.

6. When a carriage involving more than one carrier results in damage, the responsibility for which cannot be attributed to any one particular carrier though it is clearly due to negligence, a claim for damages:

(A) Must be borne by the contracting carrier
(B) Must be shared equally by all the carriers
(C) Will only be met if the claimant can show which carrier was responsible
(D) Will be shared by all carriers in proportion to the share of payment of carriage charges due to each of them

7. When a claim for damage, which was not apparent at the time of checking, is made under the CMR, it must be made in writing within how many days of checking?

(A) 3 days
(B) 5 days
(C) 7 days
(D) 14 days

8. Which of the following goods do *not* require pre-entry for Customs purposes?

(A) Goods from a bonded warehouse
(B) Goods in transit through a United Kingdom port
(C) Goods being exported under the Simplified Clearance Procedure
(D) Goods for temporary exportation

9. A TIR Carnet is obtained from:

(A) IRFO
(B) AA or RAC
(C) FTA or RHA
(D) Major Chambers of Commerce.

10. The code used on the SAD to indicate that goods are in free circulation when passing from one EC Member State to another via a third Member State is:

(A) T1
(B) T2
(C) T2L
(D) DD3

Chapter 16

1. The purpose of the ATP Convention is to ensure that haulage vehicles and their equipment comply with international standards of:

(A) Customs sealing
(B) Design
(C) Thermal efficiency
(D) Roadworthiness

2. An ATA Carnet is used in connection with which of the following goods?

   (A) The importation of perishable goods
   (B) The importation of dangerous goods
   (C) The temporary importation of goods for display
   (D) The importation of personal effects

3. An ADR vehicle certificate is valid for:

   (A) 6 months
   (B) 12 months
   (C) 2 years
   (D) 6 years

4. Tanks requiring ADR certificates may be certified by inspecting organisations approved by the Health and Safety Executive. The certificate is valid for:

   (A) 1 year
   (B) 2 years
   (C) 6 years
   (D) 6 months to 6 years according to the classification of the tank.

5. Which of the following documents must be presented to the shipping company when hazardous goods are to be carried on a Ro-Ro ferry?

   (A) Own account document
   (B) Dangerous goods shipping note
   (C) ATP certificate
   (D) CMR consignment note

6. For how long does a Certificate of Compliance issued in pursuance of the ATP Convention last?

   (A) 1 year
   (B) 2 years
   (C) 3 years
   (D) 6 years

7. In addition to road carriage, the ATP Convention covers sea journeys which do not exceed:

   (A) 50 miles
   (B) 65 miles
   (C) 75 miles
   (D) 150km

8. It is forbidden for drivers to smoke when driving in:

(A) Belgium
(B) Italy
(C) Norway
(D) Sweden

9. Vehicles with a total laden weight exceeding 3500kg must carry at least two wheel chocks in:

(A) Austria
(B) Belgium
(C) Czechoslovakia
(D) Poland

10. It is an offence to drive a vehicle in Hungary with a blood alcohol level of:

(A) 50 milligrammes of alcohol per 100 millilitres of blood
(B) 80 milligrammes of alcohol per 100 millilitres of blood
(C) 100 milligrammes of alcohol per 100 millilitres of blood
(D) Any alcohol at all

Trial Examination (International — Module D)

1. Under EC hours regulations the weekly rest period, when taken at the home base, may be reduced from 45 hours to:

    (A) 24 hours
    (B) 30 hours
    (C) 36 hours
    (D) 40 hours

2. Under EC hours regulations, when a vehicle is double-manned each driver must have a rest period of at least

    (A) 8 hours in a 27 hour period
    (B) 8 hours in a 30 hour period
    (C) 9 hours in a 27 hour period
    (D) 9 hours in a 30 hour period

3. Under EC hours regulations, where the permissible maximum weight of a vehicle exceeds 20 tonnes, a break from driving must be taken of:

    (A) At least 30 minutes after 4 hours, or 2 breaks of 20 minutes, or 3 breaks of 15 minutes during the total driving period
    (B) At least 30 minutes after 4½ hours, or 2 breaks of 20 minutes or 3 breaks of 15 minutes during the total driving period
    (C) At least 45 minutes after a total of 4½ hours, or 3 breaks of 15 minutes spread over the driving period or immediately following it
    (D) At least 1 hour after 4½ hours or 2 breaks of 30 minutes during the total daily driving period

4. Under EC hours regulations total fortnightly driving must not exceed:

    (A) 80 hours
    (B) 86 hours
    (C) 90 hours
    (D) 96 hours

5. In the event of a breakdown or faulty operation of a tachograph it must be repaired, at the latest:

    (A) Within 48 hours
    (B) As soon as the vehicle returns to its depot or en route if the journey is likely to exceed 7 days
    (C) Within 7 days
    (D) Within 14 days

6. When completed, a European Accident Statement form should be sent to:

   (A) The Motor Insurers' Bureau of the country where the accident occurred
   (B) The Motor Insurers' Bureau of the country of origin of the driver
   (C) The Motor Insurers' Bureau of the respective drivers involved in the accident
   (D) Each driver's insurance company when reporting the accident

7. A Green Card carried on an international road haulage journey relates to insurance of the:

   (A) Driver to secure release in the event of an accident
   (B) Load carried on the vehicle
   (C) Vehicle
   (D) Vehicle and its load

8. A forked tariff is one which:

   (A) Lays down maximum and minimum rates
   (B) Applies different rates to the outward and inward journeys
   (C) Gives preferential rates to "own nationality" operators
   (D) Permits the application of lower rates for return loads

9. Reference tariffs are:

   (A) Only binding if national road haulage associations have agreed them
   (B) Binding only in EC Member States which have introduced them
   (C) Obligatory among all Member States of the EC
   (D) Published for guidance only and are not binding in any way

10. International Driving Permits are issued by the:

    (A) AA or RAC
    (B) RHA or FTA
    (C) International Road Freight Office
    (D) DVLC Swansea

11. Entry visas are required for drivers visiting:

    (A) Yugoslavia
    (B) Hungary
    (C) Austria
    (D) Spain

12. A Carnet de Passage en Douane is issued in the United Kingdom by:

   (A) The International Road Freight Office
   (B) HM Customs
   (C) The AA or RAC
   (D) The RHA or FTA

13. An EC multilateral permit is required to:

   (A) Transit EC countries in order to pick up loads in countries outside the EC
   (B) Enable an operator to engage in tramping operations between Member States of the EC
   (C) Transport goods from the United Kingdom to non-EC countries
   (D) Send unaccompanied trailers or semi-trailers to EC Member States

14. Permits for own account operations are required in:

   (A) Czechoslovakia
   (B) Greece
   (C) Hungary
   (D) Norway

15. The French road/rail system (Kangarou):

   (A) Can be used for own account traffic only
   (B) Can be used for complete vehicles only
   (C) Applies to both accompanied and unaccompanied vehicles
   (D) Applies only to unaccompanied trailers or semi-trailers and must be used for both outward and return journeys

16. Vehicles which exceed the following weights (a) single axle load of more than 10 tonnes, (b) a double axle (ie less than 2m apart) load of more than 16 tonnes, are liable for tax on a sliding scale in:

   (A) Austria
   (B) Hungary
   (C) Czechoslovakia
   (D) Norway

17. Which of the following countries does not impose either a vehicle tax, or a kilometre tax, or both, on British vehicles in transit through the country?

   (A) Austria
   (B) Holland
   (C) Norway
   (D) Sweden

18. A TIR certificate of approval must be renewed:

   (A) Every year
   (B) Every 2 years
   (C) Every 4 years
   (D) Every 6 years

19. An ATA Carnet is used for the temporary importation of

   (A) Personal goods
   (B) Goods for exhibitions and fairs
   (C) Motor vehicles
   (D) Household effects

20. ATA Carnets are recognised in:

   (A) Albania
   (B) East Germany
   (C) Poland
   (D) USSR

21. An ADR vehicle certificate is valid for:

   (A) 12 months
   (B) 2 years
   (C) 3 years
   (D) 4 years

22. Vehicles requiring ADR certificates are certified by:

   (A) Organisations approved by the Health and Safety Executive
   (B) Inspectors appointed by the Chemical Industries Association (CIA)
   (C) Department of Transport examiners at HGV testing stations
   (D) RHA or FTA inspectors

23. The International Carriage of Perishable Foodstuffs Act 1976 (ATP) does not apply to which of the following

   (A) Frozen fish
   (B) Chilled meat
   (C) Fresh vegetables and soft fruit
   (D) Dairy products

24. The CMR Convention applies to:

   (A) Goods carried on own account
   (B) Mail and postal packages
   (C) Goods consigned from the United Kingdom to a non-contracting country
   (D) Funeral consignments

25. The CMR Convention does not apply to journeys between the United Kingdom and

   (A) Belgium
   (B) Eire
   (C) Holland
   (D) Poland

26. How many copies of the consignment note are required under the CMR Convention?

   (A) One
   (B) Two
   (C) Three
   (D) Four

27. Under the CMR Convention the maximum liability for loss or damage faced by a road haulier (excluding carriage charges, Customs duties and other charges incurred in connection with the carriage of goods) is:

   (A) 8.33 SDRs per kilo
   (B) 3.88 SDRs per kilo
   (C) 125 gold francs per kilo
   (D) 250 gold francs per kilo

28. Which of the following countries prohibits the transit of heavy goods vehicles on Sundays?

   (A) Norway
   (B) Belgium
   (C) Switzerland
   (D) East Germany

29. If the pound is strong in relation to the French franc a British haulage driver purchasing fuel in France would pay

   (A) Less for fuel in terms of pounds
   (B) More for fuel in terms of pounds
   (C) More for fuel in terms of francs
   (D) The same amount for the fuel as if the pound was weak

30. For which of the following countries is a visa required in addition to a British passport?

 (A) Austria
 (B) Romania
 (C) Switzerland
 (D) Yugoslavia

Answers to Tests and Examinations
(National)

Chapter	1.	2.	3.	4.	5.
Chapter 1	(C)	(A)	(D)	(C)	(D)
	6. (D)	7. (D)	8. (D)	9. (D)	10. (A)
Chapter 2	(C)	(A)	(C)	(C)	(A)
	6. (A)	7. (D)	8. (A)	9. (C)	10. (C)
Chapter 3	(C)	(C)	(D)	(C)	(D)
	6. (C)	7. (C)	8. (A)	9. (C)	10. (C)
Chapter 4	(C)	(D)	(D)	(A)	(B)
	6. (B)	7. (B)	8. (B)	9. (D)	10. (C)
Chapter 5	(D)	(A)	(A)	(D)	(B)
	6. (C)	7. (B)	8. (B)	9. (B)	10. (D)
Chapter 6	(A)	(C)	(D)	(C)	(B)
	6. (C)	7. (D)	8. (D)	9. (B)	10. (D)
Chapter 7	(A)	(D)	(D)	(C)	(B)
	6. (C)	7. (C)	8. (C)	9. (B)	10. (D)
Chapter 8	(C)	(B)	(C)	(C)	(D)
	6. (A)	7. (D)	8. (A)	9. (B)	10. (A)
Chapter 9	(D)	(A)	(C)	(C)	(D)
	6. (D)	7. (C)	8. (B)	9. (C)	10. (A)
Chapter 10	(C)	(C)	(C)	(C)	(D)
	6. (D)	7. (D)	8. (D)	9. (D)	10. (C)
Chapter 11	(D)	(C)	(C)	(D)	(C)
	6. (C)	7. (C)	8. (D)	9. (B)	10. (D)
Chapter 12	(C)	(C)	(D)	(D)	(A)
	6. (C)	7. (C)	8. (B)	9. (A)	10. (C)

Trial Examination *(National — Module A)*

1. (C)
2. (C)
3. (B)
4. (A)
5. (D)
6. (D)
7. (C)
8. (B)
9. (B)
10. (C)
11. (D)
12. (C)
13. (C)
14. (B)
15. (A)
16. (A)
17. (B)
18. (A)
19. (C)
20. (B)

Trial Examination *(National — Module B)*

1. (C)	11. (C)	21. (B)	31. (D)
2. (C)	12. (A)	22. (D)	32. (C)
3. (D)	13. (B)	23. (B)	33. (C)
4. (B)	14. (C)	24. (A)	34. (C)
5. (A)	15. (C)	25. (B)	35. (C)
6. (D)	16. (C)	26. (A)	36. (B)
7. (C)	17. (B)	27. (C)	37. (A)
8. (B)	18. (C)	28. (D)	38. (C)
9. (D)	19. (B)	29. (A)	39. (D)
10. (C)	20. (C)	30. (C)	40. (D)

(International)

Chapter 13	1. (C)	2. (A)	3. (D)	4. (B)	5. (A)
	6. (C)	7. (A)	8. (D)	9. (D)	10. (C)
Chapter 14	1. (B)	2. (D)	3. (B)	4. (A)	5. (D)
	6. (C)	7. (D)	8. (B)	9. (B)	10. (D)
Chapter 15	1. (D)	2. (B)	3. (C)	4. (C)	5. (A)
	6. (D)	7. (C)	8. (C)	9. (C)	10. (B)
Chapter 16	1. (C)	2. (C)	3. (B)	4. (D)	5. (B)
	6. (D)	7. (D)	8. (C)	9. (A)	10. (D)

Trial Examination *(International — Module D)*

1. (C)	7. (C)	13. (B)	19. (B)	25. (B)
2. (B)	8. (A)	14. (A)	20. (C)	26. (C)
3. (C)	9. (D)	15. (D)	21. (A)	27. (A)
4. (C)	10. (A)	16. (B)	22. (C)	28. (C)
5. (B)	11. (B)	17. (B)	23. (C)	29. (A)
6. (D)	12. (C)	18. (B)	24. (C)	30. (B)

Index

A
abnormal indivisible load 59–60
ACAS,
  codes of practice,
    disciplinary practice and procedures in employment 138–40
    disclosure of information to trade unions for collective bargaining 140
    time off for trade union duties and activities 140–1
  powers and duties 141
accidents, traffic,
  driver's obligations 43
  instructions to drivers 44
  procedure 43–4
  production of documents 43
acid test ratio 100
ADR Certificate (dangerous goods) 176
Advisory, Conciliation and Arbitration Service see ACAS
age limits,
  driver's mate 167
  HGV drivers 167
agents,
  compared with employees 129
  employers' liability 129–30
  function 129
AGR Convention 200
amber lights, use of 76, 80
ancient custom 123
animal, definition, Road Traffic Act 1988 43
ante-natal care, employee's right to time off 143
Articles of Association 96
articulated vehicles,
  definition 52
  maximum length 54
  maximum weights 53–4
ATA Carnet 176, 198
ATP Certificate (perishable goods) 176
attendants, when required 60
authorised insurer 44

B
bail bond 176
balance sheet 98

banks,
  accounts 118
  loans 97
  main functions 117–18
  services 117–19
bearer cheque 119
bill of lading 117
blood test, drinking and driving offences 38
blue lights, use of 76, 80
bracket tariffs 174–5
brakes 63
braking efficiency 63
breaks from driving,
  AETR regulations 168
  Community regulated operations 12
breath analysis, drinking and driving offences 38
business categories see sole trader, partnerships, limited companies

C
cabotage 172
capital, erosion 103
capital employed 99
care,
  duty of 130–1
    reasonable care 130
    to trespassers 134
    towards children 134
    visitors 134
carnets,
  ATA 176, 198
  Carnets de Passage en Douane 176, 197
  Community 197
  TIR 176, 198–200
carriage,
  contract of 128–9
  legislation 125
carriage forward 110, 128
Carriage of Goods by Road Act 1965 125, 181
carriage paid 110, 128
Carriers' Act 1830 125
carrier's liability,
  delay 185
  loss or damage 183–5, 186
cash flow 99

269

cash sales 110
cash in transit insurance 117
Central Arbitration Committee (CAC) 141-2
Certificate of Competence see CPC
Certificate of Conformity see Type Approval Certificate (TAC)
Certificate of Incorporation 96
certificate of insurance see insurance certificate
Certificate of Professional Competence see CPC
Certificate of Trading 97
Certificate of Weight 56
Certification Officer, responsibilities 142
certifying officers, powers 40, 41
charges see rates
checks on vehicle,
　annual tests 80-1
　spot checks 80-1
　TIR carnets 199-200
cheques,
　crossings 119
　description 118
　types of 119
civil liability, insurance 188
Classification, Packaging and Labelling of Dangerous Substances Regulations 1984 50
clearing house 121
closed shop agreements 151
CMR Convention 125
　consignment notes 113, 176, 182
　definition of international journey 181
　goods exempt 182
　position in UK 181-2
　purpose 165, 181
　vehicles covered 181
codes of practice 138-41
collective bargaining 137, 140
common law 123
Common Transport Policy (CTP) 164-5, 206
Community Carnet 197
Community guarantee vouchers 197
Community Transit System 195-7
company safety policy 162
composite trailer 52
compulsory tariffs 175
Conditions of Carriage, 1982 135
Conditions of Carriage, lien 110
consignment notes,
　description 112-13, 183

　noting special arrangements 187
　obtaining forms 113, 182
　recording damaged goods 187-8
　requirement of CMR Convention 113, 182
consignor, duties 187
containers 203
contract,
　breach of, remedies available 126
　definition 125
　essential elements 126-8
Contracts of Employment Act 1972 142
Convention for the International Carriage of Goods by Road see CMR Convention
convertor dolly 52
cost accounting see costing
cost centre 102
costing 100-6
　calculation of rates 106
　depreciation 103-5
　description 100
　profit level 105-6
　purpose 101
costs, types of 102, 103 Fig
costs of international haulage 201-2
CPC (Certificate of Professional Competence),
　examination 8-10
　　examining body, RSA 8
　　exemptions 9
　　topics covered 9-10
　　when held 9
　exemptions 8
　introduction of 7
　methods of study 9
　period of validity 8
credit note 112
credit sales 110
credit transfers 119
creditors 98
Croner's Health and Safety at Work 161
Croner's Operational Costings for Transport Management 106
Croner's Reference Book for Employers 162
Croner's Reference Book for Exporters 193
Croner's Reference Book for the Self Employed and Smaller Businesses 162
Croner's Road Transport Operation 190, 205
crossed cheque 119
current account 118

current ratio 100
Customs Convention on the International Transport of Goods 1975 (TIR) 165
customs conventions, sources of information 190
customs entry forms 178
Customs and Excise Management Act 1979 190
Customs Registered Number (CRN) 192
customs seals, TIR carnets 199–200
customs *see also* export declaration and clearance, import clearance

D

dangerous goods 187
  driver instruction 212
  markings on vehicle 211
  packaging and labelling 212
  regulations 210
  vehicle examination 210-11
Dangerous Substances (Conveyance by Road in Road Tankers and Tank Containers) Regulations 1981 47
debentures 97
debit note 112
debtors 98, 99
debts, factoring 99
defect notice (GV219) 83
delay in delivery 185
delegated legislation 124
deposit account 118
depreciation,
  calculation,
    diminishing balance method 104–5
    straight line method 103, 104
  definition 103
  purpose 103
dim-dip lighting devices 76
dimensions,
  Special Type vehicles and trailers 60
  vehicles 54–6
direct costs 102
direct debits 119
direction indicators 76, 77–8
disabled person, definition 158
Disabled Persons (Employment) Acts 1944 and 1958 158
disciplinary procedures, code of practice 138–40
discounts, cash and trade 110
discrimination,
  legislation,
    Disabled Persons (Employment) Acts 1944 and 1958 158
    Equal Pay Act 1970 155–6
    Race Relations Act 1976 157–8
    Sex Discrimination Act 1975 156-7
dismissal,
  employee's rights 144
  unfair, employee's rights 145–6
disqualification from driving,
  applications for removal 39–40
  calculation of period 39
  court's discretion 39
  definition 37
  removal of penalty points 40
documents, production in case of accident 43
documents used in commerce 111–13
drawbar combinations 53
drawbar trailers 53
drinking and driving offences 38
driver,
  definition 11
  obligations when involved in accident 43
drivers' hours 11–13
  AETR regulations 168
  daily, EC regulations 12, 166
  domestic operations 11
  domestic regulations, comparison with EC regulations 13
  mixed driving 11, 12
  persons covered by regulations 11
  records 13–14, 20–1, 176
    AETR member countries 169
    EC regulations 167, 169
    exemptions from British legislation 20
    information required 13
    record books 21
  use of vehicle for non-business purposes 14
  weekly, EC regulations 12, 166
drivers' mates, age limit 22
driving, definition 11
driving licences 21–8
  employer's responsibilities 23
  international transport 175
  medical conditions 22
  obtaining 21
  production of 22–3, 41–2
  provisional licence 21
  types of 21
  Unified Driver Licensing System 27–8
driving motor vehicles, minimum age limits

21-2
dual-purpose vehicles,
  definition 52
  maximum width 55
duty, breach of 130

E
EC,
  bodies,
    Assembly (European Parliament) 164
    Commission 163
    Committee of Permanent
      Representatives (COREPER) 163-4
    Council of Ministers 163
    Court of Justice 164
    Economic and Social Committee
      164
    Common Transport Policy (CTP) 164-5
EC directive, definition 163
EC Directives,
  conditions for admission to
    occupation of road haulage operator
    (74/561) 7
  insurance against civil liability
    (72/166) 188
EC law, description 124-5
EC regulated operations,
  drivers' hours 11
    daily rest period 12
    daily, weekly and fortnightly driving
      periods 12
    maximum driving periods 12
    use of ferries and trains 13
    weekly rest periods 13
EC regulations, definition 163
EC Regulations,
  drivers' hours (3820/85) 11
  harmonisation of technical standards
    (156/70) 206
  hours and conditions of work
    (3820/85) 166-7
  use and fitting of tachographs
    (3821/85) 14
ECGD see Export Credit Guarantee
  Department
ECMT (European Conference of Ministers
  of Transport) 170, 173
emergencies,
  rest periods,
    AETR regulations 168
    EC regulations 167
emergency service vehicles, lights 76, 80
employee, vital, insurance against loss 117

employees' duties, health and safety
  160
employees' rights 142-6
employers,
  consultation with trade union re
    redundancies 137
  disclosure of information to trade union
    representative 137, 140
employers' duties, health and
  safety 159-60
employers' liabilities, actions of agents and
  employees 129-30
Employers' Liability (Compulsory Insurance)
  Act 1969 116
Employers' Liability (Compulsory Insurance)
  General Regulations 1971 116
Employers' Liability (Defective Equipment)
  Act 1969 116
employers' liability insurance 114, 116
employer's responsibilities, driving
  licences 23
Employment Act 1988 149, 150-1
Employment Acts 1980 and 1982 141,
  142, 146-9
  payment to trade unions 146-7
  picketing 137, 147-9
  trade disputes 136-7
  unlawful industrial action 137
  use of employer's premises for trade
    union ballots 147
Employment Protection Act 1975 141-
  2, 142
Employment Protection (Consolidation) Act
  1978, employees' rights 142-6
end-outline marker lamps 76
endorsement,
  definition 37
  list of offences requiring endorsement
    and penalty points 37-8
  removal from licence 40
Equal Pay Act 1970 155-6
Equal Pay (Amendment) Regulations 1983
  155
equal pay and conditions 155-6
equity 123-4
EUR1 form 196
European Accident Scheme 190
European Agreement concerning the work
  of crews of vehicles engaged in
  International Road Transport (AETR)
  166, 168
European Agreement for the International
  Carriage of Dangerous Goods (ADR)

210–12
European Community *see* EC
exchange rates   201
exhaust controls   65
Export Credit Guarantee Department (ECGD)   178
export declaration and clearance,
  exemptions   191
  procedures,
    Local Export Control (LEC)   191, 192
    Local Value Procedure   191, 192
    Period Entry (Exports) Scheme (PE(E))   191, 192
    pre-entry   191
    Simplified Clearance Procedure (SCP)   191–2
  purpose of records   190

F

Factories Act 1961   159, 161
false statements   42
fidelity insurance   117
finance, sources   97–8
Finance Act 1981   190
financial accounts,
  balance sheet   98
  Profit and Loss Account   98
  ratios   99–100
  Trading Account   98
  working capital   98–9
financial resources, Licensing Authority's requirement   89
fire insurance   117
first-aid kit, countries where vehicle must carry   207–9
fiscal charges   179–80
fixed costs   102, 103 Fig
fixed penalty system   34–6
  non-payment of fine   35
fog lamps,
  requirements   76, 78
  use of   80
foodstuffs carriage   46
foreign vehicles, examiner's powers   214
forgery   42
fortnightly driving hours, EC Regulations   12
freight forwarders   121–2, 202
front axle load   54
front fog lamps   78
front position lamps (sidelights)   76, 77
fuel from bulk tank, checking use   108
fuel surcharges, international transport   180

G

goods,
  damaged or lost,
    carrier's liability   183–5, 186
    time limit for claims   186–7
  status   195–6
goods in transit insurance   116, 189
goods vehicle examiners, powers   40–1
goods vehicle operations, categories   11
goods vehicles,
  definitions   52
  maximum width   55
Goods Vehicles (Plating and Testing) Regulations 1982   69
Green Cards   176, 188–9
grievance procedures, code of practice   139–40
gross combination weight (GCW)   53
gross laden weight   53
gross plated weight   53
gross train weight   53
gross vehicle weight   53
groupage   122, 203–4
guarantee payments   142
GV160, notice re overloaded vehicle   84
GV219, prohibition notice (defect notice)   81, 83
GV3, prohibition notice   81, 82

H

hazard warning lights, regulations   76, 79
hazard warning panels   49–50
hazardous and dangerous goods,
  Approved List   47
  construction of vehicles   48
  hazard warning panels   49–50
  information required   48–9
    TREMCARD   49
  legislation   47
  marking of vehicles   49–50, 51
  operator, definition   47–8
  packaging and labelling   50–1
  parking of vehicles   51
  precautions to be taken by drivers and operators   49
  regulation enforcement   50
  requirements   47–51
  training of drivers   50, 51
headlamps   76–7
Health and Safety at Work, etc Act 1974   159–61
  employees' duties   160

273

employers' duties   159–60
  general aims   159
Health and Safety Commission   160
Health and Safety Executive   160
Health and Safety Inspector   160–1
heavy goods vehicle see HGV
heavy locomotives   52
heavy and long vehicles, vehicle marking
  regulations   74, 75 Fig
heavy motor cars   52
heights of goods vehicles   56
HGV, definition   23, 52
HGV drivers, age limits   25
HGV learner drivers,
  and ordinary learner driver   25
  special requirements   25
  Young HGV Driver Training Schemes
    26–7
HGV licences,
  application procedure   23, 24
    medical certificate   23–4
  classes   24, 25 Table
  disqualification   25–6
    return of licence   26
  Licensing Authority's refusal to grant
    24
  period of validity   23
  provisional, period of validity   23
  removal of disqualification   24
  validity in EC countries   26
HGV test, provision of vehicle   5
highway and bridge authorities,
  conditions requiring notice of movement
    of vehicle   61
hire vehicles, liability for offences
  committed while vehicles on hire   36
hired transport,
  compared with own transport   120
  contract hire   120
  public hauliers   120–1
horns   64
house bill   177

import clearance   194–8
  Community Transit System   195
  documents required   194–5
  obtaining   195
index mark see number plates
indirect costs   102
indivisible loads see abnormal indivisible
  load
industrial action, unlawful,

  legislation re damages   137
industrial relations,
  legislation   136–51
    Employment Act 1988   150–1
    Employment Acts 1980 and 1982
      136–7, 146–9
    Employment Protection Act 1975
      141–2
    Employment Protection
      (Consolidation) Act 1978   142–6
    Trade Union Act 1984   136, 149–50
    Trade Union and Labour Relations Act
      1974   136–41
Industrial Training Act 1982   151–2
Industrial Training Boards (ITBs)   151–2
insurance   113–17
  authorised insurer   44
  civil liability   188
  description   113
  Green Cards   188–9
  legal minimum   44
  Motor Vehicles (Third Party Risks
    Deposits) Regulations 1967   45
  requirements under Road Traffic Act
    1988 ss. 143–158   44, 114
insurance broker   115
insurance certificate   43, 45, 178
insurance companies,
  calculation of charges   114
  purpose   113
  risk assessment   114
insurance policy, invalidity   45
insurance see also under type of insurance
  eg employers' liability insurance
International Agreement on the Carriage of
  Dangerous Goods by Road 1968 (ADR)
  165
International Agreement on the Transport
  of Perishable Foodstuffs (ATP)   165
International Carriage of Perishable
  Foodstuffs Act 1976   212–13
international certificate of insurance see
  Green Cards
International Convention on the Taxation of
  Road Vehicles 1956   179
International Convention on the Taxation of
  Road Vehicles engaged on International
  Journeys 1957   165
International Conventions and Agreements
  165–6
international law, description   124–5
International Road Haulage Permits Act
  1975   173

international transport documentation,
  driver,
    bail bond   176
    drivers' records   21, 167, 169, 176
    driving licences   175
    letter of authorisation   176
    passports and visas   175–6
  goods
    ADR Certificate (dangerous
      goods)   176
    ATA Carnet   176, 198
    ATP Certificate (perishable goods)
      176
    bill of lading   177
    certificate of insurance   43, 45, 178
    CMR Consignment note   113, 176,
      182
    customs entry forms   178
    ECGD certificate   178
    house or groupage bill   177
    invoice   111–12, 177–8
    Single Administrative Document (SAD)
      176, 193–4
    TIR Carnet   176, 198–200
  SITPRO aligned documentation   178–9
  vehicle, list of   176
invoice   111–12, 177–8

J
*James Buchanan Co Ltd v Babco
  Forwarding* 1976   184, 189
job evaluation   155
journeys involving use of ferries or trains,
  EC regulations,
    daily rest periods   167
    drivers' hours   13
judicial precedent and case law   124

K
kerbside weight   53

L
L plates   21
law,
  principal sources,
    ancient custom   123
    common law   123
    delegated or subordinate legislation
      123, 124
    EC law and international law   123,
      124–5
    equity   123–4
    judicial precedent and case law   123,
      124
    statute law   123, 124
law of carriage *see* carriage, legislation
LCL (less than container load)   204
learner drivers,
  HGV   25, 26–7
  specific regulations   21
length of vehicle,
  maximum permitted lengths of different
    types of goods vehicles   54–5
  overall, definition   55
letter of authorisation   176
liability, methods of restricting   135
liability *see also* care, duty of Licensing
  Authorities,
  circumstances when they must be
    notified by letter   92–3
  powers re operating licences   93
licensing requirements for operators *see*
  operator licensing
lien   110–11
light bulbs, countries where vehicle must
  carry replacements   207–9
light locomotives   52
lighting   76–80
  legislation   76
  non-obligatory   79–80
  obligatory lights   76
  projecting loads   59, 78–9
  use of red light   76
  use of white light   76
  when required   80
  wide loads   59, 78
limited companies,
  Articles of Association   96
  Certificate of Incorporation   96
  Certificate of Trading   97
  description   95
  formation procedure   96–7
  liquidation of winding-up   97
  Memorandum of Association   96
  private limited company   96
  prospectus   96
  public limited company   96
liquidity ratio   100
livestock carriage   46
load restraint system, strength
  requirements   45
loading *see* parking, loading and unloading
loads,
  long   57
  projecting,
    forward   57

lighting requirements   59, 78–9
  rearward   57
projection markers   58, 59 Figs
wide,
  approval from Secretary of State for Transport   61
  indivisible   57
  lighting requirements   59, 78
  regulations   57
locomotives, maximum width   55

M

maintenance of vehicle   84–7
  frequency of inspection and servicing   85
  instructions to maintenance staff   86–7
  operating licensing requirements   84
  operator's responsibility   87
  planned maintenance   86
  records   85, 87
  statutory requirement   84
marker boards   73
markings, vehicle carrying dangerous goods   211
maternity leave   143–4
maternity pay scheme, statutory (SMP)   154–5
mechanical conditions, see individual items eg brakes
medical suspension   143
medium-sized goods vehicle, minimum age limit for driving   22
Memorandum of Association   96
Minister's Approval Certificate (MAC)   69, 71
mirrors   64
mixed driving, drivers' hours   11, 12
modification of vehicle after plating   70–1
moped, minimum age limit for driving   21
mortgages   97
motor car, definition   52
motor cycle, minimum age limit for driving   21
Motor Insurer's Bureau   114
motor scooter, minimum age limit for driving   21
motor tractors,
  definition   52
  maximum width   55
Motor Vehicle (Type Approval for Goods Vehicles) (Great Britain) Regulations 1982   71

Motor Vehicles (Authorisation of Special Types) General Order 1979   46
Motor Vehicles (Construction and Use) Regulations 1986   62
Motor Vehicles (Tests) Regulations 1981   80
Motor Vehicles (Third Party Risks Deposits) Regulations 1967   45, 114
Motor Vehicles (Type Approval) Regulations 1980   63

N

National Insurance contributions, person working temporarily abroad or in EC country   153–4
nationality plate   176
No parking restrictions, yellow markings   33 Fig, 34
noise from vehicle   65
non-payment, protection against   110
nuisance,
  definition   131
  public and private   131–2
number plates, regulations   73

O

O licence, production of   93
O licence discs   91–2
Occupier's Liability   133
off the road driving, drivers' hours   13
Offices, Shops and Railway Premises Act 1963   159, 161–2
open cheque   119
operation methods,
  hired transport   120–1
  own transport   120
  sub-contractors   121
operator, death or incapacitation   8
operator licensing   88–93
  additional vehicles   92
  appeal against refusal   91
  application form statement of intent   89–90
  application for licence   88–9
  information required by Licensing Authority   88–9
  legislation   88
  objections   90–1
operators' licences   176
  types of   8
  order form   111

overdraft 97
overhang 55
overloaded vehicles 41, 56
own account operations,
  countries requiring documentation 170
  countries requiring permits 170
owner of vehicle, liability for offences committed 42
owner's name and address, display on vehicles 72

P

pallets 203
parking brakes 63
parking, loading and unloading 31–4
  areas where parked vehicle may cause obstruction or danger 31–2
  clearways and motorways 32–3
  fixed penalty system 34–6
  general requirements 31, 32
  No parking restrictions 33
    yellow markings 33 Fig, 34
  responsibility for enforcement of regulations 34
  on road at night 32
  safe loading 45
  vehicles carrying hazardous and dangerous goods 51
partner, insurance against loss 117
Partnership Act 1890 95
partnership agreement 95
partnerships, description 95
passenger insurance 45
passports 175
pay statement, itemised 142
penalty points for traffic offences,
  disqualification 38, 39, 40
  list of 37–8
  method of operation 38, 39
perishable goods 212–13
permit and journey record 176
permits,
  bilateral 170
    countries with which UK has agreements 171
  EC 170, 173
  ECMT (European Conference of Ministers of Transport) 170, 173
  forged 174
  general information 171–2, 174
  multi-lateral 173
  obtaining 171

own account operations 170
production to examiner 173–4
quota 172
UK legislation 173
personal accident insurance 117
personal liability insurance 117
petrol tanks, legal requirements 64
PG9, prohibition notice 81, 82
PG9A, prohibition notice 81, 82
PG9B, prohibition notice 81, 83
PG9C, prohibition notice 81, 83
PG10, prohibition notice 81, 83
picketing,
  essential services and supplies 149
  lawful purposes 147
  legislation 137, 147–9
  number of pickets 148
  police role 148
  right to cross picket lines 148
  secondary industrial action 149
planned maintenance 86
plating vehicles 69–70
police,
  conditions requiring notice of movement of vehicle 61
  powers 41–2
  role, picketing 148
prices 109
private limited company *see* limited companies
private nuisance 131
profit level, aims 105
Profit and Loss Account 98
profitability, calculating 105
prohibition notices,
  appeal against refusal to remove 83–4
  forms used 81–3
  legislation 81
projecting loads *see* loads, projecting
projection markers 58, 59 Figs
provisional licence, purpose of 21
public attitudes towards HGVs, operator's position 132
public duties, employee's right to time off 143
public hauliers 120–1
public liability insurance 117
public limited company *see* limited companies
public nuisance 131
purchasing control 107

Q
quotation   111

R
Race Relations Act 1976   157–8
racial discrimination   157–8
radioactive substances, carriage   47
rail/road certificate   176
rates, calculation   106
rear axle load, calculation   54
rear fog lamps,
  requirements   76, 78
  use of   80
rear position lamps 76, 77
rear registration plate lamps   76, 78
rear retro reflectors   76, 77
rear underrun protection   67
recovery vehicles   94
redundancy,
  employer's consultation with trade
    union   137
  payments   146
  time off for retraining and job hunting
    143
Redundancy Payments Act 1965   142, 146
reference tariffs   175
registration number see number plates
regulations, responsibility for compliance
  70
rest periods,
  daily,
    AETR regulations   168
    EC regulations   12, 166–7
  weekly,
    AETR regulations   168
    EC regulations   13, 167
Restricted Operator's Licence   8
return on capital employed   105
reversing alarms   64
reversing lights   79–80
rigid goods vehicles,
  maximum length   54
  maximum weights   53
risk assessment   114
Road Haulage Association,
  tariffs   174
  trading conditions   128, 129
Road Traffic Act 1972   88
Road Traffic Act 1974, operator
  licensing   88
Road Traffic Act 1988,
  appointment of goods vehicle examiners
    (s.68)   40
  certificate of insurance (s.165)   43
  definition of forgery (s.173)   42
  insurance (ss.143–158)   44, 114
  operator licensing   88
  overloading (s.78)   56
  powers of goods vehicle examiners
    (s.166)   41
  powers of police (ss.164 & 165)   41–2
  prohibition notices (s.67)   81
  vehicle lighting   76
Road Traffic (Carriage of Dangerous
  Substances in Packages etc) Regulations
  1986   51
Road Traffic Offenders Act 1988 (Schedule
  2)   37
road trains 55
Road Vehicles Lighting Regulations 1989
  76
road/rail *piggy-back* services   172
road/rail transport, advantages and
  disadvantages   205
roll-on, roll off (Ro-Ro) services   204

S
safety glass   64
safety legislation,
  Factories Act 1961   159, 161
  Health and Safety at Work, etc Act 1974
    159–61
  Offices, Shops and Railway Premises Act
    1963   159, 161–2
Safety of Loads on Vehicles Code of
  Practice   45
sales, cash compared with credit   110
savings account   118
SDRs see Special Drawing Rights (SDRs)
secondary industrial action   149
selection of vehicles   61–2
semi-trailers,
  maximum height   56
  maximum length   55
SERPS   152–3
sex discrimination   156–7
Sex Discrimination Act 1975   156–7
Sex Discrimination Act 1986   156
share capital   97
side marker lamps   79
side retro reflectors   79
sideguards   67
sidelights see front position lamps
silencers   65
Single Administrative Document (SAD)

176, 193–4
SITPRO (Simplification of International Trade Procedures Board) system of aligned documentation 178–9
small goods vehicle, minimum age limit for driving 22
small passenger vehicle, minimum age limit for driving 22
smoke from vehicle 65
snow chains, countries where vehicle must carry 207–9
social legislation questions 162
social security legislation,
   Social Security Act 1986 152–3, 154–5
   Social Security Acts 1975 to 1988 153–4
   Social Security and House Benefits Act 1982 154
   Social Security Pensions Act 1975 152–3
sole trader 95
spare parts 108
Special Drawing Rights (SDRs) 184
special requirements for vehicles, various countries 207–10
Special Type vehicles and trailers 60
speed limits 29–31
   exemptions 31
   Special Type vehicles and trailers 60
   summary of limits 29–30
spot checks *see* checks on vehicle
spray suppression equipment 67–8
Standard Operator's Licence 8
standing orders 119
State earnings-related pension scheme *see* SERPS
statement of account 112
statement of ownership 35
statute law 124
statutory sick pay (SSP) 154
stock control 107–8
stop lamps 76, 77
sub-contractors 121

T
T forms 196
tachographs,
   breakdown and repair 17, 18, 19
   calibration 18, 19
   change of vehicle by driver 15, 17
   compulsory routine inspection 18
   entering new time zone 15
   example of completed chart 16 Fig
   information inserted by driver 15
   inspection by DOT examiner or police 17
   installation 18
   international transport 176
   items recorded 14
   law governing use and fitting 14
   maintenance 17
   method of operation 14–15
   period of time covered by one record 15
   removal by authorised person 17
   retention of records 17
   supply of copies to drivers 18
   uses of 14
   vehicles exempt,
      national and international journeys 19
      national journeys only 19–20
   when driver has more than one employer 17
tariffs 174–5
technical standards, harmonisation within EC 206
terms of employment, information required in writing 142
testing of vehicles,
   annual 80–1
   first test 69
   application procedure 70
   certificate of temporary exemption 70
   pre-test procedure for operator 70
   rectification of minor faults at testing station 70
   vehicles exempt 69
Third Party Insurance Certificate 176
three-wheel car, minimum age limit for driving 21
TIR Carnet 176, 198–200
TIR Convention,
   purpose 198
   TIR carnets 198–200
tort, definition 130
tow-ropes 55
towbars, rigid 55
towing 68
trade disputes 136–7
trade licences,
   appeal against refusal to issue 94
   description 93
   duration 94

issue 93
trade plates 94
trade union, recognised 137
Trade Union Act 1984 149–50
Trade Union and Labour Relations Act 1974 136–41, 142
trade union members, unjustifiable discipline by unions 150
trade union membership, employee's rights 143
trade unions,
  ballots
    before industrial action 150
    requirements 149–50
    use of employer's premises 147
  dues, check-off agreements 150, 151
  duties and activities,
    industrial action 141
    time off for officials 140–1, 143
    time off for trade union members 141, 143
  payments from Certification Officer 146–7
Trading Account 98
trading conditions 128, 129
traffic restrictions, various countries 207–9
traffic wardens,
  duties 34
  issue of fixed penalty tickets 35
trailers,
  brakes 63
  maximum length 55
  maximum width 55
train ferries 205
Transport Act 1968,
  drivers' hours 11–12
  licensing of road haulage operators 88
  nomination of transport manager 7
Transport Act 1982, operator's premises 88
TREMCARD (Transport Emergency Card [Road]) 49
trespass to goods 133
trespass to land 133, 134
trespass to the person 132–3
type approval 71–2
  legislation 71
  notification of alterations 72
  obtaining by manufacturer 71
  operator's copy of certificate 71–2
Type Approval Certificate (TAC) 69, 71
tyre standards 66

tyres, legal requirements 65–6

U

Unfair Contract Terms Act 1977 128
Unified Driver Licensing System 27–8
unitisation 203
unladen weight (ULW),
  definition 53
  marked on vehicles 72
unloading *see* parking, loading and unloading

V

variable costs 102, 103 Fig
vehicle, transfer from depot in one traffic area to depot in another area 92
vehicle construction, carriage of hazardous and dangerous goods 48
vehicle construction, weights and dimensions, regulations, sources of information 206
vehicle insurance,
  comprehensive 115, 189
  statutory requirement 44, 114
  Third Party 115, 189
vehicle marking regulations,
  exemptions 74
  heavy and long vehicles 74, 75 Fig
  marker boards 73
  number plates 73
  owner's name and address 72
  unladen weight 72
vehicle registration document 176
vehicle taxation 179
vehicles, acquiring new or additional, notification to Licensing Authority 91, 93
visas 175
visibility, poor, special rules of conduct 31

W

warning triangles, countries where vehicle must carry 207–9
waybill 113
weighing of motor vehicle 41
weights,
  definitions 53
  maximum permitted gross weights for different types of goods vehicles 53–4
  Special Type vehicles and trailers 60
width of vehicle, maximum permitted widths of different types of goods

vehicles 55
windscreen wipers and washers 64
work records, drivers' hours *see* drivers'
  hours, records, tachographs
work safety committees 161

working capital 98-9
working capital ratio 99-100

Y
Young HGV Training Scheme 26-7